Transmedial Resonance

TRANSMEDIAL RESONANCE

The Acoustic Afterlives of Italo Calvino

ROBERT A. RUSHING

Fordham University Press
NEW YORK   2026

For EU safety / GPSR concerns: Mare Nostrum Group B.V., Mauritskade 21D, 1091 GC Amsterdam, The Netherlands, gpsr@mare-nostrum.co.uk

Library of Congress Cataloging-in-Publication Data available online at https://catalog.loc.gov.

Printed in the United States of America

28 27 26   5 4 3 2 1

First edition

Contents

Transmedial Resonance

Introduction: Writing About Music

What's left of Calvino? There is almost nothing in the places where he lived, but there is so much of him in people's heads.

—DUCCIO CHIARINI

One Anecdote

In my first quarter teaching at UCLA, I taught a class on Italian fiction and film, and I assigned Italo Calvino's 1972 experimental novel *Invisible Cities* in translation. Calvino is a favorite of mine, but he is also a mainstay of college classes in Italian literature, as well as world literature and comparative literature. *Invisible Cities* is often assigned in such classes, not just in the US, but also around the world. Elio Baldi and Cecilia Schwartz argue that "*Invisible Cities* is without a doubt among the most imitated, copied, and adapted works of Calvino,"[1] and they might also have said, "the most widely assigned." Calvino (*Invisible Cities*, of course) was required reading for the entire freshman class at Hanyang University in Seoul, South Korea, in 2018–19, for example.[2] In a review of Calvino's global reception in 2023 (the hundredth anniversary of his birth), Lorenzo Sabatino called him "an essential figure of the twentieth century's cultural *intellighenzia*," and noted that "the success of Italo Calvino's work in Italy and around the world is, to this day, undisputed and continually growing."[3] As Francesca Rubini has demonstrated with copious hard data and many charts in *Italo Calvino nel mondo* (Calvino around the world, 2023), this "Calvino phenomenon" is truly global.

Grading the midterms for that class, however, I noticed one student's paper had used a quotation from Calvino's novel that sounded slightly off to me, "elsewhere is a mirror." I ran the phrase through Google to find the original, and while I got the quotation I was looking for, the search results were rather different from what one might expect. The first result was, as expected, the quote from Calvino (with the missing word now supplied: "elsewhere is a *negative* mirror")—but the next six results were not from the novel, nor were they from scholarly articles or even from those insipid pages of "inspirational quotes." There were two results from a Los Angeles art show by Vellum/LA dedicated to the transformations of the architectural that become possible in virtual spaces; a track of ambient music by the French musician Baptiste Martin, better known as Les Halles, from an album titled *Invisible Cities*; an album by musician Mark Vernon made up of found recordings; and a blog post by a student, Areej Medhi, from a course taught at Georgetown on networks and creativity (a course in their Communication, Culture and Technology Department).[4] The web pages about the art show by Vellum/LA discuss the different artists and the importance of imaginary architecture, but they actually never mention Calvino's name or the origin of the quote. It doesn't feel like plagiarism or even an accidental omission; it's more like everyone in the art and architecture world is just expected to know that this is a reference to *Invisible Cities*.

These results didn't surprise me because, for about the last two decades, I have been informally tracking the astonishing growth of activity (artwork, architecture, urban planning, cakes for children, dances, painting, sculpture, amateur maps and diagrams, community initiatives to combat homelessness, and much, much more) that emerges in response to Calvino's writing. Almost always this work is *inspired* by Calvino. Occasionally it is an adaptation, but for the most part, reading Calvino has triggered instead an idea for a *new* work of art, a musical composition, or perhaps an impulse to organize or help a community. This informal catalogue originally emerged from my teaching. I always refresh the images I use in my slides for lectures each year, and whenever I would lecture on Calvino, I would discover a whole new and fascinating trove of this sort of work. When I would give talks at other campuses, I would almost always find a few examples of Calvino-inspired art in whatever city I happened to be speaking in. The very first such example of these Calvino-inspired artworks that I found is sadly no longer on the internet: a set of *Invisible Cities* ViewMaster discs (those little photodiscs for children that you could slip into a tiny stereoscope and see with a 3D effect) handmade by "Vladmaster," the online identity of Vladimir Solmon, a Portland-based artist and experimental filmmaker. While *Invisible Cities* is responsible for eliciting the lion's share of this material, it sometimes seems as if any random phrase from Calvino receives an answer from somewhere else. One album of electronic music (by one of the many artists who go by the name "Invisible Cities") consists entirely of songs with titles that are odd phrases clipped from Calvino's writing, including some rather obscure ones. An album by the Italian jazz musician Vito Liturri is titled *Desires and Fears*, in English, a reference to the album's inspiration in *Invisible Cities*, while Bill Ryder-Jones (formerly of the band The Coral) has an album that ranges from the symphonic to folk music titled simply *If. . . .* It is an imaginary soundtrack for a nonexistent film version of Calvino's experimental novel *If on a winter's night a traveler.*

Some of these examples are in areas where Calvino, especially *Invisible Cities*, has had a clear professional or disciplinary impact (architecture, urban planning, thinking about communities), a ready-made toolbox that I call "city thinking" in chapter 4. Some of my examples—student projects, cakes for children, Lina Grossi's book of recipes from the *Fiabe italiane*, obscure albums on Bandcamp—are perhaps reminiscent of the creative activities typical of fans, the kind of creative reuse of culture that is part of Michel de Certeau's "practice of everyday life." There is in fact plenty of that (much of it quite wonderful and sophisticated), but much of it clearly goes well beyond this paradigm, especially in the last ten to twenty years.[5] One possible turning point might be the extensive media coverage and extremely positive critical reception of Chris Cerrone's Pulitzer-nominated "opera for headphones" of *Invisible Cities* in 2013, the subject of the second chapter.[6] Since then, a number of significant works of art that respond to Calvino have risen to critical prominence, several of which I talk about over the course of this book (Christopher Cerrone's opera, Lisa Mezzacappa's jazz suite, Ashwini Ramaswamy's multimedia dance work). What I want to isolate about this site of cultural production right away, however, is that it has happened at least as much outside Italy as inside, and more outside literature than inside, a point I'll return to shortly.

Two Calvinos

Italo Calvino (1929–1985) is Italy's most important author of the twentieth century. He lived an unusually cosmopolitan life for an Italian of his era, or even today. He was born in Cuba, where his parents worked as scientists, and was raised in Italy in his parents' free-thinking, anti-Fascist traditions in the 1920s and '30s (he was given a nonreligious education, which was very rare at the time). He fought as a partisan soldier against the Nazis in Italy at the end of World War II, and then came of age as a writer and editor for the left-wing publishing house Einaudi in Turin after the war. He published a number of politically committed realist works in the 1940s and '50s that were increasingly permeated by the fantastic.

In 1956, he publicly resigned from the Italian Communist Party after it refused to denounce the Soviet Union's brutal invasion of Hungary, and his writing appeared to shift to less explicitly political interests, such as the "science-mythology" stories in the 1965 *Cosmicomics*. After traveling for a year in the United States, he moved to Paris and joined OuLiPo (Workshop for Potential Literature), a group interested in exploring literature, mathematics, and logic. In 1972, he published the experimental novel *Invisible Cities* (it consists of fifty-five short descriptions of dreamlike cities, and a number of philosophical dialogues between Marco Polo and Kublai Khan), a work that would prove to be hugely influential, and his global reputation grew throughout the 1970s and 1980s before his untimely death in 1985.

Part of the argument of *Transmedial Resonance* is that there are really two Calvinos: One is the "Italian" Calvino, who is seen as a model for literary style (clarity, precision), but whose later works and politics fit uneasily into Italy's largely left-wing intellectual establishment. His works are regularly assigned in Italian schools (*Marcovaldo* is a typical middle-school novel in Italy, for example), but almost exclusively those works written before he left the Communist Party and Italy. Several Italian polemics against Calvino, especially his later works, published in the 1990s portrayed him as fundamentally pessimistic and escapist, incapable of confronting the hard realities of the world and preferring a melancholy withdrawal from it. Perhaps the most condensed example of this impulse is Franco Fortini's infamous one-line poem: "Cinico bimbo va Calvino incolume" (A cynical baby, Calvino goes away unscathed).[7] Even among his enthusiastic defenders in Italy, moreover, Calvino's pessimistic escapism is often a given. I don't mean that this understanding of Calvino is totally devoid of merit, but it does establish fairly clear lines within a largely Italian academic response that work to contain, even reduce, Calvino as an inspirational figure.

Meanwhile, in the Anglophone world, the burgeoning reputation of *Invisible Cities*, coupled with enthusiastic promotions of his work by Gore Vidal and Salman Rushdie in the English-language press in the 1970s and '80s, helped to establish Calvino as not just a great Italian writer, but also a canonical example of "world literature" (see Baldi and Schwartz, 5) whose imaginative and fantastic novels were playful, cerebral, and open. In a promotional quote that appeared for years on the back of Calvino's novels in the United States, John Updike compared him to Borges and Márquez, concluding that, "of the three, Calvino is the sunniest, the most variously and benignly curious about the human truth." Not only does this benign, sunny explorer seem like the polar opposite of the Italian tradition (the fearful, pessimistic, and escapist "necrophiliac" of style), but that image has also permitted an amplification and enlargement of the author's figure—not in the sense of being a great writer, but in the sense of enlarging the space Calvino might occupy, beyond national and mediatic borders.

Elio Baldi, in his remarkably encyclopedic book, *The Author in Criticism: Calvino's Authorial Image*, argues that there are multiple "Calvini" (3, his jocular Italian plural of Calvino), many more than two, and he emphatically rejects the idea of an Italian vs. non-Italian hierarchy in thinking about Calvino's authorial image (3). I agree with this impulse in theory, but in practice there really is something like an Italian institutional orthodoxy regarding Calvino, an orthodoxy Baldi himself refers to. He also describes his own book as a slow "movement from a more Italian viewpoint to a more Anglo-Saxon one" (7), and ultimately dedicates a whole section to the Italian response to Calvino's canonicity (86–102). There remain some ways to nuance this apparently inevitable binary opposition, however. We might notice that, to a limited extent, the more Italian version of the pessimistic and escapist Calvino has *also* had a global diffusion (if less widespread). We might also recognize (as Baldi does) that while the "Italian reception" I describe has happened largely in Italy, many Italian scholars and writers, both in Italy and around the world, don't recognize that negative vision of a pessimistic, apolitical, disembodied, and escapist Calvino at all. Many, like Baldi, Anna Botta, Lucia Re, or Marzia Beltrami, explicitly push back, arguing for "a more nuanced view of the author,"[8] or offer a sunnier and more engaged vision of Calvino, as Duccio Chiarini does rigorously in his documentary film, *Italo Calvino: Lo scrittore sugli alberi* (2023, Italo Calvino: The writer in the trees). That film does not use the word "melancholy" or "pessimism" even once, and insists throughout on Calvino's political engagement and value, a sentiment I also heard from the young producers behind *Silent City*, the opera I look at in chapter 4. Perhaps this is the kind of text that will set the stage for how Italy thinks about Calvino in the next generation. Indeed, another recent book, Serenella Iovino's 2023 *Gli animali di Calvino* (*Italo Calvino's Animals*, 2021), doesn't just offer a view of Calvino as environmentally aware and engaged from the beginning of his career to the end. Iovino also insists on the need to read Calvino from the "inside out" (or more outside than inside, as I say here) since he himself wrote and thought "fuori del *self*" (19, outside the self). The end result is not a reading of animals in Calvino's writing that works its way inward (what would be a mere "bestiary") but what emerges as a politically committed "guida alla biosfera del nostro presente geologico" (25, guide to the biosphere of our geological present).[9]

Lastly, scholars of the "transnational" or "transcultural" turn are quite sensitive to the fact that transnational cultural movements are also very much about political and cultural power and prestige, and Calvino's reception in both Italy and the rest of the world was clearly conditioned by Cold War politics as well as by the relative cultural weight of the English-speaking world. It was also affected by Calvino's own choices. Already by the 1960s, he was working to position himself as a cosmopolitan and global figure, writing in an Italian prose that he curated specifically to make it as translatable as possible. This move made his reception in Italy rather restricted and somewhat problematic, but made his French and Anglo-American reception much more resonant and capacious.

As I noted, the global diffusion of Calvino was relatively limited before the publication of *Invisible Cities*, but quite rapid afterward—Rubini has a detailed and quite excellent history of the global spread of Calvino's writing, and her data show that by 2020, there were over 1,500 different editions of Calvino worldwide (*Italo Calvino nel mondo*, 22), part of what she calls the "dimensione planetaria del 'fenomeno Calvino'" (23, the planetary dimension of the "Calvino phenomenon"). This is of course in synchrony with Calvino's stated desire to be a cosmopolitan rather than a national writer, unsurprising given his background that was "europeo e transnazionale" (44, European and transnational). He was a writer who, as Jhumpa Lahiri argues, already wrote in global translation and "never . . . purely in Italian."[10] So, when I say that his resonance is more outside Italy than inside, I am not referring to the number of books sold (most of the world, after all, neither speaks nor reads Italian), and I am definitely not trying to understate the Italian contributions to Calvino's "acoustic afterlives" (several of which I also examine in the pages that follow)—I am referring to the planetary dimensions of those afterlives.

Despite the at times negative stance of the Italian literary establishment, it is certainly true that Calvino has had a fairly active cultural afterlife in Italy, where there have been jazz albums (Claudio Angeleri's *Castello dei destini incrociati* [*Music from the Castle of Crossed Destinies*]) and artworks (Teatro Potlach's theatrical and multimedia *Città invisibili* [*Invisible Cities*] project, documented in detail by Kyle Gillette, celebrated its thirty-fourth year in 2024) and community initiatives as well. We don't have a unit for measuring the quantity and impact of cultural resonance (a megaCalvino?), however, so an empirical claim about comparative impact will always be a little suspect (and rightly so), even if many Calvino scholars would agree with it. What I can say, and what I argue later in this book, is that Calvino's afterlife *within* Italy is increasingly mediated by the afterlife he has had *outside* Italy. That is, even within Italy, there are two images of the author in circulation. One of them is the older, critical view I mentioned before, taught in Italian schools: Calvino as cerebral, apolitical, pessimistic, and repressed. Anna Botta has chronicled the history of this "negative" Calvino, and sees this authorial image crystallizing in the early 1990s, and other scholars have pointed out this negative reception as well (see Lucia Re's 2014 article, "Pasolini vs. Calvino, One More Time," for example). The other image of Calvino that circulates in Italy (generally outside academic institutions), however, is the Anglo-American one I detailed earlier in which he is understood as politically engaged, community-minded, playful, and creatively open. He is the author not of *Le città invisibili*, if you like, but of *Invisible Cities*. When Giuseppe Romaniello wrote his 2014 homage to Calvino and jazz, he used the English title of Calvino's Harvard lectures (*Six Memos for the Next Millennium*—the Italian title is *Le lezioni americane*, or "the American lessons") as his inspiration, and called his book *Six Memos in Jazz*, an English title for an Italian book. This is a quite deliberate turn to a cosmopolitan, flexible, transnational, and transmedial Calvino, one who can "authorize" creative endeavors in a way that the supposedly apolitical and pessimistic writer that an Italian had to read in middle school might not. Although *Transmedial Resonance* is predominantly interested in the more creative and utopian resonances Calvino has had, it is also true that this "liberated Calvino" can go literally anywhere, including places that are perhaps less playful and creative—Andrea Prencipe and Massimo Sideri coauthored an entire book (*L'innovatore rampante: L'ultima lezione di Italo Calvino* [The innovator in the trees: Italo Calvino's last lesson]) applying the lessons of Calvino's *Six Memos* to business management, an idea that Harley-Davidson Italia appropriated for a series of talks on the role of Calvino's qualities, the first of which is "Lightness: CEOs Drive the Future."[11]

As even this last example shows, the claim that Calvino is more influential outside literature than in it is equally irrefutable, if immune to exact quantification—just the field of architecture alone, where *Invisible Cities* has been referred to as "the architect's Bible," indicates how important Calvino has been.[12] There is an almost unfathomably vast catalogue of visual art produced in response to Calvino. Over the last twenty years, I have catalogued examples of paintings, drawings, etchings, digital images, installation art, sculptures, book design, and interior decorating. More than one artist has attempted to produce images of all of the fifty-five cities in *Invisible Cities*. That said, none of those visually oriented artworks rose to the same level of cultural prominence that, say, Chris Cerrone's opera did, or the musical-theatrical version of the same novel that premiered at the Manchester Festival in 2019. This is surprising, given the insistence in literary criticism on Calvino as a primarily or even exclusively visual writer (see Grundtvig et al., Belpoliti, Ricci, Almansi), a writer Daniele Del Giudice could refer to simply as "l'occhio che scrive" (the eye who writes), and that Domenico Scarpa could call "disincarnato" (disembodied).[13] It indicates that there is perhaps something that has been missed in our reception, something I hope *Transmedial Resonance* helps to supply. Equally telling is that Calvino has proven remarkably resistant to cinematic adaptation: Outside of Pino Zac's 1969 mixed live action and animation film, *Il cavaliere inesistente* (*The Nonexistent Knight*), none of his longer works have been adapted for cinema.[14]

What I am attempting to do in this book is rethink Calvino from a fundamentally acoustic perspective. I do this not only because of personal inclination (I have been a musician my entire adult life, and am perhaps a little bit obsessed by sound), but because I have become gradually convinced that sound and sound studies offer us a potent new tool for thinking about cultural influence and reception in a completely different way, one based on an acoustic model (rather than the mirror of Narcissus and the blinding of Oedipus) that privileges echo, reverberation, and resonance.

Three Sound Effects: Echo, Reverberation, Resonance

There are three related acoustic concepts that inform this project in important ways; they are sometimes used interchangeably, but they do have distinct, if related, definitions, and I will argue here that they have quite distinct connotations. I use them—we all use them—as metaphors, a point I'll return to shortly, but let's begin with a more literal and scientific description of what happens to sound as it propagates. When a sound wave first emanates from its source and encounters an object—a wall, a piece of furniture, a pane of glass—some of its energy is absorbed by the object, and some bounces away again. It will continue until all of its energy is dispersed, and the sound is no longer audible. Materials that are highly acoustically reflective, like glass or metal or ceramic, reflect back a lot of that energy, while materials that are acoustically fairly absorbent, like cloth or cushions or a human body, absorb it and reduce the reflected acoustic energy. The porous white square panels that make up the ceiling in many corporate or educational spaces (including my office) are called "acoustic tiles" for a reason: They are specially engineered to absorb reflected sound in order to eliminate distracting echoes. The molded tin ceilings and exposed brick walls that are so prized in many trendy restaurants have the exact opposite effect, however, one of the reasons those restaurants are so hard to hear in: They produce a cacophony of reflected voices.

Technically speaking, the *echo* is the first acoustic reflection that reaches the listener. So, what is the "echo" of Calvino's *Invisible Cities*, for example—the very first artistic reflection of that original signal? There is no way to know, since it was almost certainly something like an ordinary reader doodling one of the invisible cities on a piece of scrap paper, now lost forever. But I do know the first echo that I encountered, long before I was scouring the internet for lecture images, and that was while listening to National Public Radio. It was 1993 or 1994, about when physicist and creative writer Alan Lightman's novel *Einstein's Dreams* started to get significant public attention (the novel was selected for NPR's "Talk of the Nation" book club in 1998, but this was earlier, not long after it was first published in 1992). The program described the novel: a series of thirty dreams that are fantastic, short, crystalline fragments in which Einstein imagines different ways that space, time, and mass might interact. The dreams are interspersed with occasional dialogues between Einstein and his friend Besso, and as you might expect, Calvino's novel was in fact the primary inspiration for *Einstein's Dreams*.

Let us provisionally adopt that moment—Lightman on the radio—as the first audible "reflection" of Calvino's novel.[15] Again, technically speaking, the *echo* is that first acoustic "bounce" we hear when the sound we have emitted hits something reflective and returns to us. There's something appealing in the metaphor of the echo in the way it imagines cultural or literary influence as a transfer of energy, but it has a number of problems associated with it as well, perhaps most crucially a prejudice against the echo in Western culture that goes back at the least to the ancient Greeks. The mythological character Echo had the misfortune to distract Hera with mindless chatter, and Hera's husband Zeus used the distraction as cover for one of his many affairs with a mortal woman. Hence Echo was cursed by Hera to use only the last words of others and never again her own speech—she was doomed, if you like, to be derivative, unoriginal. And like the shadow images on the wall of Plato's cave, the echo is a representation of a representation, ontologically thin, deprived of the full presence of intention. To say that one author *echoes* another suggests at least some lack of original thinking or artistry, stealing the original source of light for some meager "pale fire."

As James W. Fernandez, George Lakoff, Mark Johnson, and others have argued, metaphors are not just flowery language, but also important ways of defining people, places, and ideas. They represent, to use Fernandez's term, a "strategy," a way of defining something, of associating it with certain feelings, and ultimately positioning it within a social and political hierarchy.[16] The echo is one of the most important ways of structuring our thinking about influence and artistic creation. Perhaps the best-known critical treatment of this model is Harold Bloom's Oedipal model in *The Anxiety of Influence*, where each new generation of artists must contend with the previous "masters" of the art, fretting that their own works might be perceived as derivative echoes. This book project actually originated with Philippe Lacoue-Labarthe's idea of "catacoustics" (see chapter 2), the ancient term for the study of reflected sound, the *kata-* prefix referring to the gradual dying away of sound. For Lacoue-Labarthe, reverberation could serve as an attempt to delineate a nonvisual, nonnarcissistic model of subject formation. The subject in this view is a kind of historical accretion of influential voices that make us who we are, haunting us with their obsessive melodies, phrases, and rhythms. (Ultimately, the subject is something like a rhythmic pulse, the pure form of repetition itself.) Catacoustics multiplies those reflected and repeated sounds, moving us from thinking of a singular echo that is inevitably an impoverished repetition of what came before to a larger set of reverberations that suggest a kind of acoustic wealth, and that have the potential to make us reflect on the larger cultural space we are in—just as real echoes give us the distinctive sound of the space we inhabit.

Our metaphoric use of reverberation is surprisingly close to a literal description of it: The acoustic energy that bounces off a reverberant surface will continue until it strikes another object and produces another acoustic reflection. This reverberation will also spread out until it encounters another object, and so on. As a result, when a sound is emitted, there's something of a riot of different acoustic reflections bouncing around, and they all reach our ears at different times, generally just milliseconds apart (although our hearing is excellent, and can easily discriminate very small differences in time).[17] When you put that all together, you get the acoustic world of everyday life. When you stand on the edge of a huge chasm and shout "hey!," the first sharp "hey" that comes back is the *echo*, and the spacious cloud of subsequent, ever fainter and blurrier greetings that gradually die away are collectively *reverberation* (abbreviated by musicians and sound engineers as "reverb").

Those reflections and absorptions convey a lot of information without our consciously realizing it: the size and possibly even the shape of the room we are in, how far away from the different walls we are, and even what kinds of materials are present. Different materials absorb sound differently, not only because they absorb more or less, but because different parts of the sound are reflected or absorbed, too. Some materials absorb a lot of the sound's high end, for example, like the treble knob on an old stereo—back when there were physical knobs—turned all the way down. There is a significant science and industry surrounding the management of reverberation, from the design of concert halls or the acoustic tiles in classrooms (generally focused on removing it) to the ever more elaborate digital simulations of reverb used by musicians and audio engineers (generally focused on adding it).

This is the potential in an acoustic model for thinking about influence and reception. Here one can start to see my strategic deployment of a reverberant metaphor: Rather than proceeding in a straight line of transmission from author to reader, or from Important Canonical Figure to young, impressionable, aspiring artist, a reverberative model acknowledges the lines of influence are indirect and multiple, and they come from all over. Reverberation, in other words, gives us a complex model of multiple networks of cultural *transmission* rather than cultural *influence*, whose metaphorical value is based on the water that flows (Lat.: *fluere*) in and that may recognize a host of tributaries, but only one mighty River.[18] Rather than the Origin and the Repetition of the echo, reverberation accords value to the sounds that follow. Reverberation implies a wealth and richness of sound. One of the reasons I found the idea of catacoustics so appealing is that thinking about reverberation rather than the echo confirms something I had always experienced as a musician: The sound of your instrument (classical guitar in my case) is never experienced outside some real concrete space that has a distinctive acoustic character.

What this means, practically but also theoretically, is that *the reverberation is part of the sound*. I can't actually say what my guitar sounds like "by itself," because I can never hear it being played in *nowhere*. I only ever hear it in the space it is in now (in my office, where there is little reverb, and very dry because books absorb so much acoustic energy; outside between Royce and Haines Halls, where there is almost no reverberation but a lot of noise; or in the Royce stairwell if I want a really heavy reverberation). For thinking about reception and influence, this idea that reverberation is part of the sound, not an afterthought or supplement, is a critical distinction. Where the echoing, Oedipal model thinks of Dickens, for example, as an original who is more or less imitated by other writers and later (in a perhaps fainter or less faithful echo), a model based on reverberant catacoustics might conceive of an ever-expanding Dickens-space, a space in which Dickens's novels, the parallel montage in the films of D. W. Griffith, and the television series *The Wire* are all meaningful parts. We might ask different questions, in fact: not just how Dickens influences *The Wire*, but what *The Wire* might tell us about Dickens.

Still, while reverberation is positive and spatial, and leads naturally to broader and more comparative frames of analysis, the more equal terrain of the sound and the reverberation that is part of it still promises a certain kind of primacy, and we can hear something of this in how we talk about reverberation as "enriching" (if it works well) or "muddying" (if it works badly) the sound. Reverberation follows the Derridean logic of the supplement: It is an essential and intrinsic part of the sound, and simultaneously an "extra" to the sound that needs to be managed. At one point, I called this book *Echoes of Calvino*, but one can see immediately how such a title inadvertently sends the wrong message: No matter how strongly one emphasizes how this reverberant space enriches and expands, one is left with the impression of something original, and an extra piece that is not *really* necessary. As a result, I will generally use the terms "echo" and "reverberation" indiscriminately here, as they are often used in ordinary speech—ultimately, I don't think reverberation gets us far enough away from Karmen MacKendrick's "imitative echo."[19] Part of the reason reverberation remained unsatisfying was not only that I thought the works I discuss here were amazing in their own right, but that, in speaking with the artists, it became very clear that—although they all have different relationships to Calvino—they were certainly not locked in an Oedipal struggle with a literary titan. They liked Calvino, they found him interesting, and he had sparked an idea for them, but they were not "performing" him; there was no anxiety, no hint of "Did I get it right?" It is entirely possible that part of the reason for this kind of relationship to the source of the inspiration is precisely the transmedial and transnational transmission at work. Cerrone wasn't redoing a famous opera by Britten, and Mezzacappa wasn't trying to update *Kind of Blue*. So let's instead turn to an idea that I think is better suited for thinking about futurity, and that does not privilege an origin, namely *resonance*.

Resonance is related to reverberation, but also importantly different. When the initial sound wave propagates out from its source and encounters an ordinary object like a wall or a tiled floor, that object reflects some amount of the sound (as echo and reverberation) and absorbs some of it. But some objects aren't so ordinary. Some will instead *resonate*, vibrating in sympathy with the sound energy they have received, not just reflecting the energy of the original pulse, but making a sound of their own.[20] That is, a resonant object would absorb the energy of the initial sound, but release it right back in a changed form, with a different quality of sound (what musicians call timbre) and even at a different (although related) frequency. Every object in fact has a natural frequency at which it resonates, although you generally can't predict at a glance what will resonate and at what frequency.[21]

While echo and reverberation are daily, commonplace experiences, resonance is not. On a few occasions I've happened to make a noise (a yelp when the cat startles me, a cough, a loud "Hold on!" when someone knocks at the door) at just the right volume and pitch, and my acoustic guitar has answered me with a loud musical hum. By accident, I've happened to hit just the right combination of acoustic factors to make the instrument really resonate. The sound that the instrument makes is "original" in more than one way. Stimulated to resonance, but not by being plucked, the string has a quite different sound than if I were playing it. (In fact, this sort of acoustic resonance is happening around us in a very low-key way all the time, part of the "hum of the world," as Lawrence Kramer calls it—but it is generally far too quiet to hear.)

As a metaphor, resonance does a lot of work for thinking about artistic influence, not least—following Fernandez again—the ways it organizes our feelings and how it positions the new work of art in a socio-political field. As Julie Napolin, Anne Bogart, and others who have worked on artistic resonance have noted, it is part of popular language, where it is strongly associated with positive feelings of belonging, recognition, and affiliation. A student talking in class about a story or an idea that had a powerful impact on them might say that "it really resonated for me" (or, in a related acoustic metaphor, it "really struck a chord"). We should notice here that resonance doesn't simply mean that it had an impact—it also suggests, very strongly, that the impact was *personal*. Again, although it is a metaphor, our metaphorical usage is surprisingly close to scientific fact: Resonance really is unexpected, rather unpredictable, and individual. In the real world, apparently identical wineglasses will in fact have different resonant frequencies. We don't know what will resonate with us until it actually happens, and no work of art will resonate with everyone. Resonance—like my guitar humming at me—takes us by surprise. As Bogart writes, "to be on the receiving end of resonance . . . requires a certain disposition. . . . I must be ready to hear the call, and be open enough to be altered by the interaction."[22] She thinks of her body as a tuning fork (6)—ready to be struck at just the right frequency and start humming back.[23]

In part because of its unpredictability and uniqueness, resonance also evokes something spontaneous, not studied or cultivated. This is particularly important for thinking about resonance as a model for artistic influence, because it means that the resonance is *original*. Not absolutely original, of course—artistic inspiration doesn't come out of nowhere, because literally no art comes out of nowhere. Resonance acknowledges that artists live in a space saturated with artistic energy, but that something about *this* signal produced a personal, original reaction in me. The emphasis, then, is on the *exceptional* character of the resonance, and less on the original signal (which is also exceptional, but principally insofar as it provoked a resonant reaction in *you*). One can see already why resonance is very different from influence, which is inherently suspicious of the originality of the new work of art: Is it really original, or is it mere echoing or imitation? The dreaded word "derivative" (etymologically "from the river") doesn't seem applicable to resonance at all.

Part of the reason that resonance is less suspicious as a guiding metaphor is that the focus is not on the content of what provoked the resonant response, but rather on the *energy* transmitted and emitted. Looking back at my description of my guitar's occasional resonance, the sound that provoked the response wasn't important or memorable, but the sound that resulted was. The focus was entirely on the unexpected energy transfer and the guitar's original and unique response. In our real-world scientific examples of acoustic resonance, what is most striking is how much energy can build up in resonance: enough to make a wineglass explode or a bridge collapse, as a quick survey of YouTube videos about resonance will show. When we talk about artistic resonance, however, the energy transferred is broadly more productive and less destructive, although there is no doubt something worthwhile, as Naomi Waltham-Smith argues, also in resonances that disrupt and shatter, sounds that "voice something that usually goes unheard."[24] Finally, the metaphor of artistic resonance that I am trying to deploy here has the advantage of turning away from the past exclusively and attending primarily to the present and the future, to the art and lives that come after. In a resonant space, one work of art provokes or triggers another in an unpredictable and unique transfer of energy that unleashes something original and personal—something that is, in turn, capable of producing other such responses.

There is one other advantage in turning to an acoustic model for thinking about artistic transmission. I suggested before while discussing reverberation that there was a powerful, even unique, link between sound and space. When I open up the application I use for digital audio recording, I can record in a virtual space. The software will model the typical sound of a variety of generic spaces, from a small club to a large symphony hall. I can call up simulations of quite specific real places (a particular church or famous recording studio, for example). For all practical purposes, *all* of the characteristics that create a sonic "sense of place" are essentially reverberation. Reverberation, once again, tells us the size and shape of the space we are in, what it is made of, whether it is empty or full (and what it is full of), and where we are located within that space. Logic Pro, one of the most widely used professional recording programs, calls its reverb effect "Space Designer"—to design reverb is to design space; when I change any feature of reverberation, I am effectively changing the apparent space the sound (and the listener) is in.

In her groundbreaking book on sound recording and listening practices in early twentieth-century America, *The Soundscape of Modernity* (2002), Emily Thompson argued that sound engineers severed the link between architectural space and reverberation by learning to control it (to remove it and then add it back in artificially). Logic Pro's Space Designer not only can model real spaces, but also can model ones that do not exist—what music sounds like in a room that is growing continuously larger or smaller, or what a voice sounds like inside a cavern whose walls absorb and then re-emit sound, but in ways the materials we are used to hearing do not. And yet, it remains true that, although the space may be virtual and fictional and even fantastic, it *remains a space*. Our ears and our mind were built to hear sound as space, so that even the apparent "non-space" of the recording studio has a distinctive sound (the flat, echoless, close-miked sound of the recording studio). As part of the research for this project, I visited an anechoic chamber, a room that has no echo whatsoever, used by scientists for various projects. It is the quietest space a person can ever experience. The effect is uncanny (you can hear the blood rushing through your own ears after a while), but ultimately, it is a space with a distinctive and recognizable sound of its own, like every other space.

I dwell at length on space for three reasons. The first (an issue I explore at greater length in chapter 2, on Chris Cerrone's opera of *Invisible Cities*) is that space is directly connected to, even in some ways synonymous with, the environment, a connection that I refer to here as the "echo-logical." If sound can tell us about the space we live in—and Rachel Carson certainly thought it could in *Silent Spring*—then by attending to the acoustic dimension of our cultural lives, we may also be able to think about its life, its health, and its vitality. What I'm arguing for is, in short, a different kind of environmental humanities, one that pays attention to the sounds that literature (already an acoustic art) gives rise to as a measure of the health of our cultural ecosystem. The second reason to keep present the tight connection between sound and space is that space inhabited by human beings is also political. The political valence of the "echo-logical" is probably already clear, but what becomes more salient in a sonic dimension (and one of the reasons *Invisible Cities* has been so resonant) is the fundamentally political problem of how to manage bodies in space, especially in urban space. At its most abstract level, I think this is precisely what Calvino is doing in *Invisible Cities*, and why that novel is so invested in the question of form—of how to arrange space. This receives a surprising answer in chapter 5, in which I look at dance as an acoustic-kinetic form of art that is centrally concerned with precisely the problem of how bodies can exist with other bodies in space. Lastly, all of the chapters in this book consider how the "sound" of Calvino sketches out a cultural space that is transnational in scope, and continuing to expand, sound filling up an expanding space with its reverberations. It turns out that cultural spaces may in fact work like some of those "fictional spaces" in Logic Pro's Space Designer after all, with endless expansion and weird resonances. I concentrate here on the expansion into the Anglo-American space (with some slight detours into other countries) because all of my work has been on transcultural movements between Italy and that space, but also because this has probably been the "largest" resonant space for Calvino, and as I contend in chapter 4, it is also the case that the "American" Calvino has in some ways returned to Italy in a different form: not the writer you read, analyze, and imitate in school, but the kind of writer who might inspire some of the works I look at in this book—a free jazz composition, or a community opera with a political edge.

Four Mantras

Earlier I said that we might give a provisional start to Calvino's Anglo-American resonance with Alan Lightman's 1992 novel *Einstein's Dreams*, a kind of creative homage to Calvino's *Invisible Cities*. Even in that example, we can see two distinct features that will return again and again in this book, features that eventually became something like mantras (an appropriately acoustic template for my acoustic intervention) that guided this project. The first one is, once again: "more outside than inside." I mean this primarily in a *transmedial* sense: Calvino's influence is larger and more significant outside literature than inside it. Indeed, Lightman's novel is one of the very few literary responses that seriously take up or model themselves on what Calvino did (Finnish author Leena Krohn's strange and beautiful *Tainaron: Mail from Another City* is one of the very few others, along with David Mitchell's *Cloud Atlas*). This is not to say that Calvino's literary influence is small—many writers cite him as an influence, or at least a writer they admire—but more that his cultural influence outside literature is in fact absolutely huge: architecture, urban planning, design, sustainability, arts education, as well as dance, theater, music, painting and other visual arts, sculpture, opera, and more.

Second, I mean this mantra *transnationally*. Calvino's impact has been significantly larger outside Italy than inside it, for a variety of reasons, mostly political, as we've already discussed. This is again not to say that he is not influential in Italy—in fact, Carla Benedetti's 1998 *Pasolini contro Calvino* makes the trenchant, polemical case that Calvino has been far *too* influential in Italy. Rather, the *global* resonance of his work, particularly *Invisible Cities*, is remarkable, and most of that vast transmedial and transdisciplinary influence is outside the Italian-speaking world.

The second mantra is "going out, coming back." The sounds we make propagate outward, reflecting back or dying out when they encounter obstacles, and occasionally finding objects that resonate to that original sound and generate echoes and resonances of their own. We are constantly situated by a field of sounds coming back to us from elsewhere. This has dictated the basic structure of this book, which begins with the sound of Calvino's actual voice, and a peculiar Italian reception of that voice (focusing on Silvio Perrella's claim at the end of the 1990s that Calvino "writes in falsetto") before looking at some of the most important ways that Anglophone artists have resonated to his works: Chris Cerrone's 2013 opera of *Invisible Cities* in headphones, Lisa Mezzacappa's 2020 jazz suite of the *Cosmicomics*, and Ashwini Ramaswamy's 2023 dance suite of *Invisible Cities*. But I would be remiss if I did not also chronicle the way that all this resonance also returns back to its point of origin, and Calvino's presence in Italy is very often mediated through his transmedial and transnational reception, and so chapter 4 addresses a 2019 "community opera" in Matera, Italy, *Silent City*, that shows Calvino's resonant influence on how we think about cities and their history.

The third mantra is "reverberation is space." By this I mean that echo, reverberation, and resonance are not empty or incidental features of a sound; they instead communicate incredibly important information about the space in which that resonance is expanding. A person who has been blindfolded and taken to an unknown location knows a great about the room just from listening to echoes: The short, sharp echoes of a small bare room? The short, soft echoes of a small, cluttered chamber? The slow, complex reverberation of a large space made of many materials? In this same way, attending to the reverberations and resonances that Calvino has produced tells us something about the expanding cultural spaces his resonance has unfolded in, where, over time, that signal has found a welcoming and progressively more resonant space.

The fourth mantra is, in many ways, the most important for me, since my original impetus—for learning Italian, going to grad school, becoming an academic—was the desire to read Calvino in the original (a friend had lent me a copy of *Invisible Cities* in English when I was a freshman at UC Santa Cruz, and Calvino pretty quickly became an obsession, along with classical music). That mantra is "the resonance is the source" or "the echo is part of the sound, not a supplement." Sounds actually need echoes and reverberation *to be fully themselves*. A musical instrument does not sound correct, it does not sound like itself, like it should, without at least a touch of reverb; it reveals the richness and depth of tone that were already there, but that were inaudible without it. The idea of the original is a fetish: Translations are part of the reverberant, resonant space that opens up after the original signal, and indeed, they are part of it. This is in some ways a corollary of my third principle, "reverberation is space." To have no reverberation is to be in no space at all. In a very real way, it also indicates that there are no listeners, since they would need to be in a space in order to listen. From an interpretive perspective, however, what this means is that the resonance tells us something about the original, something that was actually there, but that we did not hear, without it. I listen to each of the artists in this book to hear not only what they were inspired to say, but also what they have to tell me about Calvino ("going out, coming back"). Resonance ultimately comes back to the original source, and helps it to fill up with its own meaning. Writing about the relationship of musicology to music (or even more generally, the process of talking about music), Peter Szendy argues that there is no way of separating the two: "Music becomes the Music that it is by giving birth to other words."[25] The acoustic source (a song, a voice, a work of literature) becomes itself precisely through the resonant space that it gives rise to.

As this project has progressed, it has moved away from echo as the guiding metaphor, through reverberation, and more and more toward resonance. Although all have their uses, it is worthwhile retracing my steps so I can also talk about what each has to offer. Ultimately, however, "resonance" as a term is so rich and precisely fits so well what I am describing: how the original "sound" of Calvino propagated out and found certain artists who were in some way primed to respond to that signal. Moreover, we have a long-standing (and unjustified, even harmful) prejudice against the echo that regards it as parasitic and empty, mere repetition, derivative. Resonance, on the other hand, evinces something rich and full, a personal connection rather than a mechanical parroting, and is not so hostile to the originality of most of the works that I look at. It recognizes that they are not mere reflectors, but that they have become emitters of sound in their own right, absorbing Calvino's energy and then sending it back out again in a new form.

Five Chapters

Transmedial Resonance follows the path of sound, emanating outward from its source (in Italy) to an expanding and resonant space that is transmedial and transnational. After Calvino's untimely death in 1985, a negative assessment of his work emerged in Italy, coalescing in the Italian literary magazine *Wimbledon* putting Calvino "on trial" in June 1990, as both Botta and Baldi have argued.[26] The critics in that magazine reached the verdict that Calvino's work after he resigned from the Italian Communist Party and moved to Paris in the 1960s was inferior, false, and even "poisonous." This emerging view in Italy of Calvino as a gifted stylist but escapist and politically problematic was then solidified in two monographs at the end of the 1990s, Carla Benedetti's polemical *Pasolini contro Calvino* (1998) and the main focus of our starting point, Silvio Perrella's *Calvino* (1999). This first chapter, "Calvino's Voice: Stutter, Falsetto, Laughter," is unlike all the other chapters in the book—rather than looking at resonant art formed in response to Calvino, I look at Calvino's *voice*: His authorial voice was playful, but his actual voice as a speaker was remarkably reticent and quiet. Perrella argues, however, that something is *wrong* with Calvino's voice, famously claiming that Calvino "writes in falsetto"—a claim that he makes literal in the RAI podcast (technically state-sponsored) by having an older woman speak as Calvino's authorial voice. On the surface, this is once again about Calvino's "failure" to write acceptably realist, politically committed prose in a turn toward the fantastic and artificial (the slightly false, or *falsetto*). I try to show, however, that this claim functions to imply that Calvino's authorial voice is improperly masculine, an accusation rooted in an actual vocal dysphonia: Calvino was a lifelong stutterer, a disability that in the past was erroneously associated with male weakness and immaturity, especially "undeveloped" sexuality. And a surprisingly frequent assertion in Calvino studies is that Calvino—or at least his writing—was sexually timid, "frigid" or "virginal," descriptions not rooted in any evidence, biographical or literary. In an article looking at Calvino's authorial image, Baldi asserts that Calvino's "racconti e romanzi sono definiti come asessuali" (stories and novels are defined as asexual), and that sexuality is severely underexplored in criticism.[27] I hope it will be less underexplored after this book. As I do in each chapter, I suggest that Perrella's claim that Calvino's authorial voice is immature, not fully masculine, problematic in so many ways, is already a kind of resonance that adds something. It queers the pitch of Calvino's voice, quite literally grafting a female voice onto the authorial body in Perrella's podcast to make the falsetto real. Perrella clearly means his claim about the falsetto voice as a critique, but it still acknowledges that there is something profoundly sexual and corporeal about Calvino, something that might be best expressed in a different vocal mannerism that underscores a flirtatious irony and playfulness, visible over and over again in the actual examples we have of Calvino's voice that I end with here: his constant, self-deprecating laughter.

Of the various texts by Calvino that have found second lives, none has resonated more than his 1972 novel *Invisible Cities*. Even so, Chris Cerrone's Pulitzer-nominated 2013 *Invisible Cities* "opera for headphones" stands out, and is the focus of chapter 2, "An Echo-Logical Opera (in Headphones)." This chapter examines Philippe Lacoue-Labarthe's notion of "catacoustics," which tries to think about influence and formation not through an Oedipal mirror, but through echo and reverberation—the voices we unconsciously adopt that shape us. Chapter 2 analyzes how Cerrone's opera works to think about the echo as inextricable from space (echoes encode information about the size, layout and even material of the space that makes them). This fabric of "soundspace" is elaborated not only within the musical material (which uses the echo as a motif), but also in the careful manipulation of actual reverberation in listeners' headphones when the opera was performed (performers and spectators were all connected through wireless headphones and mics). Musicologist Nina Sun Eidsheim provocatively described this manipulation of space in Cerrone's opera as a way of forcing listeners to confront two simultaneous acoustic worlds, the real acoustic space of the opera, staged in LA's Union Station, and the manipulated acoustic space of the headphones. In this chapter I extend this idea not only to think about acoustic space, but to the ways that Cerrone's opera reverberates with Calvino's thinking about sound and physical, urban space—literally political space (*polis*, the origin of the word "politics," is the ancient Greek word for city). Ultimately, I think we can extend this thinking about space through sound even further, however, to the ecological, a form of reading I call (may the reader forgive me) the "echo-logical." In short, the resonant art that responds to Calvino showcases his continuing (and indeed, expanding) political value, especially in his work dedicated to the space of the *polis* and its impact on the space around it.

In *Un ottimista in America* (An optimist in America, the diary of the year he spent in the United States, 1959–60), Calvino claimed that jazz, particularly the "cool jazz" of that era, has a unique, positive capacity to think through modern cultural and political dilemmas without "crystallizing" into a static and unproductive image. Jazz allows us a different way to hear Calvino: playful, improvisational, and sensual. Chapter 3, "A

Jazz *Cosmicomics*," analyzes Lisa Mezzacappa's 2020 jazz suite of Calvino's *Cosmicomics* and also reflects more broadly on the role of chance and improvisation in compositions both musical and literary. Through a close analysis of Mezzacappa's "The Form of Space," I contend that her musical approach encourages us to hear Calvino's story as a critique of the purely rational, visual, and geometric. The music instead gestures toward a subject who is neurotic, perverse, and unpredictable. The improvisational nature of jazz and the geometry of spacetime both indicate that the supposedly rational and composed subject might swerve out of the predictable straight line—the "clinamen" or swerve in Lucretius's *De rerum natura*, a text that Calvino greatly valued—into surprising new territory that is boisterous, risky, and remarkably open. This reading finds substantial confirmation not only in Mezzacappa's take on "All at One Point," set before the Big Bang and the creation of the universe, but also in a broader look at some of the surprisingly perverse scenarios in Calvino's fictions. Those scenarios also resonate strongly with Perrella's depiction of Calvino's unstable and indeterminate gender in chapter 1.

Fittingly for a study of cultural reverberation, chapter 4 traces some of this cultural resonance back to its point of origin. "Desires and Fears: *Silent City*," analyzes a 2019 "community opera" staged in Matera in Italy's southern region of Basilicata. Matera is one of the oldest human habitations on Earth, but amid Italy's modernizing "economic miracle" of the 1950s, the traditional inhabitants of the old city, called the Sassi, were labeled the "vergogna d'Italia" (shame of Italy) and forcibly relocated to modern public housing. Although the Sassi were gradually repopulated (and in fact have become an upscale tourist magnet in the last twenty years), the experience is still regarded as a collective trauma that the community decided to address. L'Albero (The Tree), a women's theater group from Matera, decided that a work that would address the community's traumatic past would need to be a collective effort, one that would privilege those who directly remembered the forced resettlement (the elderly) as well as those who were so young as to have lost any sense of the historical event (the children). The resulting opera, *Silent City*, does not adapt a Calvino story or novel, but draws on the larger frame of the transnational and transmedial Calvino I have described earlier in the book, a resonant Calvino (and its title is certain to recall *Invisible Cities*). This Calvino is attuned to local history, and decidedly political—"political in form rather than in the content," as Vania Cauzillo, one of the opera's organizers, says. Instead, the collective authorship of the opera by the community of Matera was organized through what I call here "city thinking," the toolbox of European theorists we automatically use when thinking about cities:

Flaubert, Benjamin, Debord, Perec, and others. The centerpiece for that "city thinking" in *Silent City* was Calvino's often-cited phrase, "cities, like dreams, are made of desires and fears." A careful attention to the context of that phrase, however, indicates that the opera is trying to articulate something unspeakable: the tragic and ongoing devaluation of Southern Italian life by the Italian state. It is no accident that the opera's music was written by a composer best known for treating children who are victims of state-sponsored violence with music therapy—nor that the destruction of old Matera in the opera takes place offstage, and during the wordless segment of pure "electroacoustic" noise, as a truth that cannot be openly or consciously acknowledged.

Finally, in many ways dance would appear to represent the greatest challenge for a received image of Calvino as purely visual, cerebral, apolitical, and ascetic. Since John Martin's *The Modern Dance* (1935), dance's power has been understood as relying on its capacity to produce "kinesthetic sympathy," the way we automatically and unconsciously imagine our own bodies moving in sync with the dancer, binding the dance's narrative to a feeling that is both emotional and corporeal. In the last chapter, "Dancing About Architecture," I examine how Ashwini Ramaswamy's 2023 large-scale and multimedia dance suite of *Invisible Cities* dramatizes what is perhaps the novel's central political issue: how bodies can live together. Dance offers an answer to that question, finding a corporeal synchrony in the acoustic element of dance—its rhythm. Drawing on Calvino's "hyperformalism" in *Invisible Cities*, Ramaswamy weaves together dancers and dance styles that showcase how bodies and bodily movement can be different (her dancers include Indian Americans, Israelis, African Americans, and Asian Americans) and yet still find ways to be equivalent while not the same, coordinated by the formal grid of rhythm but telling individual stories and histories. To take just one example, an early part of the work is performed by breaker "MN Joe" Tran, who uses Calvino's abstract reflection on travel and foreignness ("the foreignness of what you no longer are or no longer possess lies in wait for you in foreign, unpossessed places") to fuel a dance that viscerally communicates the invisible suffering and endless labor of Tran's immigrant father, a refugee from Vietnam. This is perhaps the ideal example of a resonant response to Calvino that once again is emotional, affective, political and profoundly corporeal; it is genuine kinesthetic sympathy in the most literal sense of "shared suffering" (*syn+pathos*). I argue that this is equally true of Ramaswamy's own section of the dance, a Bharatanatyam celebration of a harmony with the cosmos, which is also the capacity of bodies to share space in harmony, a modeling of kinesthetic sympathy that brings together a space on stage that is both cosmic (the dancers are retelling the Hindu story of creation) and political. The dancers model how bodies might exist in harmony with each other as well as celestial ideals, a co-existence that emerges from our ability to move our bodies in synchrony to a rhythmic pulse. Finally, the dance's finale works to replicate the resonant lesson of Calvino's most important work, "give them space," on three levels: visually (a shift from the city to an unbounded space of nature), musically (a sonic space that offers an ambiguous music that permits two different ways of hearing the piece, and that ultimately moves from music to the sounds of nature), and kinesthetically (the chaotic movement of the dancers suddenly resolves in an open circle, a boundary of pure form, coordinated once again by rhythm).

Justifications, Stakes, Apologias

There are, of course, quite literally hundreds of other texts that I could have focused on, amazing works of music by numerous composers, from avant-garde classical to electronic dance music and jazz. I might easily have included Jevan Chowdhury's incredible, kinetic *Moving Cities*, films that feature dancers performing across a variety of cities. So why the five that I focus on: Perrella's claim that Calvino writes in falsetto; Cerrone's *Invisible Cities* opera; Mezzacappa's jazz *Cosmicomics*; Matera's "community opera" of *Silent City*; and Ramaswamy's *Invisible Cities* dance? They really resonated with me, of course, but I think there are reasons to think that these works resonated more broadly. (This is one of the potential problems with the concept of resonance, something that Calvino might say "requires constant vigilance"—if resonance is, as I suggested above, something unique to the individual, it might also be resistant to analysis, an enigmatic question of personal taste.) I chose these acoustic pieces and not others because they all have a resonance that went well beyond the local or the individual. Perrella's book on Calvino was just reissued in a third edition in Italy, Cerrone's opera was nominated for a Pulitzer, Mezzacappa's album was featured on NPR, *Silent City* was Matera's response to being selected as the European capital of culture in 2019, and Ramaswamy's dance work has been featured in the *New York Times*. In short, they all had some kind of larger resonance that clearly goes beyond just the individual.

I suggested that one of the possible drawbacks to the idea of resonance would be to treat it as a personal response that is purely idiosyncratic and hence not susceptible to analysis. The works of art that I analyze in *Transmedial Resonance* were indeed personally significant for me, but in a rather different way, one that has to do with another turn to the outside rather than the inside: Chris Cerrone, Lisa Mezzacappa, the entire Ramaswamy family and members of the dance troupe, and many of the major figures in Matera's *Silent City* (Vania Cauzillo, Andrea Ciommiento, and Ubah Cristina Ali Farah) were generous with their time and thinking in response to what I was working on. In several instances, they were also generous with the larger UCLA community of scholars and students about how their engagement with Calvino had translated into creative works. I say this not just as an acknowledgment, but to point out that this is yet another way that resonance turns to the outside, finds and fills up space, now of an extended audience. I didn't plan the book this way, but in fact each chapter also turns progressively more and more toward the *performing* arts, especially in their collective form, starting with the introspective work of a literary critic, then to a single composer, then to a jazz sextet, before moving to an opera written by an entire community and performed for that same community, and ending with a large-scale, multimedia ensemble dance piece.

Transmedial Resonance draws on a number of different kinds of thinking (gender studies, ecocriticism, psychoanalysis), but it is largely positioned at the intersection of a very old and well-defined field with a clear sense of itself as a discipline—literary studies—and sound studies, which is by contrast a loose coalition of many disciplines united primarily by, in Jonathan Sterne's words, an "orienting curiosity, a figural practice that reaches into fields of sonic knowledge and practice, and blends them with other questions, problems, fields, spaces, and histories."[28] Sterne stresses the "partiality" (4) of sound studies, by which he means it is a field that brings together partial understandings from multiple disciplines in order to find new knowledge or new approaches. Such a partiality runs certain kinds of risks, but readers open to an approach that combines multiple forms of partial knowledge will find that an engagement with acoustics, classical music, jazz, dance, and opera on the one side, and literature on the other, can shed light on all of them. In turn, I have tried to remain open to readers who will also necessarily have partial knowledge and expertise in these many areas. I sometimes include brief written musical scores, for example, but generally in ways that do not require a reader who can read music. In writing a work that combines sound studies, literary criticism, and theories of influence, I am inevitably speaking to a broad coalition of scholars who will almost certainly find one or more (or even all) of these chapters to be new territory, as several of them were for me. In other words, I am hoping that this book will take both me and its readers slightly outside our collective comfort zones—another way that it gestures to "more outside than inside." The recompense, the light shed on a number of cultural practices, might be particularly strong for the largest of the questions that interest me here: how we might understand the question of cultural "influence" in a different way, as a resonance that moves across both national and disciplinary boundaries.

Within sound studies, I am primarily interested in music in this study, but even within this arena, each chapter has a quite different focus, from the gendered politics of the stutterer as well as the high-pitched male singing voice (chapter 1) to the way that rhythmic entrainment can bring bodily movement in dance into harmony, allowing our busy bodies to feel both musically and kinesthetically how we might coexist (chapter 5). Obviously, if there is a nonpartial center to *Transmedial Resonance*, it is Calvino. Even so, this is not precisely a monograph on Calvino, nor is it a study of how Calvino inspired a group of artists. I might recall my fourth mantra here—"the resonance is the source"—and insist that the analysis and understanding has to flow both ways: how Calvino told stories and suggested ideas that were resonant with artists in other fields, but also how the art those artists produced helps us understand what Calvino was saying in the first place. We only ever hear a sound in a space ("sound is space"), and every space we hear in has some degree of reverberation that serves as a kind of acoustic signature.

Such spaces include the cultural and intellectual space in which this book was articulated, and I would be remiss if I gave the impression that I am the only scholar to have done this kind of work before. One might look to Kata Gellen's 2019 *Kafka and Noise: The Discovery of Cinematic Sound in Literary Modernism* as emblematic of a growing interest in the intersection of global literary figures and sound cultures. Julie Napolin's 2020 *The Fact of Resonance* in many ways paved the way for my project here, not only for thinking about resonance as a "form, content and method" that is "fundamentally relational" (5), but also for making clear that the pairing of sound studies and literature was a surprisingly under-explored terrain. Gellen also contends that sound studies has "shown little interest in" (7) and "largely ignored" (8) literature.[29] Napolin's work, like Gellen's, is adept at analyzing both sound *in* literature and the way that literature uses and responds to technologies of sound, including the metaphorical opportunities those technologies afford. Napolin studies, in other words, the larger *acoustic* character of literature, the way it is constituted of echoes, repetitions, voices, noises, and so on—the subtitle of her book is *Modernist Acoustics and Narrative Form*.[30] Much of the work on literature and sound has looked to see how acoustic technologies (in the broadest sense) helped to structure modernist narratives, but this text doesn't look at sonic structures or sounds *in* Calvino (although that would no doubt repay the effort) so much as it looks more outside than inside, at Calvino in the acoustic world. It aims to learn, among other things, how to read literature *through* music, and not just read the music that is depicted in literature.

I'm also not the first to notice that Calvino has played a uniquely resonant role in other fields. Letizia Modena's 2011 *Italo Calvino's Architecture of Lightness* highlighted the deep relationship between Calvino and architectural thinking, although more architecture's influence on Calvino than the reverse. Happily, Benjamin Linder's *"Invisible Cities" and the Urban Imagination* (2022) shows some of that other side, charting how "scholars of cities—geographers, urban planners, anthropologists/sociologists, architects, etc.—have found inspiration and critical insight in the pages of *Invisible Cities*" (13), which gives Calvino's novel "iconic status among literary theorists and geographers alike" (2). Kyle Gillette's *The Invisible City: Travel, Attention, and Performance* (2020) studies the yearly pilgrimages inspired by *Invisible Cities* that are made by the Teatro Potlach theater group, and this book attempts to amplify that interest in Calvino and the performing arts. Most recently (2023), Elio Baldi and Cecilia Schwartz have produced a fascinating edited volume titled *Circulation, Translation and Reception Across Borders: Italo Calvino's "Invisible Cities" Around the World*, which looks at the reception of *Invisible Cities* around the world, almost entirely through its translation, including in Africa, the USSR, China, and Brazil, although it deliberately avoids the United States.

Transmedial Resonance takes a complementary approach to this recent scholarship, arguing that resonance is a more dynamic and ultimately more productive model for how to think about cultural influence more broadly, and that Calvino is simply exemplary for how an artist's influence became a deep part of the culture. Resonance as a concept also frees us to think in both directions, both how the past shaped the present, and how the present informs that same past: not only about how Calvino has inspired geographers, architects and playwrights, but also about what the resulting works of art and study might reveal about what those artists and scholars heard—and what, in turn, we might hear in them. As filmmaker Duccio Chiarini remarks in the epigraph to this introduction, Calvino's real legacy is to be found in the minds of those he has inspired: readers, architects, musicians, dancers, and many more.

1 /   Calvino's Voice: Stutter, Falsetto, Laughter

However elegant the high male voice has sounded, it has often been heard in counterpart with a quiet but discordant ground bass. The elements of this insidious lower part may vary—notes of homosexuality, effeminacy and castration can all be heard on occasion—but the repeated theme of sexual prejudice is always recognisable. In short, the accompaniment of grumbling voices avers that the male falsettist is not a true man.

—SIMON RAVENS

I am sitting in a room

I begin by telling a story that (at first glance) has nothing to do with Calvino at all. The story is one of the founding mythologies, although completely true, of contemporary classical music, almost as well known to everyone who works on modern music as the riots that followed the debut performance of Stravinsky's *Rite of Spring* or the concept behind John Cage's *4'33"*, but directly connected to the question of resonance. In 1969, the composer Alvin Lucier recorded himself speaking the following text:

> I am sitting in a room different from the one you are in now. I am recording the sound of my speaking voice and I am going to play it back into the room again and again until the resonant frequencies of the room reinforce themselves so that any semblance of my speech, with perhaps the exception of rhythm, is destroyed. What you will hear, then, are the natural resonant frequencies of the room articulated by speech. I regard this activity not so much as a demonstration of a physical fact, but more as a way to smooth out any irregularities my speech might have.

Lucier then did exactly as he said he would: He recorded himself speaking the text, then recorded himself playing back that recording, then recorded himself playing back the recording of that recording, and again and again, until the effect of intelligible speech was completely lost. As you might imagine, noise becomes more and more of an issue as the recording is rerecorded dozens or hundreds of times. Just like the feedback that can happen during performances at live venues, however, the character of this noise is directly related to the acoustic characteristics of the room. What gets magnified is the sound of recording *in a particular space* (the Electronic Music Studio at Brandeis initially, later Lucier's own apartment). Even starting with the exact same recording, the eventual result will be the dissolution of comprehensible speech into the humming song produced by the resonant frequencies of the room you are in. As Lucier recorded and rerecorded his recordings and rerecordings, the sound that takes over is the sound of the resonant space of the room itself, and so, the piece is somewhat different in every different space. The iterative compositional process Lucier chose causes that noise to be emphasized first, and eventually to dominate completely what the listener hears. The process is slow: The full development from an initial clear recording to the end can run from 15 minutes to 45 minutes or longer. By one-third of the way in (sometimes much sooner), however, it becomes hard to understand what the voice is saying; a little further, and there is nothing resembling comprehensible speech, but a great deal of melodic and harmonic richness. The piece manages to be beautiful and somewhat disturbing at the same time.

It's not a surprise, then, that Lucier's composition holds a canonical position in discussions of modern classical music, and is often cited in connection to other significant works that cover similar territory both earlier—Steve Reich's pioneering tape loop pieces like *It's Gonna Rain* (1965)—and much later—William Basinski's *Disintegration Loops* (2002–3), which recorded him playing music loops recorded on aged magnetic tapes over and over again as they slowly disintegrated and eventually left behind just silence. Lucier's piece is compelling. It makes clear the composer's compositional process and—like so much avant-garde minimalism in late twentieth-century music—demonstrates in an intuitive, even visceral, way how extremely simple processes can lead to very complex results, while very complex initial signals can become shockingly simple. Lucier's speech eventually becomes a handful of harmonically rich pure tones that one would never guess began their lives as speech, with only some faint hint of rhythm attached.

There are many ways that this avant-garde composition speaks to the project in this book, from the ways that Lucier's composition forces the listener to "hear space" in the space of the room used for recording (which determines the resonant frequencies that eventually engulf the recording) to the sense that echoes, reverberations, and acoustic repetitions hold a kind of interpretive secret for understanding texts of the present era. But the feature of Lucier's *I Am Sitting in a Room* that interests me here is none of these, but something unusual about the text he recites. In that text, Lucier more or less explicitly disavows most of the qualities of *I Am Sitting in a Room* that critics gravitated to over the last half century: He is absolutely explicit that we should *not* be concentrating on the fascinating psychoacoustics of resonance ("not so much as a demonstration of a physical fact"), nor the innovative compositional process he has invented. Instead, he says that we should understand *I Am Sitting in a Room* as a demonstration of "a way to smooth out any irregularities my speech might have." Lucier is talking not about an abstract compositional process (typical of minimalism) nor about the complexities of sound that are becoming visible to the composer through modern electronic analysis (spectralism), but something personal about his speech.

Lucier was a lifelong stutterer, although he performed this piece so many times live that he ironically—like most stutterers when chanting or singing—eventually lost his stutter when performing the piece. In older recordings of the piece (say, 1990), Lucier audibly stutters on "the exception of r-r-r-r-rhythm," he holds the *n* of "not so much a demonstration" a little too long, and a clearly skipping "s-s-s-s-smooth out" comes at the end. These stutters sound already almost rehearsed by 1990, however: stuttering on purpose so as to not stutter by accident. By the 2017 recording, however, not only does Lucier not stutter, but he makes a significant change to the text as well: "I am sitting in a room—the *same* one you are in now." The change is a shift toward a more normative subjectivity, away from the alienation of stuttering subjectivity ("a room different from the one you are in now"), an alienation that was obliterated by the repeated overlay of the resonance of the room, one that eventually obliterates any trace of nonnormative speech. In short, already in the original version of *I Am Sitting in a Room*, Lucier contends that conceptual art, or process-oriented compositional techniques, might respond just as much to the artist's personal concerns about not performing up to standard, especially his personal concern about feeling vocally inadequate.

The Voice Can Lie

In *For More Than One Voice*, the philosopher Adriana Cavarero reminds us that the voice is an expression of the individual subject's unique existence. Her idea is that before you hear what I have to say, you will have heard the sound of my voice, a testament to a body and a life. Historically, she observes, we have always prioritized political *speech*—abstract content, material that could be quoted in a newspaper or summarized without any substantial loss—over the *voice*. The voice, however, also communicates something, even if it is not semantic content: I exist. Cavarero's opening salvo in the book is a citation from Calvino that she returns to again and again throughout the text. It is from his short story about hearing, called "A King Listens" ("Un re in ascolto"), which was also turned into an opera of the same name by Luciano Berio. Here is the passage from Calvino that Cavarero opens with and returns to throughout the book:

> Una voce significa questo: c'è una persona viva, gola, torace, senti-menti, che spinge nell'aria questa voce diversa da tutte le altre voci. Una voce mette in gioco l'ugola, la saliva, l'infanzia, la patina della vita vissuta, le intenzioni della mente, il piacere di dare una propria forma alle onde sonore. Ciò che ti attira è il piacere che questa voce mette nell'esistere. (3:165)[1]

> A voice means this: there is a living person, throat, thorax, feelings, who pushes into the air this voice so different from all other voices. A voice that puts into play their uvula, saliva, childhood, the patina of the life they've led, the intentions in their mind, the pleasure of giving a shape of their own to sound waves. What attracts you is the plea-sure this voice puts into existing.[2]

Cavarero makes a beautiful argument over the course of the book about a new and different kind of politics that would prioritize this voice as a unique expression of an individual existence, with its distinctive body and experiences, an argument that I am strongly sympathetic to—but there is an issue. Cavarero speaks as if the voice were pure sound (*phone*), without any semantic element (*logos*). That is, she argues that the voice simply *is* without (or at least, before) *meaning* something, and so it could provide a vocal alternative to the politics of speech that we have always had. The argument is grounded on the notion that the voice is natural, in-nate, and corporeal, the spontaneous and unmediated expression of one's existence. The uvula, thorax, and saliva do not lie because lies can only take place within the field of semantics, of meaning. I can lie by saying that I am a twenty-year-old 6'6" smoker from Texas, but I will still have the voice of an average-sized, middle-aged Californian who's never taken a puff. Hence, for Cavarero, my words can lie, but my *voice* cannot.

Mladen Dolar very nicely summarizes the problem with this line of thinking, however, in *A Voice and Nothing More* (2006). He deduces, quite reasonably, that the voice is precisely what "*does not contribute to making sense*" (15, original emphasis), and so far, he is in agreement with Cavarero. The voice is what is *not* a signifier, but rather what the signifier uses as its support and will eliminate once it is no longer needed. In a memorable, and rather humorous, turn, he calls the voice "the excrement of the signifier" (20)—that is, an embarrassing piece that the signifier leaves behind as quickly as it can, while it goes off and gets busy making meaning (logos). As Dolar goes on to show over the next few pages, however, there is virtually no apparently "natural" or "merely physiological" aspect of the voice that does *not* signify in some way: accent, intonation, timbre, babbling, laughter, coughing, yelling, and so forth. All of them are used as vocal signifiers, all of them can be and are cultivated, manipulated, and shaped by the speaking subject in order to produce meaning.[3] Building on Dolar's work, Martha Feldman shows how even failures of the voice, such as the crack when straining for a note slightly out of your natural range, also carry meaning, and are artfully deployed by singers to show overwhelming emotion, part of "the arsenal of extraordinary singing."[4] The apparently natural, nonsemantic voice vanishes as soon as we look for it, flushed away (let's retain, for now, this curious connection between the voice and excrement, since it will return later in this chapter).

Leaving aside the musings of high theory, even everyday experience suggests that the voice is not always a spontaneous and natural expression of the unique individual, and perhaps never fully so. We've probably all met that occasional person whose natural voice somehow doesn't "fit" with their personality or their body (or the reverse experience, where we know someone's voice quite well, but are taken aback when we meet them in person by the body that produces it). One might think of heavyweight boxing champion Mike Tyson's surprisingly high-pitched voice (Karmen MacKendrick calls it "exemplary" of a voice that does not seem to match its body),[5] or the entire plot of *Singin' in the Rain*, which hinges on the vocal mismatch between Lina Lamont's onscreen persona in silent cinema (glamorous, elegant, a paragon of feminine refinement) and her actual voice (grating, aggressive, uncouth) as the era of sound cinema dawns. Such mismatches indicate that, although waves of air pressure caused by a falling tree certainly exist, the proverbial tree *does not make a sound* unless a *person*—with all of their received ideas about race, class, gender, "normal" bodies, and "normal" voices—is there to hear it. Sound happens in our minds, which process everything within a social field.

As Nina Sun Eidsheim has pointed out in *The Race of Sound*, this is a potentially serious problem for Cavarero's desire to have us hear the existence of a unique speaking subject before we hear what they say.[6] Voices in fact already have semantic content attached to them *as voices*, and as proof that the content is semantic, the content may or may not be true. Eidsheim calls this the "myth of voice as essence" (29), and argues instead that the voice is "produced . . . heard and reproduced . . . through social relationships" (27). This is clearest in the ways the *voice*—not speech, but the voice—itself contains political or sociological content, so that we say to ourselves on hearing a voice, "This is the voice of a Black man, a middle-class white woman, a Latina, a gay man, a little girl . . ." In short, we *hear* within logos, which means all sound is at least partially semantic. If the voice itself is semantic, at least once it is heard, not only can it be misunderstood, but it can lie. The *phone* can be phony.

We might also meet people and have the impression, not that there is a mismatch between voice and body, but that there is something *deliberately* false about the voice, something deceptive. An affectation? An accent they are putting on? Perhaps someone is trying to conceal a less desirable regional accent, or emulate a more desirable one, or someone is affecting an exaggerated pronunciation of foreign language terms to showcase their knowledge. The slightly false note doesn't reveal the truth about the person, as Lina Lamont's voice does, but rather feels like artifice that conceals it. Although there is plenty to say about the voice and class, or race (see Eidsheim), the questions of artifice and the voice are particularly fraught when it comes to gender. The gendered voice is constantly policed and surveilled (uniquely so for trans people, of course), but every voice is capable of a "slip," a failure to give the correct performance, even when we are not quite certain what the role entails or whether we even want to be performing it.

Dolar notes in a long historical review that starts with Plato and runs through the Middle Ages that there is a persistent gendered anxiety about the separation of the voice from meaning, namely that "as soon as it departs from its textual anchorage, the voice becomes senseless and threatening. . . . The voice beyond sense is self-evidently equated with femininity" (43). Elizabeth Holmes, the former CEO of Theranos who was accused of defrauding investors, speaks in a surprisingly low, tenor voice that was widely viewed as unnatural, yet another fraud or perhaps a psychological disturbance, perhaps part of her purported desire to embody her management idol, Steve Jobs. It is no accident that this "deceptive" potential of the voice is consistently related to gender. It is a commonplace in sociolinguistics that young women are more likely to adopt new speech habits, including vocal affectations, and that they are also more likely to be criticized for such behavior—"uptalk" and "vocal fry," for example, are two contemporary "trendy" ways of talking that are predominantly associated with American women, ways that belie the notion that the voice is always or automatically spontaneous and authentic.[7] As one recognizes that, like all sounds, the voice is only ever heard *within* a social and semantic field, it also becomes clear that the social pressures that might make a person, consciously or unconsciously, adopt a different register or vocal mannerism are clearly part of what Calvino calls "la patina della vita vissuta" (the patina of the life they've lived). The notion of a "true voice" (and hence a "false voice" as well) begins to recede out of sight: My voice *feels* like the inimitable marker of me, emerging spontaneously from my body and my existence. And yet as soon as I speak, my voice carries all kinds of semantic information that a listener would likely infer based on my voice and speech. All of that is the "patina of my lived life," but all those traits are also semantic codes that can be imitated, parodied, recognized—and hence, can also be counterfeited and otherwise *performed*, what Judith Butler so famously called "a repeated stylization of the body."[8] Even when my voice testifies to who I really am, isn't it still just as much a performance?

Those semantic codes include received notions about many different categories, but perhaps none of them elicits as much concern or as strong a reaction as do gendered norms of speech, and those gendered norms are surprisingly one-sided. Women and men who speak with vocal mannerisms that are seen as "typically" female (uptalk, high-pitched, melodious or with exaggerated intonation, breathy or "thin" voices, quiet) are likely to be mocked or critiqued for it; both sexes are praised for avoiding overly "feminine" voices, but only women who have exaggeratedly male voice patterns (not men) are critiqued for it—the suggestion being that there is something feminine about vocal deception.[9] So while there is a higher degree of scrutiny and policing associated with the female voice, male voices are also policed to conform to a (masculine) vocal ideal, lest they too turn out to have a deceptive, feminine voice.

Calvino's Stutter

Calvino very famously thought there was something about his own authorial voice that was a little bit slippery and hard to pin down. In the novel *If on a winter's night a traveler*, when you, the Reader of the novel, get ready to recognize his voice:

> Ti prepari a riconoscere l'inconfondibile accento dell'autore [Calvino]. No. Non lo riconosci affatto. Ma, a pensarci bene, chi ha mai detto che questo autore ha un accento inconfondibile? Anzi, si sa che è un autore che cambia molto da libro a libro. E proprio in questi cambiamenti si riconosce che è lui. (2:619)

> You get ready to recognize the author's [Calvino's] unmistakable accent. No. You don't recognize it at all. But, thinking about it carefully,

who ever said that this author has an unmistakable accent? In fact, everyone knows he's an author who changes a good deal from book to book. And precisely in these changes you can tell that it's him.

Calvino's *actual* (rather than authorial) voice is readily available to us in numerous recorded interviews (there are at least a dozen at any given time on YouTube alone), and in multiple languages: Calvino gave interviews in French, English, Spanish and, of course, Italian. He speaks in a moderately low baritone that is perhaps a bit throaty (at times, slightly gravelly) and that grows a little nasal (and more throaty) as he gets older. He has one fairly distinctive vocal quality, however, which is more or less noticeable in different interviews: He stutters.

After Calvino's death, the Italian writer Natalia Ginzburg recalled that Calvino had stuttered quite badly as a young man when she first met him, then much less as he got older and learned various ways to compensate for it.[10] The older Calvino uses a great deal of filler sounds as he is speaking, and often repeats the first word of a sentence or phrase again and again before moving on. In fact, he shows all of the typical traits of stuttering compensation: syllable repetition; what are called "fixed postures," such as a propensity for prolonged noises indicating thinking ("hmmm-mmmmm"); and "superfluous behaviors," such as the unusually frequent (and repeated) use of filler sounds like "uh," or "ah." At times, the stutter becomes quite evident, as in a 1974 interview with Franco Maria Ricci and Valerio Riva. Discussing the fantastic in literature, Calvino says (and here I transcribe phonetically for the sound, not for the content):

> . . .si, si, si, si cerca di, di scoprire che cosa c'è sotto de, dei, dei fatti. E, e, eh, probabilmente il tipo di lettura della letteratura fantastica ci, eh, eh, ci dà questo, uh, uh, que, que, uh, uh, questo mo—uh, questo modello di, di, di conoscenza, una conoscenza da interpretare.

> . . .you, you, you, you try to, to discover what's behind suh–, some, some facts. And, and, uh, probably the kind of reading of fantastic literature guh–, uh, uh, gives us this, uh, uh, the, the, this mm–, uh, this model of, of knowledge, a knowledge we must interpret.[11]

Calvino did not talk about his stutter often, but he was upfront about it when he did. In at least one interview (in English, from 1984, included in Damian Pettigrew's documentary about Calvino, *Dans la peau d'Italo Calvino* [In Calvino's skin]) the author said:

> For me to, to, to, to talk—I, I had always problems, uh, with speech. Not, uh [smiling ironically], not only in a foreign language; also in

my own, uh, language. And so, uh, problem of, uh, the problem of speech and of silence is a. . . is a. . . is a problem. I, I, I always need to. . . um, to write, uh. . . to be sure to express myself, uh, completely.

Like many stutterers, Calvino often preferred to stay silent, was even in some sense known for it. Ernesto Ferrero's *Italo* states the author's "mutism" was "leggendario a scuola e con gli amici" (25, legendary at school and among his friends). There is a famous story that, at a 1984 conference in Seville, Calvino's wife Chichita went to talk to the blind Argentinian writer Jorge Luis Borges. After she chatted with him for a while, she mentioned that Calvino was with her, and Borges replied, "I know. I recognized him from the silence."[12] Calvino sometimes even understood his difficulty with speaking as a kind of a virtue, albeit in a complicated way. In one autobiographical passage, he discusses why he can only write in Italian (although strictly speaking, he wrote and published some essays in French as well):

> Ciò che conta è il rapporto nevrotico che si ha con la lingua, e io posso averlo soltanto con la lingua italiana. . . . Per dirla tutta, ho difficoltà di parola e mi esprimo male in tutte le lingue. Balbetto anche nella mia lingua madre. . . . È una battaglia con la lingua, nella quale io devo conoscere alla perfezione il potenziale delle forze nemiche, coglierlo a colpo d'occhio, e questo sono in grado di farlo solo con l'italiano. (*Sono nato in America*, 645)

> What counts is the neurotic relationship that you have with language, and I can only have it with the Italian language. . . To be completely honest, I have trouble speaking and express myself poorly in every language. I stutter even in my mother tongue. . . . It's a battle with language, one in which I must know perfectly the potential of the enemy forces, seize it in the blink of an eye, and I am capable of doing this only in Italian.

Stuttering is largely a male phenomenon, both in reality (some 80 percent of stutterers are male), but even more so in literary and audiovisual representations of stammering.[13] Could Calvino's stutter and disfluency have made his authorial voice somehow less commanding and masculine, especially among critics who knew him and had seen him speak? This certainly seems possible: Jeffrey K. Johnson offers a review of stuttering in literature, film, and television, and *all* of the stutterers he discusses in the article are male, and stuttering in almost all of his examples is utilized as a shorthand for weakness and a lack of self-confidence. Sophia Stewart, in an insightful discussion of stuttering, gender, and literature, argues that "most male characters who stutter do so as a sign of arrested development; they are weak, infantile, dull, debilitatingly nervous or shy, and this is the cause of their disfluency. They usually overcome their stuttering through a masculinity-affirming feat or a radical perspective shift." Chris Eagle in *Dysfluencies: On Speech Disorders in Modern Literature* (2018) also offers a thorough account of the history and representation of stuttering as "male weakness," and it is worth looking at his account in some detail, because many twentieth-century accounts of stuttering have a number of common features, and by the end of this chapter, they will be quite familiar.

Eagle contends that from the end of World War I on, there is remarkable consistency in understanding stuttering as belonging to a specific personality type, rather than, say, as a response to shell shock, and that personality is "neurotic, timid, and sexually repressed" (14). The psychosexual model of stuttering was essentially Freudian in character, although Eagle points out that it did not emerge from Freud, but rather from Sándor Ferenczi and others (81) who connected stuttering to a personality type modeled on Freud's "anal retentive" personality, but this time connected to the genitals. Ferenczi actually called it "genital stuttering," and contended that this personality type suffers not only from verbal stuttering but erectile dysfunction and "disturbances of ejaculation" (Eagle, 82). The stutterer's throat and genitals were tight, clutching, unable to dilate and release, just like the anal retentive's sphincter. The model may sound absurd today, but it was very influential for a very long time, and as it diffused through popular culture, it is clear that it retained its sense of masculine sexual inadequacy, at least at an unconscious level. Eagle looks to a number of literary representations of the stutterer that were well known in the middle of the twentieth century, starting with "Billy Budd," and all of the accounts Eagle discusses depict male stutterers as "cripplingly timid, with a childlike or feminized form of weakness that prevents them from mastering their own tongue" (83). It's worth noting already that in the autobiographical passage from earlier, Calvino figures his stutter as a kind of virtue, but he also implicitly connects it to neurosis, saying that what really matters is having a neurotic relationship with language, one that leads him to a mastery of it, albeit one acquired with great difficulty.

It's clear from Marc Shell's *Stutter* that there is also a curious link between stuttering and writing, and even mastery of other languages. Many stutterers, when they begin to anticipate a difficulty in saying a word, not only make use of other words, developing "unusually large vocabularies" (22) as they grow older, but also use alternate languages in contexts where multiple languages are spoken. Shell also notes that writers who stuttered include Lewis Carroll, Margaret Drabble, John Updike, Somerset Maugham, André Bazin, and Henry James. Shell details some other strategies that stutterers use, which include "learning to stutter voluntarily" (27) as a way of gaining mastery and simulating fluency. Several of Calvino's close acquaintances thought that there was often something deliberate in his stuttering, as when the actress Elsa de' Giorgi (Calvino's lover for a time in the 1950s) says that Calvino "gestiva momenti di meditata balbuzie" (would perform moments of premeditated stuttering),[14] and Ginzburg says the same thing. Shell also makes a point virtually everyone who studies stuttering notices: Stutterers do not stutter when singing or chanting (30), and he discusses in detail one very famous stutterer who controlled her stuttering by adopting a high-pitched "breathy singsong" (142) for speaking—Marilyn Monroe. This technique is so effective that, according to Shell, certain kinds of stutterers regularly make use of the "Marilyn Monroe voice" (142) as a way of avoiding the stutter. This last technique, however, indicates that the "unmanly" stutter might have a curious medicine, namely an artificial voice, one that might have somewhat unpredictable gendered consequences.

There are two larger points that I want to bring out here. The first is that there was a fairly widespread understanding throughout most of the twentieth century (often unconscious and filtered through popular consciousness) of the male stutterer as timid, feminine, and sexually blocked. While it should be obvious, it is worth reiterating that, although this psychosexual understanding of stuttering is certainly false, it was nevertheless an influential and pernicious notion, one that permeated Calvino's culture and time—and the mere fact that it is false and absurd doesn't mean that it is not, on some level, still part of our larger cultural imaginary. The second is that stutterers in reality often learn a variety of ways to compensate for their stutter and to simulate fluency: large vocabularies, multilinguistic competence, writing as a means of expression, covering involuntary stuttering with voluntary stuttering, and even, in some cases, adopting the "Marilyn Monroe voice." I argue in this chapter that all of these features relate to Calvino as he has been understood by some of his most influential critics, often in surprising ways, and there is much to learn about the space of his reception and the space in which the resonance of his body of work continues to expand.

In turning to criticism, I am—at least at first glance—heading into territory quite different from that of the rest of this book, which concentrates on musically driven works of art that help us understand the catacoustic space that Calvino's voice has given rise to over the last fifty years or so. That said, criticism is very much part of the afterlife of the voice, not only limiting and shaping the voice's echoes (by claiming that we should understand an author in this or that particular way), but also sustaining and repeating it. And as Francesca Rubini argues (*Italo Calvino nel mondo*, 88, 108), Calvino eventually became understood, especially outside Italy, as the sort of writer people read in a university class—in other words, in the reading world most directly shaped by criticism. That sustaining function certainly prolongs the echo, most importantly in the classroom. Thousands of college students, in the United States alone, will be assigned Calvino every year (whether they all read him is a different question), and certainly one of my hopes in writing this book is to help open up critical awareness of how the "Calvino-space" has expanded and changed.

I also turn to criticism because at least one Italian critic, widely read in Italy, has repeatedly and influentially argued that there *is* something gender nonconforming about Calvino's voice. I am referring to Silvio Perrella, whose book on Calvino (titled simply *Calvino*) came out in 1999. The book was rereleased in an updated edition (an easily affordable paperback) some ten years after its initial publication, and was rereleased again in a third affordable paperback edition in 2023. It contains appendices for students who are in school and blank pages for the notes they might take during class. In short, Perrella's book is highly regarded and widely read (and probably also widely assigned). Moreover, it is more of a work of art than one might expect: *Calvino* received an honorable mention for one of Italy's top literary prizes (the Viareggio), a prize more typically associated with novels. Marco Belpoliti also states on the cover that it is more a work of creative imagination than of traditional literary criticism. Even so, when RAI Tre (the educational and cultural branch of Italian state media) made a podcast about Calvino for their "Wikiradio" project that covers notable cultural figures from around the world, they chose Perrella as the narrator, giving his voice an unusual (and effectively state-sponsored) stature among Calvino critics. In all of these venues, the claim Perrella makes is that Calvino writes in falsetto.

This claim has become widespread in Italian criticism, so much so that it seems to have become part of the background. A recent (2023) volume of essays by Italian linguists about Calvino has a very fine piece by Chiara De Caprio on the linguistic architecture in Calvino's works.[15] She observes his preference for combining and contaminating forms (such as the dialogue) and then says that, in the play of forms and voices in his works, one can discern a "vocazione per l'ibrido e il *falsetto*" (20, vocation for the hybrid and the *falsetto* [original emphasis]). The notion of Calvino as writing in falsetto is so diffuse, then, that not only is it familiar to a linguist, but it is in fact so familiar that De Caprio does not cite Perrella or anyone else for this claim. She also does not explain what a vocation for the falsetto might mean or explain how it might be connected to the notion of hybridity, nor does she ever refer to it again. It is something that one says about Calvino that everyone "just knows." Ferrero, too, describes one of Calvino's unfinished novels, *Il bianco veliero*, using Perrella's terminology—"il linguaggio è tutto un po' in falsetto" (58, the language is all a little bit in falsetto), again without any overt nod to Perrella. Most tellingly, Domenico Scarpa's monumental (over 800 pages) 2023 biography/interpretation of Calvino repeatedly uses Perrella's falsetto to describe Calvino, always as a characteristic or technique that is obvious and well known to the reader: "il suo caratteristico falsetto" (117, his characteristic falsetto), "quel suo falsetto finto-svagato" (233, that fake-dreamy falsetto of his), "il falsetto che ben conosciamo" (494, the falsetto we know so well), and so on. As with De Caprio and Ferrero, there is no explicit reference to Perrella, whose name appears in the acknowledgments, but not in the bibliography. The impression given by these authors is that one can argue about how falsetto Calvino's voice is, or which phrases or works are in falsetto, but *everyone knows* that Calvino writes in falsetto. It is a concept so commonplace it never needs a citation, so obvious it never needs to be defined.

Calvino's Falsetto

According to Perrella, Calvino's genuine and natural writing voice appears only in its pure form very early on (13). He gives as an example of this authentic, non-falsetto voice an emotional letter Calvino wrote to Eugenio Scalfari, his high school friend, in which he recounts his adventures as a partisan guerrilla soldier fighting the Nazis (Calvino was about twenty years old at the time). If you are curious to read this letter written in Calvino's authentic voice, however, you will be disappointed, because it does not exist. Calvino did send the letter to Scalfari, but it was lost in the war, and so Perrella instead imagines in the conditional mood "la voce che avremmo trovata, se [la lettera] non fosse andata perduta" (13, the voice that we *would have* found if the letter hadn't gone missing; my emphasis).[16] Such a letter would have given us the "rarissimo Calvino 'frontale'" (13, most rare, "frontal" Calvino), rather than the "riflesso e innaturale" (13, twisted back and unnatural) falsetto. Readers hoping for a definition of this falsetto, or examples that clearly demonstrate what is and is not a falsetto, will also hope in vain. It is never defined (part of the book's novelistic character), but that doesn't mean that we can't infer some things about it.[17]

To start off with, Perrella says the natural voice is "frontal," presumably meaning direct, without artifice and, in Calvino's case, without playful irony. The falsetto, by contrast, does not proceed in a straight line (it is "riflesso," reflected, but also turned back), it approaches indirectly, and it makes use of artifice, irony, and play, but it can be even more artificial—on the following page, Perrella uses a different but related musical metaphor, arguing that Calvino's writing passes through "una sordina immaginaria: il falsetto" (14, an imaginary mute: the falsetto). A *sordina* (literally, "a little deaf" in Italian, but called a "mute" in English) is a device used on musical instruments that reduces volume but that also changes their timbre, the distinctive quality of sound that makes a flute sound like a flute rather than an oboe or clarinet, even when they are all playing the exact same note.[18] Perrella knows something about music, and the idea of an "imaginary mute" is especially potent: He is not saying that the mute is fictional or unreal, but rather that it literally works by way of the image. What makes Calvino unnatural is his constant recurrence to *images*, a use that in some fashion "artificializes" his voice, changes its timbre, reduces its intensity. In this view, what should have been a natural, honest, and direct voice speaking to us became an image, which in turn mutes and distorts the voice into something unnatural: a falsetto.

Perrella's musical knowledge is even more extensive, in fact, since he also puns on the idea of Calvino's voice as "una voce di testa" (14, a head voice), meaning that it is entirely inside the head (cerebral, detached from reality, solipsistic). In vocal practice, the term "head voice" (in both English and Italian) refers to where a singer primarily feels the resonance inside the body: in the chest, in the throat, or in the head, generally moving upward not only in the body, but also in pitch. It is a synonym for falsetto. We should pay attention to the many valences Perrella's falsetto might have: its musical uses; the etymological suggestion that there is something not truthful about it; the fact that the falsetto is almost exclusively used in music (here writing), not in speech. The falsetto is both like and unlike Calvino's stutter, and I will argue that, for Perrella, the two are related. A spoken disfluency becomes a musical fluency (Marilyn Monroe's breathy singsong), even as direct and honest speech about the real world (the lost letter) becomes a falsetto "head voice" of someone trapped in their own head.

Perrella's contention that Calvino's writing is artificial and divorced from reality fits in with a larger (mostly Italian) narrative about Calvino that I discussed at some length in the introduction. In that narrative, he is a writer who turned away from a promising and politically committed form of writing (his early neorealist novels and stories) to an escapist literature of the fantastic, or even postmodern games, aimed primarily at an international market. Anna Botta has dated this narrative to a 1990 issue of the Italian literary magazine *Wimbledon* that assembled ten Italian critics and put Calvino "on trial" (81), finding his work starting with the *Cosmicomics* (when he moved to Paris) to be inferior, false, or worse. James Butler, writing in the *London Review of Books*, cites Franco Fortini's broadside in that issue of *Wimbledon*, in which Fortini characterized Calvino's "later works as 'deadly, destructive,' the encounter with Oulipo as a 'poisoning,' [and] *Six Memos* as an exercise in banality contrived for idiot Americans. . . . Fortini charged him with involution, with substituting a pallid theoreticism for his *italianità* and with a retreat from history, politics and relevance."[19] Botta contends that this sentiment became widespread in Italy, even among Calvino's admirers, and that Italian critics frequently understand his move to Paris as a "betrayal of his *italianità*" (82, Italianness). Fabio Gambaro, in a book dedicated exclusively to Calvino's Parisian years and their aftermath, is equally unsparing describing the Italian reaction to Calvino's international success (and note the acoustic metaphor he uses): "Naturalmente l'eco del successo internazionale giunse anche in Italia . . . [dove] l'autore veniva spesso considerato uno scrittore formalista . . . una sorta di sapiente e fredda ingegneria letteraria, lontana dalle passioni quanto dall'impegno e dal mondo reale" (naturally, the echo of his international success also reached Italy . . . [where] the author was often considered a formalist writer of . . . a sort of cold, erudite literary machinery, as far removed from the passions as it was from politics and the real world).[20] In this same vein, Perrella's "falsetto" would be not just about the fundamentally false character of the writing, artificial because it is not oriented toward the real, but also about a national and political betrayal. A close reading of Perrella indicates that there is perhaps something even deeper at work, however, and a much broader range of anxieties implicated in the claim that Calvino's voice is falsetto.

I began this discussion by critiquing the idea that the voice is ever a completely natural, spontaneous expression of unique existence; instead, it is in fact always captured in a network of social and ideological relations, gender not least among them. Here, I think it is almost self-evident that, when Perrella says that Calvino writes in falsetto, there is an implication that his voice is not only artificial, but also not "typically" or "correctly" masculine. The distinctive traits of the stereotypically "masculine" voice and "feminine" voice are much the same in English and Italian: The masculine voice is pitched lower, is less marked in intonation (more monotonous), and is louder; while the feminine voice is higher pitched, with more musical intonation, and comparatively quieter (loudness is much less stressed as a gendered marker in Italian speech than in English, however, and "uptalk" is not typical of any gender in Italian). That said, high and low pitch are relative, and singers of various sexes, genders, and ages might all sing in the same range. Marc Matter, for example, discusses an installation piece by Imogen Stidworthy titled *Castrato* in which three singers—a boy, a male countertenor, and a female soprano—sing together, with the three projected videos generally making it totally unclear whose voice we are hearing. The lack of difference between them forms what Matter calls "a tension between merging and separation,"[21] but also illustrates that voice and sex do not have a clear one-to-one correspondence at all. Eidsheim makes a convincing case that the primary marker of gender in the voice is not pitch, since typical male and female singing voices in fact overlap in pitch as much as they differ (*Race of Sound*, 102–5), and any number of male and female signers have overlapping or even nearly identical ranges. While male voices are lower *on average*, listeners still readily identify high-pitched male voices as male. Eidsheim argues that male singers who sing exclusively in falsetto might also maintain a male identification through "strong masculine cues" (108) in *speech*. This last point is telling, since Calvino writes in falsetto but also stutters in speech, according to Perrella. There would seem to be no way for Calvino's voice to signal normative masculinity in this view, since either way he does not conform to the gendered stereotypes of a voice, whether it is speaking or singing.

Falsetto is gendered in complex ways. While it is definitely not stereotypically masculine, it is nonetheless a singing style associated only with men. Cathy Lane provocatively calls falsetto a form of "vocal drag" and associates it with "ambiguous gender roles,"[22] and the epigraph to this chapter from Simon Ravens (*The Supernatural Voice: A History of High Male Singing*) indicates that the high-pitched male voice is a highly charged and contested site that only the whole signals an "incorrect" performance of masculinity that is normatively understood as cisgender and heterosexual.[23] As for women, they can and do sing in falsetto, but the change in timbre and volume when they shift into falsetto is comparatively slight and it is rarely heard as such. Moreover, we don't normally think of falsetto as applying to the spoken word, but rather only to singing, which makes Perrella's claim about Calvino *writing* in falsetto uniquely interesting. It may be gender nonconforming, but there is something fundamentally artistic about it. This may be why the falsetto is simultaneously both male and unmasculine—it makes the voice into a *technique*.

Falsetto is physically different from one's normal singing voice, also called chest voice or modal voice. In falsetto, the vocal cords vibrate only at their edges, producing a higher pitch with a somewhat thinner, less reso-nant sound, usually (at least in an untrained singer) quieter as well. In this regard, the falsetto really does function the same way the *sordina*, or mute, does. A falsetto voice, despite the name's intimation of falseness and artifi-ciality, emerges naturally and spontaneously from both men and women. Ravens observes, for example, that men at a sporting event who whoop do so in falsetto without realizing it, as do men (or women) who give out a "hoo" in a cave in order to hear the echo (6). Almost everyone uses falsetto or head voice when speaking in singsong to a baby or a pet, and they do so spontaneously ("Who's a good boy? That's right! You are!"). Despite its spontaneous and near-universal use, falsetto has long been associated with something false and artificial, and it is telling that the very first known writer to describe it with the term "falsa" (Bernard of Clairvaux in the twelfth century) also characterized it as "feminea" or "womanly" (qtd. in Ravens, 9). Today, singers of classical music who primarily use this register are likely to avoid the term falsetto and describe themselves as "counter-tenors," in part because, although the use of the falsetto register is often desirable, the word itself has negative connotations, as the epigraph to this chapter attests. As Ravens is careful to observe, those connotations have changed over time and place in important and nuanced ways, but even so, terminology surrounding the use of falsetto has almost always suggested an artifice or unnaturalness, not to mention a deviation from received norms about gender and sexuality. For instance, in Italian, the term that corresponds to countertenor is "contraltista"—a term that still indicates a man in a female vocal space (the space of the contralto), and that is pri-marily associated with the *castrati* of the eighteenth century.[24]

Falsetto becomes markedly unpopular by the middle of the nineteenth century, a development Ravens convincingly attributes to powerful and highly differentiated gender roles that emerge as part of Victorian culture. Ravens argues that this had a profound impact on vocal types, with a vivid hostility by the middle of the nineteenth century, openly "couched in terms of gender" (184), to the use of falsetto. Lastly, Ravens then turns to mid-twentieth-century figures like Alfred Deller (an early counter-tenor), and Michael Tippett and Benjamin Britten (composers who wrote groundbreaking works for countertenors), and an embrace of the falsetto starting in the 1940s and '50s that "was seen by the wider public to be part of a gradual breaking up of rigid gender identities" (184), a return that was eventually part of a shift in popular music and the sexual revolution (185).

In short, Perrella's use of the term (especially given his evident famil-iarity with music) is not innocent or merely whimsical or playful. Calvino himself comes of age precisely at the moment in which the use of falsetto returns and finds a new foothold of approval within classical and popular music, one understood more broadly to be consonant with a questioning and breakdown of rigid gender binaries. It had long been erroneously associated with effeminacy and homosexuality, as Ravens notes in the epigraph, and more recently—especially in popular music—gender-bending and androgyny. The association of the falsetto with homosexuality has perhaps diminished in recent years, but Ravens still contends that Tippett and Britten might have been more open to the use of falsetto because they were homosexual (184), an idea that now appears rather reductive, not unlike Susan McClary's doubt about her colleagues' similarly reductive suggestion that Tchaikovsky modulated by thirds rather than by fifths because he was homosexual (77).[25] These are all indications that, simplistic and reductive as these sorts of readings may sound today, the linkage between specific musical techniques and sexual orientation was and perhaps still is widespread in critical circles. Perrella's contention that Calvino's use of the falsetto is absent or understated in his early, wartime works (and more broadly, in the writings he produced while living in Italy), and most exaggerated and pronounced in the works he composed while living in Paris is hardly incidental here, either. It is impossible to avoid the conclusion that Perrella is not simply saying that there is something artificial (playful, cerebral, ludic, postmodern) about Calvino's voice: It became unmanly.

This is even more unavoidable in Perrella's episode for RAI's *Wikiradio* podcast about Calvino, precisely because the medium is audio, specifically voices. Initially, Perrella avoids mentioning the falsetto in the podcast, but when he turns to Calvino's *Cosmicomics*, about nineteen minutes in, he follows the "*Wimbledon* verdict" that this book is *fully* marked by a tendency that was previously only "filtrato" (filtered) in Calvino's early writing: writing in falsetto. He pronounces his famous phrase with a kind of dramatic reluctance, with many pauses and hesitations before it. It is the first time he mentions the falsetto, a big reveal of Calvino's shameful secret. Calvino has a "tendency," we are told, and that tendency is to construct a literary language . . . in falsetto. There is a brief pause in the podcast, a musical flourish, and then an androgynous voice speaks.

Now, Perrella is playing a clever game here, because the story is one of the *Cosmicomics* ("At Daybreak"), and Calvino does say that the narrator of those stories, a certain Qfwfq, speaks in the falsetto of an old man (men's voices often do change in old age due to falling testosterone levels, rising in pitch and becoming thinner and less loud, the hallmarks of the falsetto). Qfwfq is very old indeed, having been present before the

Big Bang and still with us today, but Perrella does not mention the story or Qfwfq, or quote the part where the narrator of the story informs us that Qfwfq speaks in falsetto. He simply says that Calvino elaborates a literary language in falsetto, and then we hear an androgynous voice: a woman speaking the part of an old man who speaks in falsetto, written by a middle-aged writer who speaks in a stuttering baritone but who, evidently, writes in falsetto.

Sound theorist Michel Chion, probably the foremost theoretician of film sound, posits a faculty he calls *synchresis*, an automatic and immediate tendency to "synchronize" sound and image.[26] The most prominent example of synchresis is the tendency to seek out and find a visual cause for sound within the image, but this also happens even when a "cause" is not strictly present. If we see footage of a jet plane while an announcer says "the well-trained pilot directs his aircraft toward the conflict zone," then we will perceive the image as just that; if the announcer says "the pilot, bored and distracted, falls out of formation and flies off aimlessly," we will see precisely that, even though the footage may be exactly the same. The same syncretic faculty applies to acoustic "footage," as well: Perrella's authoritative voice-over effectively grafts a contralto female voice onto Calvino's "body." The voice that reads for Qfwfq is not definitively attributed to anyone in the credits (it is probably that of Antonella Borghi, who also worked on the podcast), but the effect is deeply syncretic in Chion's sense. We are told to expect Calvino's falsetto, and then we literally hear a female voice, giving the impression of gender ambiguity that the listener will, unfailingly, attach first to Calvino, before realizing it is the narrator. This vocal grafting inevitably makes the expression of Calvino's gender complex and indeterminate, suggesting that Calvino, between stutter and falsetto, is not satisfying the normative expectations of traditional masculinity. (As we will see, this plays out in some surprising ways that resonate with my "jazz" readings of the *Cosmicomics* in chapter 3 that emphasize Calvino's "swerve from the straight line.")

When Perrella first introduces the notion of the falsetto in Calvino, he contrasts it with the "rarissimo Calvino 'frontale'" (13, most rare "frontal" Calvino).[27] I pointed out before that Perrella's falsetto was indirect or bent rather than direct or straight, but we should also take seriously Perrella's term "frontal"; the falsetto Calvino is not frontal, so it is something opposed to the frontal. Dorsal? Perrella exercises his novelistic approach to Calvino's lack of frontality or straightforwardness when he speculates about the name "Italo." According to the standard account of his naming, given by Calvino as well as by his family members in interviews, Calvino's mother chose this somewhat unusual first name for her son because he was born in Cuba, and she did not want him to forget his Italian roots. Perrella, however, declares that it is not a real name. It does not have, he says, the "felice arbitrarietà dei veri nomi, che non alludono a nulla" (43, the fortunate randomness of real names, which don't refer to anything), since Italo clearly alludes to Italy. He goes on to speculate that such a name is really "un'invenzione onomastica di un artista. . . . Il vero nome di Calvino non sia mai stato pronunciato, se non, forse, in segreto" (43, an artist's onomastic invention. . . . Calvino's true name has never been uttered, if not, perhaps, in secret). Calvino is not "frontal," then, starting with his true nature, which is something secret; he calls himself by someone else's name, as it were. In his RAI podcast, Perrella refers to Calvino's first name as "un pseudonimo" (a pseudonym), which it is not—perhaps he is unconsciously thinking of another ironic, slippery Italian writer, Italo Svevo, whose "Italo" really was a pseudonym.

This is a surprising and obviously untrue claim about names, since virtually all names have meanings, sometimes quite obvious ones (Claire, Taylor, Faith, Benedict, Felix, Vincent, etc.; or in Italian, Cesare, Pasquale, Chiara, ecc.); in fact, the link between "Italo" and "Italia" (Italy) is almost exactly the same, and just as clear, as the link between "Silvio" (Perrella's first name) and "silva" (the word for forest in Latin), which is where it comes from. Perrella is being whimsical and playful here, but also determined to find something false(tto) about Calvino that is at the core of his identity, something that transcends his lived experience and that belongs to his essence—not what he did, but what he was, even before he was born. I might also point out that this claim about the name Italo doesn't just emphasize Calvino's artificiality or falseness as fundamental, even ontological, but also suggests that the connection between Calvino and Italy is unstable, and even artificial. Calvino is not properly true and masculine (falsetto), not fully Italian (not really Italo).

Much of this converges when Perrella returns to Calvino's stutter. He recalls Natalia Ginzburg's observation that Calvino spoke as if he were imitating or making fun of himself, and Perrella contends that this impression "derivava forse da un problema ritmico legato a una sua leggera balbuzie che mimetizzava. . . . Un fenomeno simile avviene nella sua scrittura, l'esecuzione della quale è spesso in falsetto" (73, derived perhaps from a problem with rhythm tied to a slight stammer of his that he camouflaged. . . . A similar phenomenon happens in his writing, the execution of which is often in falsetto). In short, Perrella confirms that the stutter and the falsetto are related, outgrowths of each other or perhaps a kind of reciprocal compensation for each other. Calvino is hiding something about his "real nature."

The Calvino who emerges from Perrella's portrait is remarkably non-normative, even queer: stuttering to mask his stuttering, writing in falsetto, concealing an artistic secret about his true self, "twisted back," "unnatural," and not "frontal."[28] In Perrella's third chapter, which follows directly on the heels of his suggestion that Calvino's falsetto emerges from his stutter, things take an even more remarkable turn, since Perrella explicitly turns to the falseness and unnatural character of Calvino's *body*. We should recall here Cavarero's notion that the *voice*, precisely because it emerges from the body, is supposed to carry a kind of ontological truth that *speech* does not necessarily carry. For Perrella, Calvino's voice, even his name, is nothing but falsity: Perhaps even Calvino's body is a lie.

Calvino's Body: Head and Intestine

The first section of the chapter in Perrella in question is titled "Il corpo di uno scrittore magro" (The body of a skinny writer), and he begins by claiming that Calvino's body was "apparentemente immune dalle leggi dell'invecchiamento" (83, apparently immune to the laws of aging). He instructs anyone who doubts it to look at photographs of the older Calvino, photographs of a fit, active man who, it is true, does not gain much weight over the years. His jowls sag a bit in his sixties, and his hairline recedes somewhat (he is, after all, *calvino*, a bit bald), but the body is always slender. Perrella does not make an *explicit* reference to Dorian Gray here, but he does argue that this fit, slender body also conceals a secret truth, a truth that he locates in a surprising part of that body that indicates precisely in what way Calvino's voice is not "frontal" with us: the rectum.

Perrella's investigation of Calvino's strangely skinny body leads him to a surgical procedure that Calvino had in the fall of 1962, an experience Calvino recounted in a magazine story about the experience of contemporary health care in Italy. The story never says why he needed surgery, but Perrella discovers in the original manuscript a sentence that was eliminated from the published version of the story: Calvino's physician was the top local specialist in vasal surgery—that is, hemorrhoids (84).[29] Calvino's lifelong slenderness had less to do with self-control or a magical painting in the attic, and more to do with severe digestive issues that plagued him for his whole life. Now we know what the opposite of "frontal" is—it is rectal.

I do not exaggerate when I say that Perrella goes on to make this rectal secret about Calvino the secret truth about him and his writing. I also think he is perhaps right, if not precisely in the way he imagines. Perrella makes a literary reference in revealing this "hidden" rectal truth; he calls Calvino a "cittadino onorario di Bersabea" (122, honorary citizen of Beersheba), one of Calvino's *Invisible Cities*. Let us recall that city, because this is the only specific connection that Perrella draws between Calvino's strangely skinny body and his writing. Beersheba is a doubly mirrored city in Calvino's novel: The city dreams that it has a celestial reflection, in which everything is made of gold and silver and diamonds, and the inhabitants, moved by lofty virtues, "elaborano forme di composita compostezza" (2:454, elaborate forms of composite composure). At the same time, however, the inhabitants of Beersheba also believe that their city has a subterranean reflection, a "città fecale" (2:454, fecal city) whose "sostanza sia quella oscura e duttile e densa come pece che cala giù per le cloache prolungando il percorso delle viscere umane, di nero buco in nero buco, fino a spiaccicarsi sull'ultimo fondo sotterraneo" (2:454, substance is one dark, ductile, and dense as pitch that flows down through the sewers, prolonging the route of the human viscera, from black hole to black hole, until it spreads out across the last, subterranean bottom).

Perrella reads this city as an allegory for Calvino's secret being: Calvino has constructed an artificial and imaginary world that is all head (the head voice, the falsetto) when we could have had the ugly, but real, truth of the intestine (122). Like the inhabitants of Beersheba, Calvino's head is stuck in the celestial city of gold and diamonds, dreaming of perfect forms. Perrella's placement of Calvino into this scene from *Invisible Cities* does not work, however. Calvino is absolutely clear that the inhabitants of Beersheba *have made a terrible mistake* in believing that their best selves are to be found in the celestial city. On the contrary, that aspiration toward the purity of the celestial makes them uptight, rigid, greedy, even morally repellent. The city can be honest and straightforward, but "solo quando caca" (2:455, only when it shits).

Freud's influence on Calvino is much greater than is generally understood, particularly since Calvino is apt to cite Freudian ideas or structures without explicitly mentioning Freud's name. That is the case in Beersheba, where Calvino contrasts the two possible dispositions a city can have toward its waste: an uptight, rigid denial or a generous and relaxed acceptance. Beersheba, in other words, is a clear allegory of Freud's hypothesis about the anal phase of childhood, and the child's two possible stances toward its excretions, which were later taken up in popular psychology as two opposing personality types.[30] The first is the anal retentive (now a fixture of popular psychology and popular culture), a type that is rigid, obsessive, controlling and stingy, or as Freud puts it, given to "avarice, pedantry and obstinacy" ("Transformations of Instinct," 127). This is what the citizens of Beersheba aspire to and take pride in—and they should not.

The second (a type that did not enter popular consciousness to nearly the same degree) is the anal expulsive, who is disorganized, easygoing, and generous. Implicitly, but importantly for Freud, the two types also express political attitudes. The retentive type is meticulous about rule following, while the expulsive type is politically unruly. More exactly, both types can present oppositional political behaviors: The retentive type tends toward a conservative obstinance, wishing to keep things as they are and have always been (so, strictly speaking, politically conservative, but not necessarily obedient), while the expulsive personality has a disinclination to follow rules at all (hence anarchic).[31]

Calvino is quite explicit in his language, as well as about which side he is on. The city's "soli momenti d'abbandono generoso sono quelli dello staccare da sé, lasciar cadere, spandere" (2:455, only moments of generous abandon are those when it breaks away from itself, lets go, expands).[32] The city's best version of itself is a dilated anus that no longer tries to hold back or keep everything inside, and it puts the pretentious city's "head" to shame. Beersheba's aspirations of perfect geometries and composed exactitude are nothing more than a show that conceals the city's most impressive architecture and achievements, which are in fact its sewers. Perrella is correct that we should read the city in a moral key, precisely because Calvino is absolutely explicit about his moral rejection of the "celestial" version of the city. "Intenta ad accumulare i suoi carati di perfezione, Bersabea crede virtù ciò che è ormai un cupo invasamento a riempire il vaso vuoto di se stessa" (2:455, intent on accumulating carats of perfection, Beersheba believes to be virtue what is by now a dark possession that drives it to fill the empty vessel of itself). The "invasamento" (possession, like a demonic possession) and "vaso vuoto di se stesso" (empty vessel of itself) are also explicit recollections in Italian of the bodily vessels of the vasal surgery Perrella was so eager to catch sight of earlier. The body here becomes a chamber pot (*vaso di notte*) that is morally bankrupt and empty, precisely because of its maniacal desire to remain pristine and clean, and because of its mistaken pride in that desire. Calvino is indeed an honorary citizen of Beersheba, but the subterranean city of sewers, not the celestial city of diamonds.

This is hardly the only moment in which Calvino attends to the opposition between the anal retentive and the anal expulsive. It is also the structuring opposition between Agilulfo and Gurdulù in *The Nonexistent Knight*, or between the two women who literally rule two halves of the moon in "The Meteorites" (one of his "cosmicomic" stories). It is the entire movement of Calvino's meditation on taking out the trash in Paris, "La poubelle agréée" (French for "garbage bin"). In almost every instance,

Calvino works to at least destabilize our automatic assumption that order is superior to chaos, and in the case of "La poubelle," the story moves from Calvino at his most maniacally rigid and geometric, a kind of parody of order, logic, and cleanliness, to the final pages in which the story dissolves into just a series of fragments of sentences and literary material that, unlike the kitchen trash bin, cannot be assimilated into the story or neatly disposed of. Even Calvino's writing prizes its moments of generous abandon, of expansive dilation.[33]

Remarkably, Perrella's concern with Calvino's voice and his concern with Calvino's intestines emerge from exactly the same psychic underpinnings. Whether it is his "intestinally retentive" mind or his "vocally retentive" stutter (see again Eagle on Ferenczi's idea of the stutter as a genital-vocal block, 81–83), both produce a subject so wound up, so tight and rigid that when he speaks, all that can emerge is a high-pitched squeak, from one end of the GI tract or the other. The voice really is the excrement of the signifier, in Dolar's memorable phrase.

While Perrella misunderstands the point Calvino is making in Beersheba, he is one of the very few echoes of Calvino in literary criticism to call attention to the writer's body and the bodily dimension of Calvino's thinking at all. Perrella is in fact willing to take the logic of his own conceit about Beersheba and Calvino's intestines to its logical conclusions, conclusions that again, may be wrong, but that reveal much more than he realizes:

> Calvino era un loico viscerale. In un certo senso, aveva trascinato il suo intestino dentro la testa e aveva cercato di geometrizzarlo. Ma . . . la sua testa era labirintica e buia almeno quanto il suo intestino. È anche per questa ragione che il paragone [di Calvino] con Pasolini è così stimolante per l'immaginazione critica. (124)

> Calvino was a visceral logician. In a certain sense, he had dragged his own intestine into his head and tried to geometrize it. But his head was at least as labyrinthine and dark as his intestine. It's for this reason, too, that the comparison [of Calvino] to Pasolini is so stimulating for the critical imagination.

Implicit in this is a tendency in Italian criticism to associate Calvino with the disembodied eye (essentially a floating mind), and Pasolini instead with the body (see Baldi, *The Author in Criticism*, 96, on this frequent dichotomy). But perhaps Perrella, who clearly wants to make the same point here, is strangely correct in the basic coordinates of his analysis: Calvino *is* a visceral logician, albeit in the opposite sense of the one Perrella means. Calvino understands that geometry may gesture toward a world of perfect, logical forms, but it does so in a field that is saturated by desire, perversion, and anxiety, and those forms themselves (as we will see) become emblematic of desire and fear. Calvino's logic reveals that the geometrically straight and smooth is always actually textured and twisted (as in "The Form of Space," analyzed at length in chapter 3). Moreover, one doesn't need to geometrize the intestines to make them straight, since the straight line of geometry can already be found there—precisely in the *rectum*, which literally means "the straight part" in Latin. The geometrizing body is always a body, one that has intestines, an anus, and genitals, as well as an eye and brain, and Calvino is constantly at pains to remind the reader of that, perhaps because the twists of his obstinate intestine would never let him forget it.

Perrella indicates his own intestinal fantasy in the "visceral logic" passage as well: There is something "stimulating" for the critic's imagination in putting Calvino and Pasolini together. The critic has a fantasy that the two writers share some quality, something that Pasolini was open about (homosexuality), but that Calvino kept hidden, betrayed only by his falsetto.[34] Calvino wasn't betrayed *only* by the falsetto, however. Perrella turns to another critic, Paolo Monelli, who describes a major transformation ("metamorfosi") in Calvino in the 1960s, when supposedly Calvino began to flaunt "giacchette sportive con i tagli laterali, vistosi gilé" (sporty jackets with side vents, showy vests), as well as a white Giulietta Sprint, a two-seater.[35] Perrella archly observes that the car was meant to be used "per andare con le ragazze—e sembra che Calvino piaccia alle ragazze molto" (89, for going out with girls—and it seems that the girls quite like Calvino), but neither Monelli nor Perrella is willing to say if Calvino liked the girls.

The question of Calvino's actual sexual orientation (exclusively heterosexual as far as it is known) is irrelevant here. What is instead revealing is the persistence of critics (including, as I argue in chapter 3, Perrella, Benedetti, Hume, and others) who insist that there is something non-normative about his sexuality, but without ever saying quite what it is. In other words, a queer space is opened up but left undefined, vaguely metaphorical without any sense of what has been substituted. Is Calvino asexual, "pure," "frigid"? Or is he more interested in clothes than in girls? As I do throughout this study, I want to contend that Perrella's vocal intervention is also a form of echo that actually enriches the original signal, however, and it does so in a way that is once again creative (recall Belpoliti's claim that Perrella's book is essentially a novel) and acoustic. It brings into play Calvino's voice, at the end of the 1990s, now with a queered pitch, sharpened into a falsetto.

Conclusions: From Falsetto to Laughter

Let's briefly summarize before I offer a different way in which Calvino's voice might resonate after his death. I argue throughout this book that, in the half century since his death, Calvino's voice has also echoed onward and outward, both filling and creating a space that has been remarkably open and inspirational, but also, for some, problematic. Calvino spoke with a stutter, and like many stutterers, he elaborated a number of ways to manage that disfluency. For much of the twentieth century, however, the stutter functioned as a marker of weakness, specifically of masculine insufficiency. It is a voice, then, which fails to correctly perform its gender, or which, alternatively, reveals a more ambiguous gender performance, one not altogether masculine. Perrella has claimed that Calvino's stutter is linked to his tendency to "write in falsetto," an intriguing claim that indicates a failure to adhere to vocal norms. Both vocal "disfluencies" (falsetto, the stutter) stem from the same psychological problem: a fundamentally *retentive* (anally, genitally, vocally) character, a subject who keeps everything on the inside and whose maniacal dedication to order leads him to straighten up everything, from the tangled coils of his own intestines to his presumably less than straight sexual orientation (not frontal, but rather "riflesso e innaturale," curved back and unnatural).

As in my discussion of Calvino's less-than-straight trajectories in chapter 3, I would argue here that Perrella's falsetto might be telling us something about how Calvino has resonated with readers, however. Perrella's reading may come to conclusions opposite to those Calvino is trying to convey, but the coordinates that he is offering are perhaps the right ones: He is arguing that at its core, there is something fundamentally *sexual* about Calvino's geometric fictions, and that a key to understanding Calvino might lie in the tension between the retentive, controlling, hierarchical instinct and the expulsive, liberal, rebellious one. Ultimately, Perrella is like most critics of Calvino when he tries to demonstrate that Calvino is the former type (retentive) and not the latter type (expulsive); he is all control and order and geometry. Unlike most critics, however, Perrella at least raises the question, briefly allows—if only to close it down again—a new set of critical dimensions for Calvino, a set of critical dimensions that gesture in an entirely different direction. Suddenly Calvino might be no longer a dour, unhappy, escapist intellectual. Instead, he is on stage wearing a flamboyant gilet and singing in falsetto. To return to Feldman's essay on the crack in the voice as it tries to sing higher than it usually can, the most accomplished singers "*toy* or flirt with vocal failure" (189, original emphasis), making it part of their arsenal of expressive techniques and transforming an emotional trauma (such as, say, the isolation and self-consciousness of a stuttering young man) into a dramatic, even theatrical "restaging of [that] trauma" (189).

Such a reading, I've argued here, would allow us to hear something in Calvino's voice that we didn't hear before. A remarkable number of critics—particularly, but not exclusively, in Italy—have insisted that Calvino is an apolitical pessimist obsessed with geometry rather than politics and an embodied, lived life—a sexless, disembodied cerebellum. Although few say so openly, it is Calvino's 1957 public resignation from the Italian Communist Party, after it required all members to publicly approve the Soviet invasion of Hungary, that made Calvino increasingly problematic for many Italian intellectuals. On some level, when Perrella says that Calvino's early neorealist stories are honest and real, but that everything else is tainted by the falsetto, it is part of that critical tradition. And yet, Perrella's reaction to the *falsetto* is an attempt to pin it directly to Calvino's body and his dysfunctional intestines, bringing us back to the body and its desires.

Like any form of the voice, the falsetto can have some political value (contesting, for example, self-evident norms about the male voice), but Perrella makes Calvino's falsetto voice into a pathology, one that sounds rather fatal, in fact, when Calvino drags his intestines into his own head in order to attempt to impose order on them. And yet, Perrella is actually one of the very rare voices in literary criticism to have ever suggested, however briefly, that there is a different register (falsetto) in which we might hear Calvino's voice. He might not only be rational and rigorous, but also comic, exuberant, expressive, and less strictly obedient to norms than we thought. That way of hearing Calvino's voice is, I think, not at all rare *outside* literary criticism. As I've already suggested, Calvino's writing has given rise to an extraordinary explosion of art, music, architecture, ethical urban planning, community-based culture, and much more, which is what the rest of this book will pursue. I am not quite sure I can square Calvino's real voice, that serious, gravelly baritone, with Perrella's deceptive, intestine-strangling falsetto, but as a *positive* idea of what Calvino's voice might mean, I think we could do worse.

For my part, I would like to look at a quite different vocalization, one that Natalia Ginzburg identified as the actual way Calvino dealt with his stutter, one that Perrella does not attend to. It is a vocal feature that, to my ear, is far more constant and important than any kind of disfluency in Calvino's speech: laughter. I will say at the outset that while there is no evidence that Calvino ever made use of a Marilyn Monroe falsetto to deal with his stutter, there is evidence for the laughter that Ginzburg observes:

"quella sua balbuzie in parte vera e in parte simulata m'aveva colpito per un'allegria straordinaria che ne emanava" (188–89, that stuttering of his, in part real and in part simulated, had struck me for the extraordinary happiness that would emanate from it). Despite the insistence of Italian critics who so often stress Calvino's pessimism and melancholy, it is difficult to find an interview in which Calvino does not laugh, a laughter that is spontaneous and delighted, almost always with the implication that he is laughing at himself, laughing at his own speech and thought.

In a very early television interview in French (Cravenne), Calvino discusses *The Baron in the Trees*, which had just come out in French translation (*Le Baron perché*), with Raymond Dumayet. The interview is extremely awkward, almost painful to watch. When it begins, Calvino is visibly uncomfortable, and he begins to lean away from Dumayet as much as possible (fig. 1a). At the start of the interview, he twice makes furtive and fleeting eye contact with Dumayet and then steadfastly stares at the floor or ceiling while nervously twisting his hands (fig. 1b). He also speaks French slowly and rather haltingly, and begins to stammer about two minutes in. It doesn't help that Dumayet's questions are tone deaf, and it is doubtful that he has actually read the novel. Dumayet asks, for example, if, instead of refusing to eat his snails for dinner and going to live in the trees, the novel's protagonist, the eleven-year-old Baron Cosimo, might have killed himself instead as a similar act of protest or rebellion. Calvino is justifiably aghast at the idea, and at a loss as to how to answer.

At several points later in the interview, however, Calvino takes on an introspective look and smiles to himself as if at a private joke. At the end of the interview, Dumayet asks him about *I nostri antenati* (Our Ancestors), Calvino's trilogy of fantastic novels set in the past, published in English as *The Cloven Viscount*, *The Nonexistent Knight*, and *The Baron in the Trees*. Dumayet asks which of the three main characters in the trilogy Calvino feels most directly descended from. Calvino answers without any hesitation that it is certainly the Baron who spends his life in the trees. Dumayet then asks him, absolutely seriously, if Calvino would want to live in the trees like the fictional Baron. Calvino starts to answer him seriously, but breaks off after a few words and suddenly begins to really smile. Now making full eye contact, first with Dumayet and then the camera, he turns relaxed and playful, even as the stammer remains. He says, "peut-être, peut-être je, je, je, je vis . . . je vis là- là- là-dessus" (perhaps, perhaps I, I, I, I do live, I do live, live, up, up, up there). "Dans les arbres?" (In the trees?) asks Dumayet, confused. "Oui," replies Calvino with a laugh, now grinning and looking directly into the camera (fig. 1c). This direct look is perhaps also a very Calvinian challenge, asking Dumayet, but also his

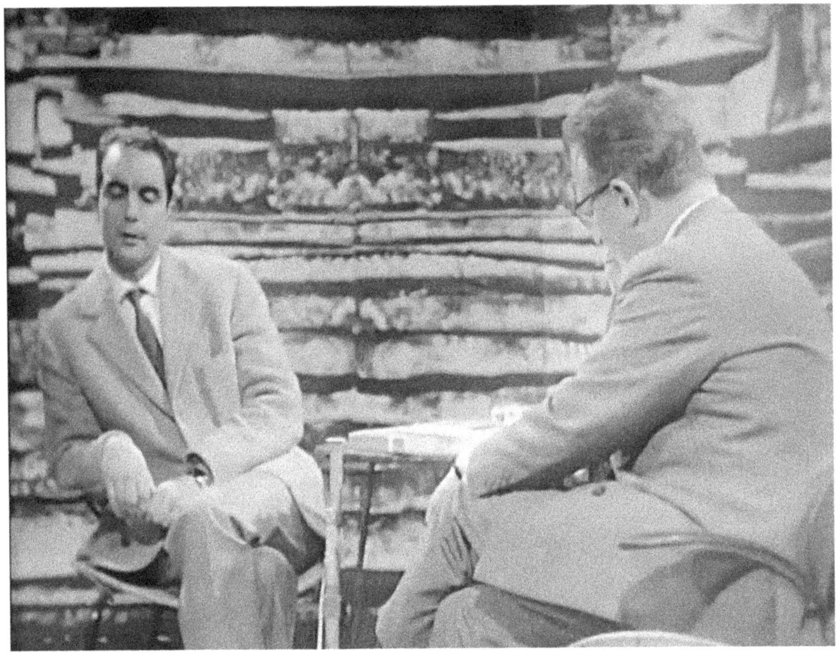

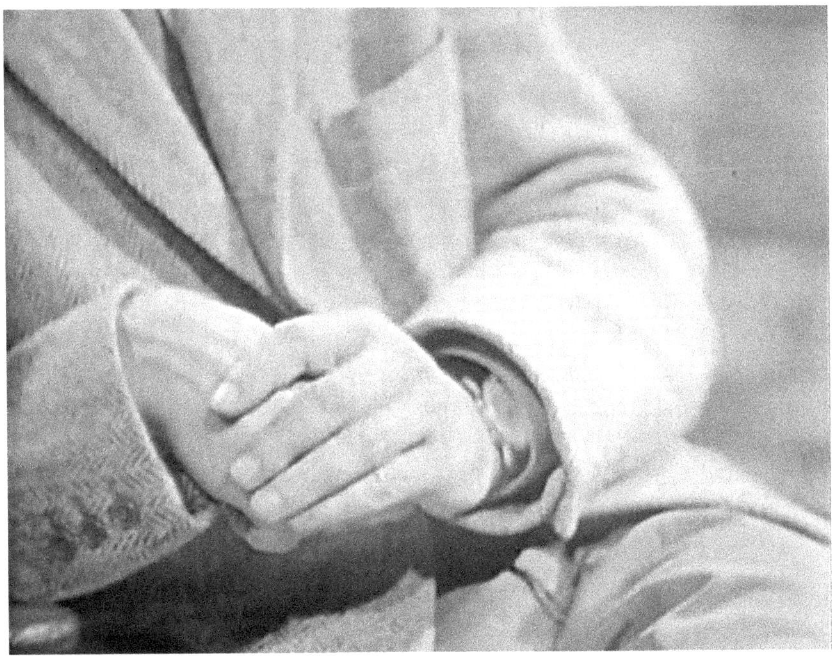

FIGURE 1A, B, C. The two sides of Calvino: awkward and reticent, then direct.

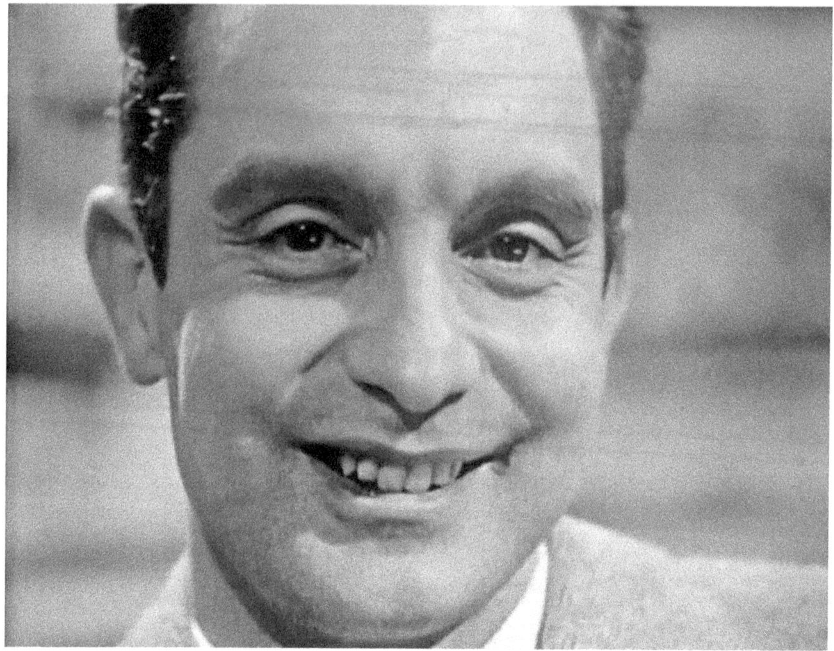

FIGURE 1A, B, C. Continued

readers: Can you see my ideal, imagined world (the author living in the trees), beyond the mundane author in a television studio?[36]

This is precisely what Ginzburg says about Calvino's stutter, that it turns into joy (189). By the time he was older, it was at least partially a way for Calvino to make a show of himself that was also self-conscious, ironic, winking—a falsetto performance, playful, theatrical, motivated by joy. From that early television interview in 1960, when Calvino laughs at his own fantasy of living in the trees as something both delightful and impossible and yet somehow real, turning to the interviewer and the whole audience to get them in on the joke, the self-ironizing smile and laugh are a fixture of Calvino's embodied speech. Ginzburg marks this laughing stutter as a delightful spontaneous bodily emission of happiness rather than a strangling retentiveness, a generous gift that has clearly opened up a space for other artists, other thinkers; a space that is still expanding, resonant with Calvino's laughter.

2 /   An Echo-Logical Opera (in Headphones)

Catacoustics

Of all of Calvino's novels and other projects, none has resonated more with readers than his 1972 *Invisible Cities*. It would be difficult at this point to catalogue all of the works inspired by this novel about Marco Polo and Kublai Khan, but responses have been particularly noteworthy in architecture (Hong Kong architect William Lim calls it the "bible of architecture students"[1]), while in urban planning and design courses it is not unusual to assign students the book and projects based on it. (At every university where I've given a talk on Calvino, it has been trivial to find examples of student design and art projects there that were based on *Invisible Cities*.) It has even found its way into discussions of educational policy, as when the Yale National Initiative, a collaboration between Yale and the New Haven Teachers Initiative, published a curriculum unit on "Invisible Cities: The Arts and Renewable Community."[2] Even more numerous, however, have been the responses of other artists to the novel. Those responses include popular (and amateur) arts and crafts: Patricia Slavinski, a Canadian high school teacher, ran a contest for her students to build an invisible city out of gingerbread in 2015 (the winner was Baucis). They also include more professional visual artists: David Fleck, Colleen Corradi Brannigan, and others have done series based on the novel. One finds sculpture (by Liu Wei and Diana Al-Hadid), installation (by Nadia Lakhani), book design (by Zoey Liangzhang), urban dance movies (Jevan Chowdhury's *Moving Cities*), interior design (the Hotel Tres Sants in Menorca was originally designed with each guest room referencing a city from the novel), and more.[3]

Examples of community-based public-facing art and initiatives are far too numerous to mention (I have found dozens of them over the last two decades), but I offer a few to give some sense of their character: Designer Christian Schmidt and artist Liangjie Xia took real-time geocoded data of activity from Twitter and Flickr in 2010, and used it to distort the topography of Manhattan, changing its flat topography to show mountains and valleys of internet usage; in 2011, two Italian filmmakers (Gianpaolo Bucci and Beatrice Ngalula Kabutakapua) set out to document the lived experiences of the African diaspora across the world, from Los Angeles to Tokyo; in 2017, the European urban studies program 4CITIES explored Brussels looking for the "thousands of other Brussels both real and imagined";[4] while today online activist Sheryl Chan organizes linkups for those suffering from invisible but chronic illnesses and disabilities. What unites these very different projects is that they all reference Calvino's *Invisible Cities* as a point of departure.[5]

The majority of these interventions have focused on visibility, aiming to bring out a part of the city that was heretofore invisible: an invisible structure, especially a community within the city, a community that is in some sense an "invisible city" of its own. It is worth noting that the rhetoric of visibility is itself potentially exclusionary, however; rendering something visible does not automatically grant it dignity, and unwanted visibility falls more heavily on some groups than others. (As one of my students once asked, "invisible to whom?") Moreover, sight is not the privileged sense for everyone. Studies of Calvino have often replicated this insistence on the visible (see Grundtvig, Belpoliti, Ricci, or Almansi on Calvino's predominantly visual or geometric nature), and to be sure Calvino does seem at times obsessed with the visual, especially its abstract and geometrical dimension.[6] This is so much the case that Alberto Carli could title his 2018 book on Calvino and Pasolini simply *L'occhio e la voce* (The eye and the voice), and every reader could be expected to know that Calvino was the eye.[7] Even so, there is another side to Calvino, and it concerns the *acoustic* dimension of his work.

I want to think about the "afterlives" of *Invisible Cities* as echoes that delineate an expanding cultural space. If Calvino's ideas live on and find new life in these new works—and they often do—we could understand them in light of what Philippe Lacoue-Labarthe calls *catacoustics*, an archaic term for the science of reflected sound. Lacoue-Labarthe's argument is lengthy and complex, but is essentially that the subject perceives itself as caught in a rhythm, not an artificially imposed one, but the naturally occurring rhythm of the reverberation or echo. To grasp ourselves as emergent figures in a historical flow is to understand ourselves as echoes of what came before, to work backward "from Narcissus to Echo" (146).[8] Although the narcissistic and masculine register receives all the attention, the first figure in the story and in the chain of reflections is Echo, an acoustic model of arrested development (or so it is usually thought) rather than a visual one.

A conventional view of the echo indicates that it is a "mere" repetition or copy of the original, without its full acoustic richness. Catacoustics might initially seem to do the same, since *kata-* in Greek suggests a downward movement, a loss or degradation, as virtually all of the English words that make use of it show: *cataclysm, catacomb, cataleptic, cataract, catastrophe, catatonic* . . . But Lacoue-Labarthe has something a bit more oppositional in mind, something that goes up as well as down, like the *kata-* in *catapult*, which would aim at "l'écoute en écho ou l'interprétation catacoustique" (249, listening by echo or a catacoustic interpretation). Such a listening presupposes that what one is listening for is not a concrete object, certainly not a word or a phrase, but the quality of the sound itself, its timbre, color, resonance, the rhythm not of the notes, but of the melody's echo.

For Lacoue-Labarthe, the subject is built around a deep rhythmic sense of an echo that is connected to the voice and the rhythms of the mother's body, but a rhythm that also manifests what biologists call "entrainment." This is the (almost) uniquely human ability to be captured by or fall in with a beat, as when we begin to sway or tap along with a piece of music (and I'll return to entrainment in the last chapter, as well). Our entrained feel for rhythm is not entirely voluntary, and this is true of the catacoustic echo as well, which is why you might find yourself tapping your foot even to a piece of music you actively dislike. Amittai Aviram argues that Lacoue-Labarthe is fundamentally Nietzschean in his regard for the rhythmic as a "state of being outside of and prior to the social, verbal, thinking subject" (197), and notes that the term "catacoustic" derives from a Greek verb (*katakoúein*) that means "to listen to" but also "to obey" (217). In fact, the English "obey" also comes from the Latin *ob+audire*, "to listen to." For Lacoue-Labarthe, the language I use, the ways I think of myself and present myself to others, the language that others catch coming from me without my conscious awareness—these are all echoes of figures who preceded me in time. In some sense, I am an echo of those who came before me (and others who come after me might very well echo me in turn), but an echo that exceeds my volition. I don't choose what will resonate with me—it resonates inside me, whether I want it to or not.

That said, catacoustics (and the modern study of acoustics) tells us that the echo is never (just) a partial and degraded repetition of an authentic, rich original: While it is true that an echo repeats only a portion of the original signal, it does so in a way that conveys a huge quantity of *additional information* that was not in the original signal.[9] When a harpist playing in a cathedral plucks the strings, the sound that we hear is in fact primarily composed of echoes (and equally important, echoes of echoes). The complex of reverberations that arrives to our ears tells us the distance from us to the harpist, the distance from the harpist to the walls, and the overall interior dimensions of the cathedral. But we also hear the material that the cathedral is made out of (one material may reflect the "treble" end of sounds, another may absorb them), and the changing character of sound might reveal how the space is changing over time. In short, a catacoustic approach indicates that it is only in and with the echo that the sound is fully realized, and this realization or repletion of the origin happens in a way that demarcates and defines a space—something the mirror image does not gesture at.

"To register sound," writes Brandon LaBelle, is "to mark it as spatial and architectural . . . integral to the built environment."[10] Every sound, then, carries a complex of reverberations that are indelibly marked by the space that produces them.[11] As Emily Thompson argues, historically, "reverberation [was] a direct result of the architecture that created it. . . . [Architecture] sounded the acoustic signature of each particular place."[12] This linkage between sound and space as we "listen by echo" means that sound offers a kind of "echo-logical" perspective, one that I'd like to use to explore not just Calvino, but the larger reverberant space that *Invisible Cities* has opened up. The echo-logical suggests a different way of thinking about reception, since following the logic of the echo lays at least equal stress on what comes after the work, and not exclusively the value of the work "in itself." Just as we always hear an instrument in a specific sonic environment, we never hear a work "in itself," but always and only the work within an expanding complex of cultural reverberations. The work becomes and fully realizes itself in its cultural echoes.

Invisible Cities clearly provided a powerful formal model that subsequent artists could follow (it had a certain kind of "echo-logic"), but the political valence of many of those echoes indicates that the reverberant space opened up by Calvino was in fact a way of thinking about community and what is excluded from the community in a surprisingly concrete and practical way. Moreover, the innate linkage between sound and space (where the echo carries with it the sound of the space in which it was created) means that the echo and the eco- share a meaning that goes beyond their accidentally similar sound in modern English. The echo, in other words, also tells us a great deal about the space in which we dwell, our political and cultural ecology. My approach here is unusually broad, as well as inevitably partial, as I noted in the introduction (Sterne favors the term *partial* as a positive way to describe the incomplete but multi-disciplinary approach to sound studies). I draw on critical theory, sound studies, literary studies, reception theory, the environmental humanities, and even some musical analysis in this chapter and the rest of this book, but this breadth is a necessary one if we are going to try to get a handle on a phenomenon (the echoes of *Invisible Cities*) that is characterized precisely by its expansive reach, its ever-growing volume (a term we use to describe both the architectural dimensions of a space and the amplitude of a sound).

Hearing Space

To illustrate this connection between sound and space, I turn first to one of Calvino's stories. He had planned to write five stories about the five senses (likely setting them in some kind of larger frame narrative), but managed to complete only three before his untimely death in 1985— smell, taste, and hearing—today collected in the volume *Under the Jaguar Sun*. I'd like to take as my point of departure the story about hearing, "A King Listens" (the Italian title is "Un re in ascolto," which is something a little more receptive and static than "listens," perhaps something more like, "A King, Listening"). Calvino's story is addressed to "you," but you are a paranoid king who is determined at all costs to maintain the image of power and sovereignty—this king remains at all times perched on his throne, scepter in hand, crown on head (at *all* times, the story emphasizes: He sleeps there, makes love there, defecates there . . .). He has learned to mistrust everything he hears, knowing that the courtiers may be lying to him, but sound is really the only meaningful sense available to him, since he can never leave the throne to actually inspect the troops, see the people, look at his city. Like the prisoners in Plato's cave, his perspective is painfully limited to what may be a false charade designed to beguile him. Unlike the prisoners in the allegory, however, the king recognizes that, while his eyes have little to offer him, he has another sense at his disposal:

Se il tuo palazzo resta per te sconosciuto e inconoscibile, puoi tentare di ricostruirlo pezzo a pezzo, situando ogni calpestio, ogni colpo di tosse in un punto dello spazio, immaginando intorno a ogni segno sonoro pareti, soffitti, impiantiti, dando forma al vuoto in cui i rumori si propagano e agli ostacoli contro cui urtano, lasciando che siano i suoni stessi a suggerire le immagini. Un tintinnio argentino non è solo non è solo un cucchiaino che è caduto dal sottocoppa in cui era in bilico ma è anche un angolo di tavola coperto da una tovaglia di lino con frangia di pizzo. . . .

Il palazzo è una costruzione sonora. . . . Puoi percorrerlo guidato dagli echi. (3:156)

If your palace remains unknown and unknowable to you, you can still try to reconstruct it bit by bit, locating every shuffle, every coughing fit in a point in space, imagining around every sonorous sign walls, ceilings, flooring, giving form to the void in which sounds spread and to the obstacles they bounce off of, letting the sounds themselves prompt the images. A silvery tinkling is not simply a teaspoon that fell from the saucer it was balanced on, but is also a corner of a table covered by a lace-fringed linen tablecloth. . . .

The palace is a sonorous construction. . . . You can traverse it guided by the echoes.

This is precisely catacoustics, the cognizing of space and environment through an attentive study not of the signal, but of the signal's echoes. Ultimately, the king is able to reconstruct his palace, discern plots against him, and intercept secret messages, all through the reverberations that carry through the palace and the city beyond it. The acoustic world is inherently political for Calvino.

The overall value of sound in Calvino's story lies in the way that sound and its reverberations allow us to perceive the space in which they occur; this is a space that is not only physical, but also thoroughly political in the oldest sense of the word, which refers both to the physical city as well as to the community that lives in it, the *polis*. The argument that there is something inherently or deeply political about Calvino's later works (those of the 1960s onward) is meant to challenge the view that Calvino's works were politically disengaged after he abandoned the Italian Communist Party, particularly after his move to Paris in 1967.[13] This debate has continued, and indeed, intensified in recent years, as Lucia Re indicates in an extensive review in 2014, with major broadsides attacking Calvino as politically disengaged, even actively harmful, coming from Carla Benedetti (1998) and Alessia Ricciardi (1999, 2012), among others.[14] The literature on both sides is quite copious, and the terms of the debate have affected, in ways both subtle and overt, how Calvino's novels have been read. For my part, I am hoping that this catacoustic or echological approach, which looks to the larger cultural resonances as a way of understanding the original, might offer a different way of understanding the importance of the political for Calvino.

As I mentioned in the previous chapter, the political philosopher Adriana Cavarero uses "A King Listens" to open her book about the political value of the human voice and vocal expression. Essentially, she argues that Calvino's story is an extremely rare text in the history of a Western metaphysics that has historically separated the *voice* (traditionally coded as feminine, irrational, incidental, immanent, decorative) from *speech* (masculine, rational, central, transcendent, meaningful). Calvino's story could be read as reinforcing this separation: The king falls in love with the singer's voice. That voice is decorative and alluring, especially since the words of her song cannot be made out, and thus seem irrelevant, leaving us the pure voice. Cavarero argues, however, that Calvino's story persistently associates this pure voice with political revolution, in part because the voice is embodied in a way that emphasizes its radical difference, and further, the radical difference of all subjects. In short, there is something in Calvino's thinking that connects "acoustic thinking" and political awareness, even a disposition to political change.

Cavarero does not exaggerate Calvino's emphasis on the embodied uniqueness that a voice gives to us. Calvino's phrase, "throat of flesh" (*gola di carne*), returns again and again in Cavarero's book as a phrase that is emblematic of an embodied and relational politics. That voice is not just a sign of the political subject's embodiment, but also a lifetime of experiences of other people, especially infancy, a subject that is quite important for Cavarero's feminist politics. I have some reservations about this project, as indicated in the previous chapter. We cannot escape that we always hear the voice within a social field (we hear each "authentic" individual voice inside social and political categories like race, sex, age, class, and so on), but a focus on echo-logic tells us that the converse is also true: Both the voice and speech always emerge in a particular space (the throat, the chest, the body) and then reverberate in some space that is both literal (my voice, amplified or not, in the lecture hall) and larger, metaphorical (academic space, institutional space, the space of discourses inspired by Calvino, and so on). In other words, the logic of the echo is that every sound is always a sound in a space, so that the materiality of the voice, the (political) speech it produces, and the presence of a body are inextricable. Every sound that we hear, no matter if it is digitally altered or even generated, is a sound in a space.[15] Voices are embodied in a larger sense than just our corporeal bodies; those bodies exist within a larger space that we are part of and that is part of us, our ecology. There really is something radical in the voice once we recognize that we never hear a voice "by itself"—it always sounds in some particular place, a place that is an environment. This is what I mean by an "echo-logical" understanding.

As outlined in the introduction and elaborated in the first chapter, there is a substantial stereotype of Calvino as a disembodied and cerebral author—Silvio Perrella's view of Calvino as a head strangled by its own intestines. This understanding tends to go hand in hand with the idea of Calvino as a predominantly visual or "geometric" writer. Like the insistence on Calvino's ocularcentrism, the language used to describe Calvino's geometric visuality can become quite exaggerated, especially on the Italian side. Guido Almansi refers to Calvino's "follia" (madness), "sfrenata passione" (unbridled passion) and "ossessione" (obsession, 100–102) over geometric thinking, while Marco Belpoliti refers to Calvino's "passione scopofila" (scopophilic passion, 250) and "l'occhio-mente" (eye-mind, xii).[16] At its most extreme, it can become something like the caricature of Calvino as "pure" given by Carla Benedetti in *Pasolini contro Calvino*, where "pure" means apolitical and so cerebral as to be bodiless (more "Puritan" than "pure"). (These descriptions frequently also hint at the idea that a normal sexuality has been replaced by a passion for something else.) But in Calvino's "A King Listens," we find a very corporeal depiction: a throat of flesh, coated with saliva, encased in a chest that is filled with feelings, a childhood, a lifetime of experiences (3:165). This is not a "pure" or abstract voice, not a geometrical abstraction or reduction of a complex world. It comes from a throat coated with saliva.

As for the space that surrounds us, we could return to the passage where the king attempts to make a mental map of the shape of his palace just from the sounds around him. It would be easy to read this passage as a flight from the real and embodied world—all of that concrete reality becomes just another abstract network of signifiers.[17] But what motivates the king's sonic experiment is quite the reverse. He wants to move from the apparently immaterial world of sound (immaterial in both senses—disembodied and unimportant, the irrational and trivial register of coughs, shuffles, and dropped spoons) to reconstruct the phenomenal world specifically in its dirty, political complexity. He wants to hear if his enemies are on the move, and where he might hide. He wants to not be killed, and his survival depends on his knowledge of and his ability to *hear* the space around him and the political valence of that space.

If Cavarero uses Calvino's homage to the embodied voice to show the ways in which it has been hidden behind a disembodied and abstract speech, I want to argue here that a similar (although not identical) metaphysical occultation has taken place in this passage. Calvino suggests that the apparently trivial and meaningless dimension of echoing sound—what would ordinarily be called noise—carries a certain political value for the king. Specifically, it allows him to reconstruct space. Here, Calvino specifically subordinates the visual register to the acoustic. The acoustic is now primary and *permits* a secondary visualization of space, giving "form to the void in which the sounds spread and to the obstacles they encounter, allowing the sounds themselves to prompt the images." This is a process that takes place within the mind, but also within the body, within the ear (in an earlier passage, the narrator calls the entire palace the king's ear, a "palazzo-orecchio" [3:153, palace-ear]). What Calvino describes when the king reconstructs the space of the palace is not some abstract game or cerebral, theoretical exercise, but in fact the way that sound operates in the real world (and the way that it is processed in our brains): The echo produces space.

In certain cases, too much reverberation can make the signal hard to make out, and we might complain about the acoustics. In *Sensing Sound*, Nina Sun Eidsheim argues that there is effectively an ideology (unconscious, unrecognized, normative) about what constitutes "good sound" in music and acoustic media more broadly. She calls this the "figure of sound," the presupposition of certain "dominant concepts" (11–12, 17) about how music is "normally" experienced, and it includes very exact limits to what are considered "acceptable" levels of reverberation (58–69).[18] This is essentially a metaphysics of sound, and as Cavarero also argues, it is about privileging the essential communicability of a message. Too much reverberation would blur the comprehensibility of the words, "degrading" speech into pure voice. In other words, we have learned to listen only ever for the message and never to the sound itself (with all of the many messages it, too, encodes). Likewise, Lacoue-Labarthe's "inner echo" (150) is not repetition of a message or an abstract idea, but takes place at the level of the "*musical* part . . . the *voice*: intonation, elocution, tone, inflections, melisma, rhythm, even timbre (or what Barthes calls 'grain')" (159, original emphasis).

In other words, Lacoue-Labarthe is listening for, and the subject is sonically constituted within, a specific space, a cavity whose matrix offers special acoustic (or catacoustic) qualities. This is why Lacoue-Labarthe's notion of the catacoustic is so useful for breaking down a metaphysics of sound that presupposes an originary sound that could be isolated and abstracted away from the particularity of its concrete enunciation or performance, as a textual transcript does to the spoken voice, or as a musical score does to the performance. As any musician knows, even the best musical instrument needs a proper space in which to be played for it to fully display its "true sound," to have the best sound it can have. Like different organisms inhabiting different niches, the "ideal echo," if it exists at all, changes from instrument to instrument and from piece to piece (slow-moving Medieval plainchant works wonderfully in large church spaces, but faster and more complex vocal music can turn into acoustic mud in the same space). Reverberation plays a crucial role in our reception of sound, not only making an instrument or a voice sound richer, but also allowing a mental reconstruction of the space of the performance. If you were blindfolded and led into an unknown room, the quality of a sound's reverberation would convey by itself a wealth of information: Is the room large, medium, or small? Filled with objects or mostly empty? Are the walls and other surfaces acoustically reflective (marble, steel) or sound absorbing (wood, fabric)? Are the walls or other surfaces near or far away?[19] The king's notion that he could reconstruct the space of his palace, and ultimately his city, entirely through reflected sound is not at all absurd, even if the suggestion that he can perceive the lace fringe of a linen tablecloth from the tinkle of a spoon that's fallen to the floor is surely an exaggeration.

In what follows, I want to attempt a catacoustic reading of *Invisible Cities*—not the 1972 novel by Italo Calvino, but the 2013 opera by Christopher Cerrone, understood as a way we can hear a larger catacoustic echo, a part of the resonant space opened up by Calvino.[20] I think there's a good deal at stake in this echo-logical reading, particularly a certain image of Calvino, who is, in Benedetti's eyes, so attentive "al visibile e alle superfici" (to the visible and to surfaces) that he is stricken by a "narcisismo cagionevole" (feeble narcissism) that makes him into an "autore immagine" (author-image) rather than an "autore in carne e ossa" (author in flesh and blood) (24–27). We can ask, along with Lacoue-Labarthe, "what happens when one goes back from Narcissus to Echo" (146), what happens when we turn away from the idea of Calvino as a "feeble narcissist" dedicated entirely to the visual (and its concomitant tendency toward the abstract and schematic), and instead investigate the acoustic dimensions of his work? Is he still so superficial, or is there a deeper and more politically committed element that becomes *audible* in Cerrone's opera? What happens when we hear Calvino once more within the catacoustic dimensions of his work, that is to say, along with the cultural echoes that it has produced and that have enriched it, as well as the space that is opened up and delimited by those reverberations. The overall effect, I hope, will be to restore a sense of materiality and concreteness to the entire resonant complex, a sense of "flesh and bone" as well as a sense of its political impetus. Ultimately, I think that catacoustics as they are delineated in Lacoue-Labarthe still leave traces of an Oedipal model of the anxiety of influence, but I hope this analysis will show that a more resonant model of catacoustics can go beyond the echo and instead amplify, enrich and make it more fully what it is.

An Opera for Headphones

As I noted at the start of this chapter, there are many visual echoes of Calvino's novel, but there are also a number of compelling acoustic interventions that follow or cite *Invisible Cities* in some fashion, both popular (a Bay Area indie rock band named "The Invisible Cities," another from Leeds, and many dozens of songs with that title, including an instrumental by The Police guitarist Andy Summers) and more rarified (an orchestral work by the Swedish composer Britta Byström, an avant-garde piano piece by British composer and installation artist Alwynne Pritchard, a sound installation documenting the sounds of Baltimore by US artist Teri Rueb). The most significant of these works so far, however, is Christopher Cerrone's opera based on the novel (libretto based on William Weaver's English translation), which was staged a few times in 2009 and 2010, but then radically reinvented for its Los Angeles run in 2013 when it gained significant media attention; it was nominated for a Pulitzer in 2014, and a PBS documentary about the opera's LA performance won an Emmy.

What made the reinvented opera so newsworthy was its technologically dispersed modality of reception and site-specific performance. It was staged in Los Angeles's Union Station, and both audience and performers experienced the music entirely through wireless microphones and headsets. Since Union Station is the city's main hub for rail transport, and the opera was held during normal operating hours, this meant that both the performers and the audience were dispersed throughout the station among passengers, and moved (more or less) freely throughout (the orchestra remained in one space throughout, since it's rather difficult to move freely about with a cello or piano).[21] It is evident how the venue reflects the novel's central concern with travel and exploration of both literal and philosophical geographies. Yuval Sharon, the opera's director, cleverly echoes these concerns by presenting Marco Polo as a baseball cap–wearing backpacker, who commemorates the places he's been with tourist patches on his bright-red sleeveless hoodie (see fig. 2; his signature baseball cap is marked with his initials on the front and his birth and death dates on the sides; note also his wireless earbud, with his lavalier microphone taped to his jaw on the other side). Kublai Khan, by contrast, is a distinguished, somewhat older man with diminished mobility (he spends most of the opera in a wheelchair; see fig. 3). So far, these are clever

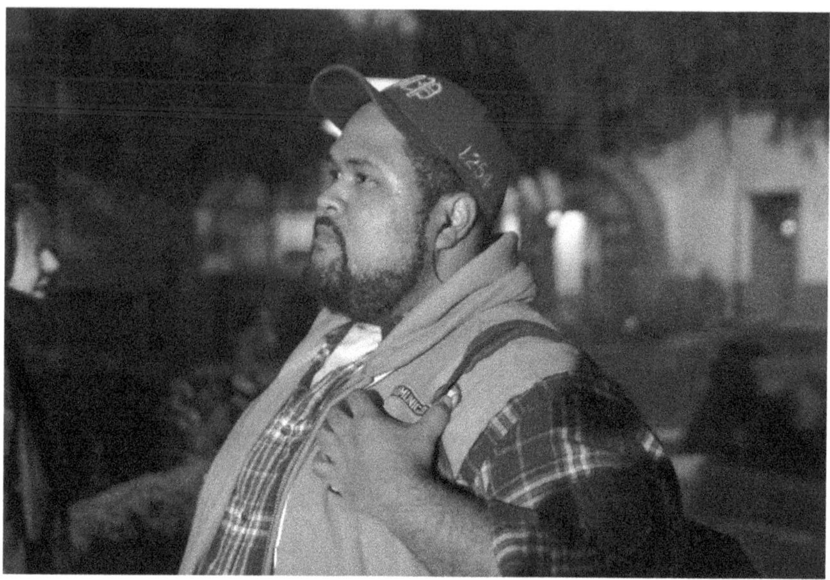

FIGURE 2. Marco Polo as modern backpacker. Courtesy Dana Ross (danaross.com)

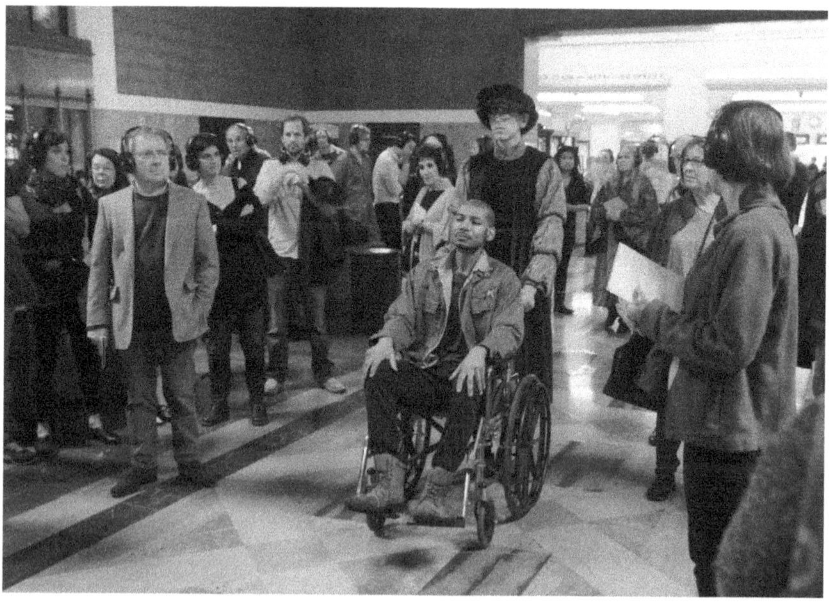

FIGURE 3. Kublai Khan and attendant. Courtesy Dana Ross (danaross.com)

modern-day projections of the two characters' fundamental functions in the novel: mobility and stasis. Audience members could hear the opera's acoustic entirety in their headphones, but could watch what they wished: instrumentalists, singers, dancers, or perhaps the passengers rushing to catch their trains, since the normal business of Union Station continued throughout the performance (although station "employees" and bystanders would also occasionally turn out to be singers or dancers).

The opera's form is a much-shortened version of the novel. There is an instrumental overture, and then four of the italicized "dialogue" sections of Calvino's novel: the opening about Kublai Khan's desire to rescue his empire from "the termite's gnawing," one of the dialogues about Marco Polo and Kublai Khan attempting to communicate, the dialogue in which they discuss Venice, and the final one about how to oppose the inferno of urban life. These sections are interleaved with just three of Marco Polo's "invisible cities"—Isidora (the city of the traveler's dreams that he reaches, alas, only in old age), Armilla (the city that consists only of plumbing, inhabited by water nymphs) and Adelma (the city populated by those we know who have died).

I. Overture (instrumental): A sudden musical slide up, and an even faster drop back down, a minor third. This movement, suggesting an unreleased tension, is shattered from time to time by fortissimo explosions of low dissonance. The overall mood is threatening, ominous. The ringing of crotales (a kind of tuned cymbal), which serves throughout the work as a kind of punctuation, brings the music to an end.

II. Prologue: A delicate, melancholy motif on piano, intervals that close and then open, folding, unfolding; Nadir calls it "the heartbeat/anxiety rhythm" (190). Kublai Khan sings of the desire to save his empire from "formless ruin" (the music becomes cacophonous) by finding a "a pattern so subtle" (quieter, a single note). We first hear the three-note "Ku-blai Khan" motif, rising and then falling.

III. Isidora: According to the score, this is a lyrical and evocative "Venetian boat song" in 6/8 rhythm (probably a reference to Mendelssohn, op. 30, no. 6, but heavier, more plodding), as Marco Polo sings of the city of the traveler's dreams that he only reaches, alas, in old age.

IV. Language: The Khan and Polo attempt to communicate, without speaking each other's languages. The music is dark, chaotic, cacophonous, recalling the Overture, and accompanied by

> prerecorded passages of rapid speech in Turkish, Croatian, Farsi, Urdu, Italian, overlapping; the singing privileges sound over sense, even once Polo and the Khan find a common language.
>
> V. Armilla: A distinctly minor tonality, lyrical, in a marked triple meter. Marco Polo sings of a city that consists only of plumbing without walls, ceilings, or floors, inhabited by water nymphs.
>
> VI. Venice: A haunting piano part that is strongly reminiscent of the Prologue's "heartbeat" opening and closing, as the Khan and Polo discuss Venice. The clearest articulation of the two-note motif (a falling minor second in most cases) for "Mar-co" and "Ve-nice" (as well as the word "si-lence").
>
> VII. Adelma: Dissonant and melodramatic. Marco Polo recounts in spoken word the city populated by those we once knew who have died; the music primarily reiterates music we have already heard (the Venetian boat song of Isidora, the low bass explosions of the Overture, the "heartbeat" of the Prologue), but in ghastly, dissonant versions.
>
> VIII. Epilogue: Beginning with the chaos of the "Language" music and a fortissimo "Ku-blai Khan" motif, the Epilogue gradually works its way toward that "pattern so subtle," the spaces and moments that we find that are not inferno, so that we might "give them space." The crotales once more serve as a lingering punctuation that marks the end.

It is clear from numerous details that Cerrone and Sharon (as well as Joris Debeij, who is responsible for the filmed version) are very familiar with the novel—Cerrone read the novel in both English and Italian (see Nadir, 173), and he clearly knows Calvino well. He references Calvino's work on "Lightness," for instance, in explaining why the opera is relatively short (Nadir, 171), and he composed a much earlier piece, "Reading a Wave," for three trios playing slightly out of sync with each other, based on the first short story in Calvino's *Mr. Palomar*. I will point out other ways in which Cerrone and Sharon demonstrate a deep understanding of Calvino as I go along, but it is absolutely clear that any sort of "literal" adaptation was never on the table (as Nadir points out [188], a brief section of the lyrics in the final epilogue are not Calvino at all, but taken from T. S. Eliot).[22] Cerrone's work, in other words, is neither a repetition of nor an Oedipal challenge to Calvino, but rather a way to expand what the original did into a new space.

Cerrone is, broadly speaking, a "postminimalist" composer. Unlike other "post-" terms that indicate a rejection of what came before, post-minimalist music is strongly influenced by minimalist music (such as Steve Reich or Terry Riley), often adopting its techniques and procedures. Those include a steady, driving pulse, sometimes mechanical in feel; a move away from atonal and serial music back toward compositions with diatonic harmonies and recognizable tonal centers; multiple musical phrases that move in and out of phase with each other; additive and subtractive processes, such as partial melodies that are repeated, gradually becoming complete; and combinatorial compositional techniques. I began chapter 1 by discussing Alvin Lucier's *I Am Sitting in a Room*, which gradually transforms a recording of speech into musical tones simply by recording it again and again, a typically minimalist additive process. In postminimalist music, those techniques are still used, but less rigidly and with greater complexity, now aiming for a subtler, more personal effect.[23]

Each of the sections in Cerrone's opera has a distinct musical character, but with an emphasis on the Emperor's melancholy, often interspersed with sections that depict wild chaos, both musical and linguistic. As I'll go on to discuss, the work is permeated by echoes, not only in its echoing of Calvino, but even compositionally. Four "names" echo throughout the opera, appearing and reappearing in different sections: "Marco" and "Venice," "Kublai Khan" and "Inferno." Each is a distinctive motif (arguably they are leitmotifs, since they are associated with names and places): "Ku-blai" leaps up an octave for the second syllable of his name before descending for "Khan," as does the three-syllable "in-fer-no," while "Mar-co," "Ve-nice" (and "si-lence") are sung to the same two-note melody (typically a falling half-step, B down to A♯). All of the "echo phrases" of the opera are falling in pitch (the *kata-* of catacoustics) for the final syl-lable. This echoing helps to bind together an opera at risk of a potentially destabilizing dispersal in space. At times, the motifs are echoed as part of an "additive process" of minimalist and postminimalist composition until echoes of echoes produce a canon-like "in and out of phase" effect (see fig. 4)—echoes of echoes, cascading down (a different sense of the *kata-* of catacoustics).[24] That additive process can also be reversed (as it is at the end of the Epilogue) to create a progressive simplification and lightening of density.

Some listeners may also hear yet another echo in the repeated de-scending melody of the name "Marco," namely the children's game that seems all too germane to my argument here about sound and space (or the paranoid king in his palace), in which one child in a swimming pool,

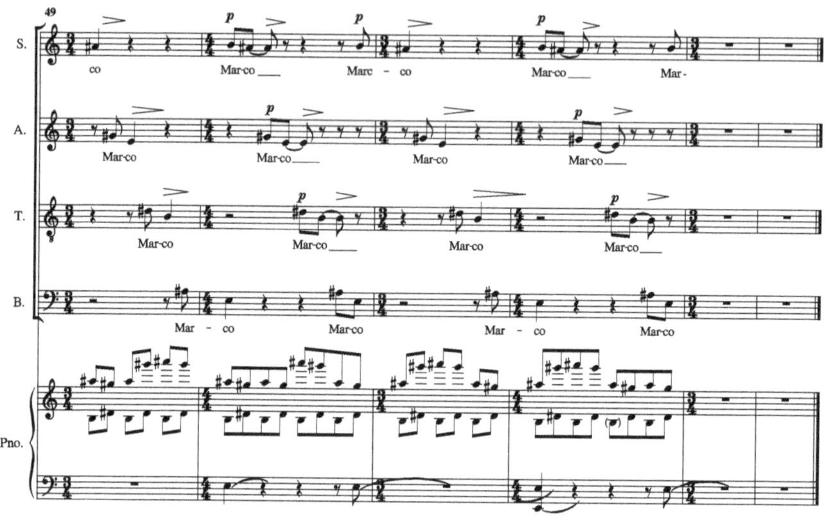

FIGURE 4. Contrapuntal "echoing." (Cerrone, scene 5, measures 49–52)

eyes closed, tries to locate the other children through sound alone, calling out the name "Marco" and waiting for the echoic response "Polo."[25]

The opera's truly audacious innovation is, of course, its wireless and networked means of registering and distributing sound. Eidsheim discusses this feature of the opera at length in *Sensing Sound*, arguing that the experience creates "two simultaneous acoustic worlds" (89) that are in a productive tension with each other, and that crucially, the listener is free to choose between.[26] You are hearing the music, live, but always more than what you can see. The singers are generally not in the same room as the orchestra, and may not even be in the same room as the other singers. You are also hearing something less (which may also be more); you are hearing the music, but perfectly mixed, from a kind of "bird's-ear" vantage point, just as you listen to professionally recorded music through headphones at home. In this opera, there will be no irritating unwrapping of a cough lozenge or that telltale cell phone ring that someone forgot to silence! The musicians and singers are closely miked with microphones that mostly pick up sound from directly in front of them, and don't let through much ambient sound. In a normal concert hall, if you are seated in the far-right front corner, you might be overwhelmed by the sounds of the instruments on that side (say, the basses and cellos), and strain to hear those on the other side (the violins and the woodwinds, perhaps). In this opera, the sound is all correctly checked and balanced, as in a professional recording rather than a real space.

Some readers and listeners might find something disturbing and artificial in this. The classical music world has in fact long resisted forms of electronic amplification and alteration in favor of the natural and the authentic. This ideology is generally followed in public, but not always behind the scenes where the audience might not notice the use of audio technology, and virtually no classical recording is made without some (often substantial amounts of) "touching up" in the studio. Although more digital manipulation of recorded classical music goes on than some would like to admit, the governing conceit is still that one is hearing the "real thing," a largely faithful replica of the actual performance. Cerrone's opera of *Invisible Cities* effectively demolishes this paradigm, however, since the sound of the "authentic performance" is either the carefully curated mix that was heard by spectators in 2013, or the "authentic sound of being there" that would have been picked up by an omnidirectional microphone in Union Station: a lot of passengers running around, some (apparently) unaccompanied singers, and perhaps the muffled distant sound of an orchestra. Compellingly, however, almost every account of Cerrone's opera that I have read (including Eidsheim's) mentions that listeners sometimes took their headphones off, either to share them with the passengers transiting the station who wanted to know what was happening, or to experience the sound *in situ*, the singer without the musical support.[27] Even some of the publicity photographs for the opera show listeners with the headphones half on and half off, experiencing both reality and a kind of augmented reality at the same time, and in the portions of the filmed performance of the opera that are live, you can see several listeners with headphones half on, half off, or sharing their headset with others (see fig. 5, where most of the audience members are wearing their headsets, but not the blondish man on the right side; this is also visible in fig. 3, in which the man wearing a light shirt and jeans, dark jacket draped over his arm, to the left of Kublai Khan has taken his headset off).

A clear goal was to problematize the idea that one can clearly separate performance and "ordinary life," especially in public spaces, where it's not unusual to find someone wearing headphones, or for that matter, loudly singing or talking to themselves. While some of the dancers and singers wore clothing that was more clearly costume-like (see Kublai Khan's attendant in fig. 3, wearing a Venetian Renaissance–like outfit with mask), this was no guarantee: The performances were all clustered around Halloween, so it was not unusual to see audience members or ordinary train passengers also wearing costumes. Moreover, the opera made visible the simultaneity of two very different kinds of spaces in Union Station: In figure 5, one can see a surprising contrast between the performers (most

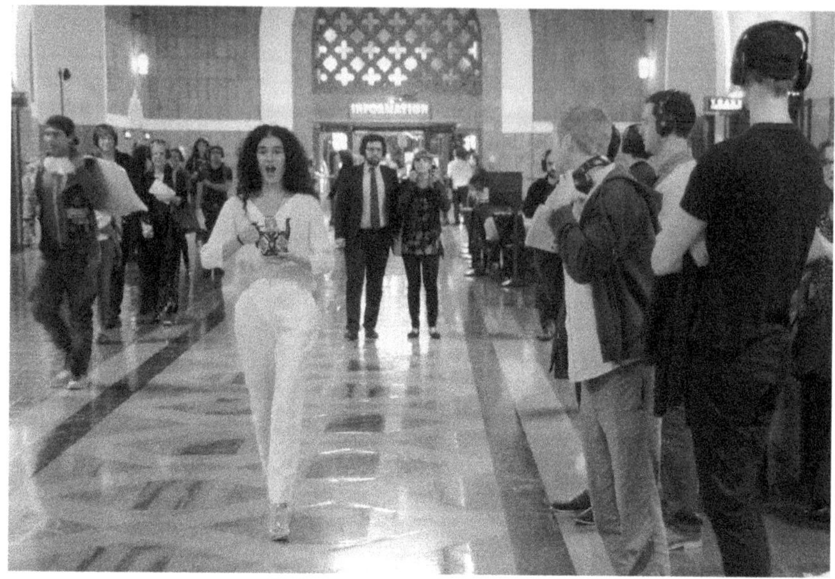

FIGURE 5. Performer, composer, audience, public. Courtesy Dana Ross (danaross.com)

notably the soprano carrying a teapot), the audience members with their headphones (particularly the man walking behind her in a suit and tie, who is in fact Chris Cerrone), and the public (the man on the left-hand side of the image with a backward baseball cap and his belongings stuffed into a white plastic garbage bag slung over his shoulders).

"90 percent of operas are about getting together and seeing a big spectacle," says Cerrone in the *Artbound* documentary, "but my opera is about getting together and being by yourself." This is an experience that is typical of the Calvinian subject, and perhaps also typical of a contemporary digital, networked life. Indeed, most contemporary thinking about mobile headphone use emphasizes the sense of neoliberal autonomy and separation that it creates (an "autonomous 'head space'" in Hosokawa, or a "privatized sound world" and "an illusion of omnipotence" in Bull), but it is clear this is not actually how headphones functioned in Cerrone's opera.[28] Indeed, it seems to have rather the opposite effect. Here, the audience is watching a performance in a particular space, an inhabited public space, and the sound of the space in the headphones does not match what is seen. This clearly disrupts that sense of starring in your own movie, living in a private sound world, and listeners appeared to have *enjoyed* that disruption. A much more fitting model might be the one developed by Angela Frattarola in *Modernist Soundscapes*, especially in her chapter on Joyce's *Ulysses* as a kind of "headphone novel." There she refers to a modernist *auditory cosmopolitanism*, since "headphones correlate with stream of consciousness in their shared capacity to bring cosmopolitan sounds from different cultures and classes into one's headspace" (107). This is an accurate way of describing what happened in the Union Station performances of *Invisible Cities*: different cultures and different soundscapes brought into a "cosmopolitan" (literally, "city-space") experience that is constituted more by difference and alterity than by an idealized fiction of an autonomous and private self.

Eidsheim discusses reverberation at some length in her chapter on Cerrone. The composer and director were in fact extremely aware that they were not simply presenting a performance, but also creating and manipulating an acoustic *space* through reverb. The tiny lavalier microphones that were used to capture the singing are so close to the performer (taped to their jawline), and directional (different kinds of microphones can pick up sounds from all around, or only from a given direction), that they do not capture reflected sound. But recall that "the figure of sound" cuts both ways: Too much reverb is very bad, because it would muddy the singing and could even render the melody hard to make out, but no reverb at all would also sound unmusical, dry, flat, lifeless, and artificial, strongly associated with the ultra-controlled acoustics of a recording studio. As a result, reverb was added digitally—meaning that it could also be manipulated digitally. As I discussed briefly in the introduction, modern digital audio recording programs are able to model reverb (and hence space) in very sophisticated ways. A typical professional audio recording program offers the user spaces both generic ("concert hall," "city street," "deep canyon") and quite specific ("Price Hall," "Aranno Chapel," "Michaelis Nave"). One can also choose from among a wide variety of imaginary spaces when using the program, and the user is not necessarily limited to Eidsheim's "figure of [good] sound." Some of the spaces are not actually physically possible in the ordinary world, such as "moving spaces," which model the reverberation of a room that is constantly changing in size, distance, and reflective character. With a few clicks of the mouse, the user can place a recorded sound underwater, or on a cave on another planet, a cave made of some exotic material that not only reflects the sound, but sustains and amplifies parts of it.[29]

Cerrone has said that he is "obsessed with reverb," so it is not surprising that he and Sharon were particularly attentive to the question of reverberation.[30] Cerrone worked closely with the sound designer, E. Martin Gimenez, to create a specific "sound world": "Each scene [has] a different acoustic, a different reverberation. Some scenes are dry and dead and not reverberant. Other scenes feel like they're in the middle of a cathedral" (Margolies). This wasn't a bug, but a feature, one trumpeted in the production company's clip book, where the same quote appears. In the PBS documentary about the opera, Gimenez describes the real-time manipulation of reverb during the performance to recreate a cinematic experience, moving in the opening section from a "bone-dry" sound (short, unreflective, as if we were right next to the singer, close up) to a huge "cathedral reverb" (very long echoes, around seven seconds, according to Gimenez) to show that Kublai Khan, while master of a vast empire, is also all alone (qtd. in Eidsheim, 81). In the recorded version, one can hear something similar in the Prologue when Kublai Khan sings the word "planispheres" (no significant reverb, close miked, centered in the stereo mix, so neither left nor right). Some six or seven seconds later, his voice now panned to the left, triple piano, with big "cathedral reverb," echoes "planispheres" again. The effect is, as the score indicates, of a distant singer, "offstage." The offstage Kublai Khan and Marco Polo (who is panned hard right, same reverb) then sing the words "sandalwood" and "emptiness," but out of sync, splitting the syllables of the words between the two voices. The overall effect is to suggest a huge "offstage" space, but a lonely one, ricocheting with voices that don't connect.

The difficult solitude of the male subject is a constant feature in Calvino, a thread that runs throughout his work. Two or more people may be together—physically in the same space—but the Calvinian subject remains trapped in his head, in his thoughts (I use the male pronoun advisedly), and the dominant affect in many of Calvino's fictions is solitude, often mourning for the lost other he can't connect to. This is particularly true of men and women trying to be together, but it is also true in many other sequences. In other words, characters in Calvino are, we might say, always in a different place, both literally and metaphorically, united in a network of communication that is also a sign of their incommensurability.

In some ways, this is actually *more* true in Cerrone and Sharon's *Invisible Cities* than it is in Calvino's novel, however. Throughout the novel's dialogues, Marco Polo and Kublai Khan are in a constant struggle over how to understand the Khan's empire and its cities (a constant duel over how to understand: the infinite diversity of the singular thing, or the vast pattern that encompasses all, but loses the details?). Cerrone's opera effectively realizes—that is, renders literal—the philosophical distances that separate them. Here, the two sing what are effectively duets in which they are not in the same space at all. In fact, Sharon's staging keeps Polo and Kublai Khan in completely separate spaces until well over halfway through the opera, and afterward, he repeatedly stages their encounters as near misses; in the "Venice" dialogue, for instance, they are about to encounter each other when Polo suddenly swerves and exits the building (although the singing continues, since the listener inhabits the acoustic space of the wireless headphones). In the opera's finale, Marco Polo, still a contemporary backpacker, approaches the Emperor, now dressed in thirteen-century Mongolian finery, begging him to "make them endure, give them space." They walk slowly toward each other but do not even make eye contact, moving along parallel paths in opposite directions. They pass each other by, but have they shared a moment, or missed one? What Sharon and Cerrone have understood in their solitary-yet-together, dispersed-yet-community opera is what Claudio Milanini calls Calvino's "utopia discontinua" (scattered utopia), for which his governing metaphor is the mosaic whose fragments, once apprehended, manage to convey a whole.

Cerrone and Sharon's production of the opera also grounds Marco Polo's and Kublai Khan's voices in specific bodies, namely the two singers of the principal roles, both African American: the boyish Marco Polo (Ashley Faatoalia); the slender, dignified, wheelchair user Kublai Khan (Cedric Berry, not actually disabled). This happens in any musical performance, of course, since the music must be produced by an actual body, with its specific timbre, range (Barthes's "grain of the voice"): Faatoalia's uniquely sweet and rounded tenor, Berry's authoritative and forceful baritone. Every singer has a more or less distinctive voice, but Cerrone's music effectively reminds the spectator of the unique body of the singer. For example, in the "Language" section of the opera, when Kublai Khan first begins to sing it is the first-person pronoun "I," loudly and, in the score, "with an air commanding" (38, measure 28) primarily on the note of A♯, over many bars—the note, however, constantly flutters between A♯ and B, occasionally diving an octave down and then returning, in brief flurries of vocal glissando, that are punctuated in the score by marks that indicate that he is to "inhale loudly" (38, measure 31). This continues for about 11 seconds, just the single syllable "I." When he finally begins the word ("remain"), he continues in this same fashion, wavering on and around the notes, and this style continues for almost a full minute. What is happening here is somewhere between an extreme form of vocal vibrato and a technique called melisma, in which singers sing many notes for a single syllable (rather than a precise correspondence of one note per syllable). Like excessive reverb, melisma can have the effect of making the words essentially incomprehensible—one loses track of the language in the flurry of soaring vocal melodies—and Lawrence Kramer refers to it in *Musical Meaning* as an example of "overvocalization . . . a rupture, a wrenching of song beyond the terrain of symbolizing language" (63). Mladen Dolar also argues that "voice [can] take over in its own jubilation, melisma without a support" (*A Voice*, 49), a further detachment of pure vocality from the sense of the words. Unlike reverb, which is produced by space, melisma tends to make us aware of the singer's bodily presence since it indicates an excess of emotion (one well-known example in pop music is Whitney Houston's cover of "I Will Always Love You"). It is also difficult, however, a kind of vocal athleticism, and it involves singing long melodic sections, taking a quick breath and then beginning a new syllable and new melodic line. This is amplified in Cerrone's score, which calls for the singer to loudly emphasize the sound of his breathing, highlighting what Cavarero calls the "corporeality of breath and voice" (*For More Than One*, 62).[31]

At the same time, there are other features of the opera that tend to "disembody" the performances (again, we are hearing the same fundamental dynamic that Milanini describes, a simultaneous fragmentation and unification). The opening of that same "Language" section, for example, consists of rapid-fire speech (banal geographical information), reciting texts in Turkish, Croatian, Urdu and Farsi, the modern languages of the ambassadors who visit Kublai Khan in the dialogue just after Isaura. On the one hand, the texts are read in ways that do emphasize the bodily presence of the speaker. The Turkish and Croatian are high-pitched and nasal voices (with "halting, gasping breaths," according to the score), while the Farsi and Urdu are "whispered ("as fast as possible"), incomprehensible with frequent breaths ("like Morse code")" (25, measure 3). The frequent breaths call attention to the embodied performance, but both the quality of the sound (close mike, no reverb, whispered voice) and the fact that the voices are prerecorded, electronically triggered and never attached to any visible body indicates they are disembodied.[32] Other moments in the score also call for prerecorded voices, including Marco Polo's and Kublai Khan's (see Scene I—Prologue, measures 24–33, the example I mentioned before of deep reverb used to create an "offstage" space without any stage).[33] What this means during the performance is that not all sounds can be visually "pinned" to a body. As a spectator with wireless headphones, I might search throughout Union Station looking for the source of a voice or instrumental sound, but I might not always be able to find it. Again, the sound experience is perhaps closest to film sound, with certain voices remaining "acousmatic," in Michel Chion's terms[34]—voices that are never tied to an "onscreen" body. Even *within* the headphones, Cerrone's opera replicates the "cosmopolitan" experience of multiple worlds crowding the audience's headspace.

Give Them Space

So, does this opera dissolve the embodied performance, the pure voice, that Cavarero believes has an important (even revolutionary) political valence, or does it represent its maximum intensity? As Eidsheim observed in *Sensing Sound*, the genius of Cerrone's opera, and what makes it so destabilizing for our acoustical norms, is that it does *both* at the same time. In Cerrone's *Invisible Cities*, when we hear a sound, we must choose whether to "hear it non-normatively" or to "reject the challenge to our [more typical] experience as wrong" (93). For Eidsheim, this is ultimately an ethical choice between whether we will "explore" (94) or reject acoustic difference (and ultimately, whether we explore or reject human difference and alterity). I might frame it as a choice between the exploration of an inner world (the private, autonomous "headphone space") and a relational world, with the recognition that anything like utopia will be found scattered in all kinds of spaces, internal and external, normative and other. Still, the visible record of so many audience members choosing to explore multiple acoustic spaces is promising—they are following, even before hearing it, Calvino's final injunction to readers at the end of *Invisible Cities*: "Seek and find who and what, in the midst of the inferno are not the inferno, make them endure, give them space." Exploration is of course one of the principal themes of *Invisible Cities*, particularly the exploration of spaces that are not simply unknown, but *invisible*, those that do not fit into the categories that have habitually rendered our world legible in the past, including the auditory. We might also recall that the novel takes as its starting point an emblematic encounter between West and non-West, between mutually incomprehensible languages and cultures, a rare historical encounter with alterity and difference that seems to have led to at least some comprehension.

And this is where I would like to return to the notion of "catacoustics," but now working to move beyond thinking of the echo as a repetition that haunts and insists, or worse, that demarcates the dying away of a defective copy. Calvino's novel has acquired a certain resonance; its echoes are very much still continuing today, echoes that—like all reverberations—create a cultural space, articulated by echo, for us to explore. The catacoustic, in other words, is about creating and recognizing an acoustic space—recognizing one's own self as part of a space composed of echoes and repetitions. This is a space in which something—an idea, for example—can not only endure but grow, just as Calvino's novel has grown into some decidedly non-infernal forms over the last half century: people working on the intersection of art, sustainability and community; others documenting a global African diaspora; still others recognizing disability and chronic illness as its own form of potential community. And some are making music that not only understands, but enhances, amplifies, and enriches Calvino's original ideas, scattered moments in which we might recognize the tracery of a pattern so subtle that it might survive our worst impulses and most reductive ways of thinking.

In offering this rather hopeful notion of the catacoustic, we might want to emphasize a different sense for that Greek prefix *kata-*. Rather than a something gone bad, dwindling away, or degrading, we might take the more energetic sense that it can also have: *against*, as in the example I offered earlier in this chapter, *catapult*. At least implicitly (often explicitly), works like Cavarero's and Eidsheim's are fundamentally political, arguing *against* a repressive sonic regime that has gone largely unnoticed (a privileging of discursive and semantic speech and concomitant marginalization of the voice in Cavarero; a normative "figure of sound" that is imposed on our listening practices without us ever even realizing it for Eidsheim). Calvino's position as a political artist has been quite fraught, however, as I indicated in the introduction. While Calvino was primarily interested in art as a means of thinking, this does not mean that his works do not have something to say to and about politics. Indisputably, Calvino's most political work is *Invisible Cities*, and an echo-logical reading that attends to the space in which Calvino's works have resonated makes this clear in the most literal way possible. A UK social enterprise initiative called Invisible Cities trains people struggling with homelessness to become walking tour guides to their cities, working to alleviate homelessness, change perceptions of the homeless, and make visible parts of the city that remain invisible. Meanwhile, John Moody's Invisible Cities Studio is a "collaborative design studio" in the US that uses film to "help communities shape their surrounding environments by telling stories that communicate what is meaningful about places and what is possible for their future," collaborating on media campaigns and other video interventions that foster "inclusive urban spaces." *Le città invisibili* (*Invisible Cities*) is a long-running theatrical project by Pino di Buduo's Teatro Potlach based in Italy but ranging all over the world that aims to rediscover and make visible the historical cultural identity of places, while "Le nostre città invisibili" (Our Invisible Cities) is an initiative by Migrantour that aims to make cultural diversity and new models of citizenship visible in Italy, in part by organizing intercultural walking tours with migrants as tour guides. The root of the word *politics* is the Greek word *polis*, or city. These are just a handful of the ways that Calvino's novel has clearly resonated in a political space and not just a literary one. Indeed, its resonance appears to be increasing over time, and I will have more to say about Calvino's role in developing "city thinking" in chapter 4.

When I state that Calvino is political it is actually to say something indisputable, even slightly obvious: *Invisible Cities* is ultimately a novel about how we explore the world, encounter other people and places; how we speak to each other and negotiate our different languages, understand those differences and the world we inhabit; and most especially how we can live together—as couples, in communities, in cities—without the space of that shared life turning into hell. What Cerrone's opera brings to the fore (what this catacoustic echo adds to the mix) is precisely what Cavarero indicates is essential about political life, about life together: a recognition that the voice always speaks in a social, political, and cultural space, a space that includes that "throat of flesh," in Calvino's phrase "saliva, infancy, the patina of experienced life, the mind's intentions, the pleasure of giving a personal form to sound waves" (3:165). Here we might suggest that it is precisely in a musical form, then, that Cerrone's *Invisible Cities*—that is to say, the acoustic rather than the visible dimension of the political—not only keeps the past alive, but amplifies it and makes it grow.

Sound and the Ec(h)ological

Finally, I'd like to extend this catacoustic "echo-logic" a bit farther, to talk about how the linkage of sound and political space might also bring us to consider natural space, ecology. Although "ecology" derives from the Greek word for home, *oikos*, the German zoologist (Haeckel) who coined the term in the nineteenth century meant for it to refer to the relationship between organisms and their environments, the *space* in which they live. Since the 1960s, however, the word has acquired a slightly different connotation, evincing an activist intervention that is concerned with human effects on the environment, the *oikos* or dwelling space of plants and other animals, particularly the effects of human pollutants and toxins released into that environment. This sense appeared in the 1960s, but we can in fact give a much more precise date for the beginning of this sense of the ecological: September 27, 1962, the publication date of Rachel Carson's transformative book, which began the modern environmentalist movement and led to the creation of the Environmental Protection Agency, a book with a conspicuously acoustic title: *Silent Spring.*

An attentive reading of Calvino—the child of two botanists—reveals a lifelong concern for the natural world and how human beings dwell in it and disturb it. This concern is particularly visible in his earlier works ("La formica argentina," *La nuvola di smog, Marcolvaldo*), as indicated by Serenella Iovino, Monica Seger, and Adele Sanna, but it remains a constant concern throughout the 1960s and 1970s as well, especially in the form of a concern about the human production of trash and pollution (Angela M. Jeannet, 134–54), and human overpopulation.[35] Calvino consistently frames these two issues in terms of space. For example, the ever-clean, ever-renewed city of Leonia generates so much trash that it gradually forms walls and ramparts that would conquer the globe if not for all the other cities doing the same thing: "Forse il mondo intero, oltre i confini di Leonia, è ricoperto da crateri di spazzatura, ognuno con al centro una metropoli in eruzione ininterrotta. I confini tra le città estranee e nemiche sono bastioni infetti in cui i detriti dell'una e dell'altra si puntellano a vicenda, si sovrastano, si mescolano" (2:457, Perhaps the whole world, outside of Leonia's boundaries, is covered by craters of trash, each one with a metropolis in constant eruption at its center. The borders between the alien, hostile cities are contaminated ramparts where each one's detritus supports the other, overlapping, mingling). In the city of Procopia, Marco Polo always stays at the same inn so he can admire the view of an ideal harmony between humans and nature: "un fosso, un ponte, un muretto, un albero di sorbo, un campo di pannocchie, un roveto con le more, un pollaio, un dosso di collina giallo, una nuvola bianca, un pezzo di cielo azzurro a forma di trapezio" (2:481, a ditch, a bridge, a little wall, a rowan tree, a field of corn ears, a blackberry bramble, a chicken yard, a hill's yellow round, a white cloud, a piece of blue sky shaped like a trapezoid). The following year, however, he spies "una faccia tonda e piatta che rosicchiava una pannocchia" (2:481, a round, flat face that was gnawing on a corn cob)—then the next year, three of them, then six, sixteen, twenty-nine, forty-seven, and then too many to count. "Un anno dopo l'altro ho visto sparire il fosso, l'albero, il roveto, nascosti da siepi di sorrisi tranquilli" until "la finestra inquadra solo una distesa di facce: da un angolo all'altro, a tutti i livelli e a tutte le distanze, si vedono questi visi tondi, fermi, piatti piatti, con un accenno di sorriso, e in mezzo molte mani, che si tengono alle spalle di quelli che stanno davanti. Anche il cielo è sparito" (2:482, Year after year, I saw the ditch vanish, the tree, the bramble, hidden by hedges of tranquil smiles. . . . The window frames only a sea of faces: from one corner to the other, at every level and distance, you see those round, still, utterly flat faces. Even the sky has vanished). The Anthropocene here erases the natural world with an endless series of idiotic human faces.

At times, pollution and overpopulation appear together, as in the city of Olivia, which "è avvolta in una nuvola di fuliggine e d'unto che s'attacca alle pareti delle case. . . . Nella ressa delle vie i rimorchi in manovra schiacciano i pedoni contro i muri" (2:406, is wrapped up in a cloud of soot and grease that sticks to the walls. . . . In the crowded streets, the trailers bouncing about crush the pedestrians against the walls), a grim city that is revealed primarily through the sound of its factories, "lo stridere di ruote" (2:408, the squealing wheels). There is a problem, in short, with space, and this is perhaps the central problem for *Invisible Cities*, which offers at its very end a suggestion about how to make our world more livable, surely the point of ecology in a more political sense. In Weaver's translation (used by Cerrone for the libretto): "seek and learn to recognize who and what, in the midst of the inferno, are not inferno, then make them endure, give them space" (165). For an organism to endure, let alone thrive, it must have space—and sound and space are co-constitutive.

As I argue throughout this book, space and sound share an intimate relationship in which each produces the other. In our cities, our political spaces par excellence, we must pay to hear silence or the natural world (in the nice restaurants, or an upscale cafe with a garden patio), and the greatest incidence of hearing loss is among those who work with heavy machinery or in factories.[36] Naomi Waltham-Smith, in *Shattering Biopolitics*, goes further and argues that "listening is intimately bound up with the power over life, the power to make some lives more or less livable than others" (13). The basic lexicon of politics is largely acoustic (wanting to be heard, having a voice, even the oral vow that is at the heart of "vote"). In Cerrone's remarkable sonic meditation on Calvino's novel, it's clear that he understands the novel's final ethical injunction about the rare space of the non-infernal in our cities ("make them endure, give them space") to be an acoustic one. In the opera's closing movement, three of the four singers take up Calvino's political imperative ("give them space"), chanting on the note of C. Although there is no key signature anywhere in the piece, this section has a typically minor sound (sometimes described as "sad," but more accurately as "serious" or "solemn"), and the insistence on the note of C makes it the tonal center, at least for now (in fact, the notes we hear do all belong to the key of C minor). The tenor voice (Marco Polo), however, continues to sing about the inferno with a melody that moves from beneath that C (A♭) that leaps to G and then descends along the notes of C minor to a D, not dissonant, but indicating that a real resolution has not yet arrived (see fig. 6), since the melody is hovering just above the note that would give the strongest resolution (C).

Eventually, however, Polo also joins in what is a fully unified call for action, with four voices, all distinct, but all chanting on the same note: "make them endure, give them space." If Cerrone has temporarily ousted

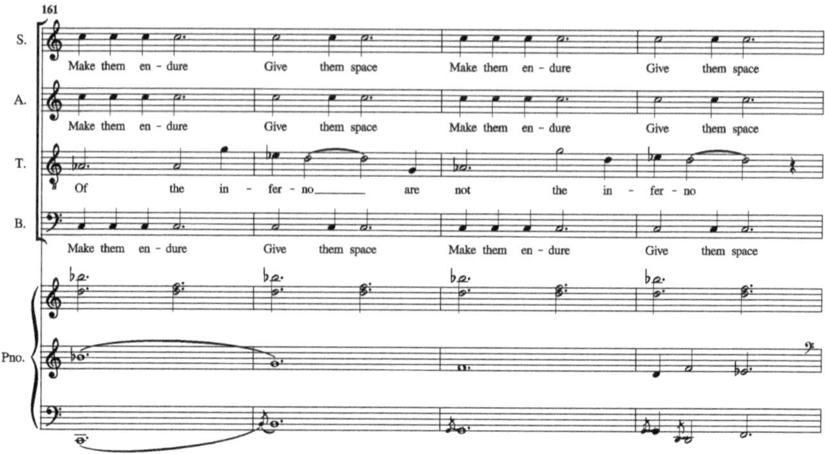

FIGURE 6. Near unity. (Cerrone, scene 7, measures 161–64)

the infernal from the opera, he makes space for harmony with the nonhuman environment; the human voices retreat and leave just the piano. The musical environment continues to echo the Calvinian imperative "make them endure; give them space") now by pedaling the bass in the same rhythm (see fig. 7, where the lower staff keeps the same rhythm that was previously employed by the bass, soprano, and alto voices in fig. 6). In the opera's final measure, we end once more on a suspension, but a consonant one (a perfect fifth moving to a perfect fourth, the same motif that opens the opera's Prologue, and played on the same instrument, the crotales, a fixture in Cerrone's compositions). The final direction in the score

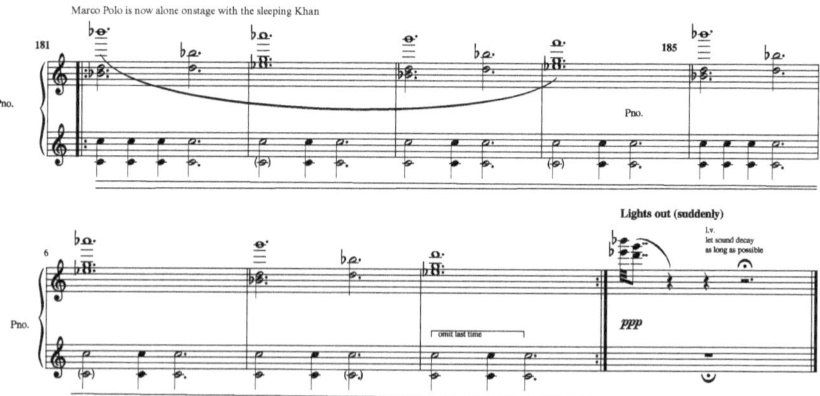

FIGURE 7. Making a space through echo. (Cerrone, scene 7, measures 181–89)

gestures precisely to the capacity of reverberation to open up the space of the possible, the invisible cities that lie beyond the borders of the novel and the opera's score, but also the nonhuman environment beyond those cities: "l.v. [laissez vibrer], let sound decay as long as possible" (p. 125, measure 189; see fig. 7). There is a subtle but significant shift in how we might hear the opera's ending, however, that is visible in the written score: The fermatas (the signs that indicate to the musician to hold a note well past its nominal length) are placed over the *rests*, not the notes, meaning that it is the silence of the space itself that we are supposed to hear and prolong.

Conclusions

What I am proposing here is the notion of a "catacoustic reading" that attends to the echo as a fundamental part of the sound, not as a debilitated and less significant repetition, but as a source of acoustic and interpretive wealth. Moreover, I want to emphasize the connections between the echo and space. Sounds don't come to us in isolation, but rather they come to us with their spatiality and materiality attached. I don't just hear the distinctive sound of a shoe scraping on pavement; I hear it from behind me, low to the ground, perhaps off to the right side. Virtually all of that spatial information is produced by the echoes of the space I am in (a parking garage, a hallway, a hiking path). More broadly, reading by echo demonstrates that we understand the meaning of a text not only "in itself" but through its reverberations, that we "hear" a larger cultural space opened up by an initial vibration. This is uniquely compelling in the case of Calvino's *Invisible Cities*, whose subsequent reverberations have echoed not only through space across national and cultural boundaries, but across media and disciplines, with a pointed political resonance that I am calling "echo-logical." Chris Cerrone's opera is perhaps the most salient example yet of one of those reverberations.

Lastly, the impulse in Calvino (and in the various cultural resonances that *Invisible Cities* has given rise to) to hear sound and space as inextricably joined is often also ecological in the broadest sense, a concern with how we can live in the space of our environment, how we might degrade or even destroy that space, but also how me might make it grow, expand, and become more livable over time. As Niccolò Scaffai observes in his volume on literature and ecology, Calvino understood the book as a textual space, but quite often more literally as "uno spazio vero e proprio, in senso geografico o topografico" (151, a true and proper space, in a geographical or topological sense). If Calvino understood literary space as real space, Cerrone's opera brings its audience to understand acoustic and musical space as geographical and topological space as well, space perceived through sound: an echo-logical reading. What I am calling the "Calvinian imperative" at the end of *Invisible Cities*—find what is not hell in your world, "make it endure, give it space"—is not just about breathable air and drinkable water (although it definitely is about such things), or even social and economic justice (although it definitely is about that as well): It is also about how literature, art, architecture, and music can actually create the spaces of the non-infernal. One of the goals of a catacoustic or echo-logical reading is to help us hear space itself, beyond the roar of the infernal city.

3 / A Jazz *Cosmicomics*

La coscienza americana riesce a esprimersi solo con reazioni che non si cristal-lizzano in immagini: la pittura informale e lo jazz. Lo jazz "freddo" è una razionalizzazione del nervosismo attuale che direi più fondata e storicamente utile.

American consciousness can only express itself with reactions that don't crystal-lize into images: informalist painting and jazz. "Cool" jazz is a rationalization of the current neuroticism that I would say is more historically useful and grounded.

—ITALO CALVINO, *UN OTTIMISTA IN AMERICA*

I've already shown that Calvino has been a source of inspiration for many artists (works of music, painting, dance, opera, installation art, multime-dia, sculpture, and so on) but also in fields much farther afield: archi-tecture, urban planning, caring for the homeless, art education, social networks, and even a handful of video games. This transmedial, transdis-ciplinary, and transnational influence is in fact growing larger all the time, and in my discussions of it I have made recourse to a metaphor which is not simply apt, but which I think helps make clear what is at stake in such a project, namely reverberation and resonance. As a result, I have been drawn primarily to music as one of the most important ways in which this Calvinian resonance has continued to grow and expand. In chapter 2, I looked at Chris Cerrone and Yuval Sharon's opera of *Invisible Cit-ies*, staged in Los Angeles's Union Station in 2013 as a work that adapted Calvino while also revealing the degree to which Calvino's text is about the political value of space and environment (the "echo-logical" reading). While Cerrone's music is a delicate but profound postminimalist explora-tion of that resonant space, in this chapter I want to look instead at a more boisterous, risky, and playful musical approach to Calvino (although equally transmedial, transdisciplinary, and transnational), namely Lisa Mezzacappa's eponymous jazz suite of the *Cosmicomics* from 2020. The album refers to a collection of short stories Calvino began publishing in the mid-1960s (he continued adding to that collection for the rest of his life), for which he coined the word "cosmicomica" (cosmicomic). They are stories inspired by science, but quirky, humorous, or even absurd.

The central character is named Qfwfq, present from the beginning of the universe, sometimes as a black hole, sometimes a dinosaur, but always watching epochal moments in the universe's history. Mezzacappa understands that Qfwfq is not a dispassionate, intellectual eye whose scientific gaze provides us with an objective account; he is rather a charmingly neurotic character, deeply flawed, and driven by the same bodily appetites as the rest of us. Moreover, at the level of form, as well as in more specifically musical questions of orchestration and technique, Mezzacappa develops a "form of space" (the title of one of Calvino's stories) in her music that is not a rational, controlled, and orderly space, but rather one charged with possibilities that are musical, cognitive, and sexual. These possibilities include, rather crucially, some queer potentialities that are raised as logically possible if never realized—but also never foreclosed. (In this regard, this chapter picks up the thread from chapter 1 of a Calvino who may not write in falsetto, but who is more corporeal and flamboyant than we might have expected.)

Mezzacappa is very attentive to the question of form. For many of her pieces, she creates visual diagrams to guide the band's improvisations and to give a kind of bird's-eye view of the musical process (these do not replace, however, traditional "lead sheets" of written music for the musicians, but they are an effective way to convey the spirit of a piece). If we take as a guiding principle that the reverberation of the musical space not only enhances but is in fact constitutive of the original sound, we find that Mezzacappa's playful improvisations are indeed responding to something that is already there in Calvino. As I argued in chapter 1, Calvino's geometries are in fact surprisingly perverse, and the logic that orders his stories is always suffused with paranoia and sexual desire. Ultimately, this isn't about a queer reading of Calvino, as valuable as that might be, but rather about working against a certain kind of static, "crystallized" image of the author that I think is profoundly misleading: a rigid, geometric brain without a body, besotted by the Enlightenment and withdrawn from the world. This is an image of Calvino that is almost unrecognizable in the space that has opened up around him, where he is seen as an irreverent and playful inspiration. That understanding of the *Cosmicomics* is not unique to Mezzacappa, but is part of the transnational, "resonant" understanding of Calvino—as Ildiko Nemeth, who did a stage version of the *Cosmicomics*, observes, the stories are "playful . . . tales of obsession, neurosis, love."[1] As I argue throughout, Calvino is actually consistently *opposed* to images and geometric orders that do not constantly change, including this static and fixed image of the author himself—what Nemeth in that same interview calls "constant transformation."

Program Music

Musical works do not seem to have meanings that are semantically "translatable"—that is, you can't transcribe a series of musical notes and chords into a sentence, like "this movement from F to F♯ over a C9 chord means that the composer is outraged by the breakdown of modern gender roles," or something similar. Music can evoke images, but in a rather unpredictable and indeterminate way (you and I will probably imagine different things in response to the same evocative piece of music, although perhaps fairly similar things); most often, it evokes *feelings*, sometimes very strongly: feelings of nostalgia, longing, sadness, joy, energy, and many others. If one were to finish listening to Miles Davis's cool jazz composition "Blue and Green" from *Kind of Blue* and ask "What is Davis trying to say about the colors blue and green?" we might respond that that's not the right kind of question to ask about such a piece. This is not to say that music doesn't have meaning, but rather to emphasize that its meaning is not primarily or exclusively semantic in character, a feature Adriana Cavarero gestures to in her work on the voice.[2]

And yet, music is not meaningless, either, not only in the sense that it is meaningful (i.e., emotionally important) to us, but also in the ways that musicologists, music critics, and ordinary listeners constantly insist on interpreting music, from electronic dance music to supposedly "ineffable" works by Beethoven, often convincingly and without any recourse to highly technical language (see Lawrence Kramer, *The Thought of Music*, 22–43 or *Musical Meaning*, 1–9). We also learned in chapter 1 that we should be wary of the idea that pure sound is without semantic content. Vibrations may be a purely material fact, outside of logos, but we *hear* inside logos, and so we can ascribe all sorts of meanings to sound. Moreover, at least from the Romantic era onward, it is actually fairly rare that a sense of meaning in music is not at least suggested to the listener, often through the title. As much as "autonomous" music (such as an instrumental classical piece titled "Musical Work No. 47") may have a certain artistic prestige, the musical universe we mostly inhabit constantly tells us that it is about something, that it tells us a story, or opens up a space in which we tell ourselves a story.

The term "program music" derives from the practice of explaining in a musical program how a piece is structured by a narrative, sometimes in a very rigorous way, as in Richard Strauss's *Don Quixote*: The cello represents Don Quixote, the bass clarinet his squire Sancho Panza, the first variation depicts the famous tilting at windmills sequence, and so on. Sometimes, however, the title alone is sufficient to suggest a kind of interpretive lens (say, Beethoven's "Eroica" symphony, his third), even without a detailed background to the piece being given in the program; the listener might very well imagine heroic battles, marches, funerals, and the like.[3] Although "program music" is primarily associated with nineteenth-century Western art music, the practice is in fact common in film music, which is almost always intended to both depict and enhance the impact of events shown in the film, as well as in instrumental jazz. Duke Ellington, for example, in collaboration with Billy Strayhorn, composed a number of jazz suites that were intended to convey a musical rendition of narratives from Shakespeare (*Such Sweet Thunder*) to Steinbeck (*Suite Thursday*).[4]

Here we might return to this chapter's initial epigraph from Calvino, who finds something promising in art forms that don't "crystallize" into images. This is not to say that Calvino objects to the visual register, but that a concrete and static image (in painting or in poetry or in prose) does not manage to capture the essence of the American spirit, which is a vague and shapeless unhappiness in the face of a mechanized modernity (Calvino was writing in 1959–60 and has in mind the "organization man" of the era right before *Mad Men*). Instead, he turns to two forms of art that both have the capacity to express something without its being reducible to stable and fixed semantic content. Of the two, he finds that jazz has a greater capacity to "rationalize" that neurotic dissatisfaction. "Rationalize" is a term with a number of possible meanings, but here it is clearly positive: a thinking through, even if it does not find settled or final terms, an "image," for that thought. This "noncrystallized" thought does not eschew either form or image, but attempts to render them provisional, continuously in progress, even "live," and this is where jazz particularly excels.

Calvino clearly understood that jazz's capacity to remain free and uncrystallized was strongly linked to the provisional and the improvisational. This in turn leads us to a certain "cosmicomic" story by Calvino, "Crystals." It is set in New York and features one of these dissatisfied, restless organization men (Qfwfq, once again) whose life is a tedious routine, a kind of maniacally regulated order that has intruded even into his psyche. He dreams of a life that is in perfect order, one giant crystal, uncontaminated by the tiniest disturbance or imperfection, but concludes that the world is an impossible mixture of both crystallized forms and their flaws and impurities. He prepares to share this revelation with his partner, but decides to wait "che finisca il disco di Thelonious Monk" (2:256, for the Thelonious Monk record to finish). That is literally the last line of the story, leaving Qfwfq, his romantic partner *and* the reader on the verge of a crystalline revelation, but one that is suspended by jazz.

Giorgio Rimondi, in *La scrittura sincopata* (Syncopated writing), perhaps the only book on jazz and modern Italian literature, claims that Calvino was so visual, he may be partially excused for his "sordità" (191, deafness) toward jazz even when he was in the US. This claim is for me emblematic of how the insistence on Calvino's visuality obscures his acoustic resonance (although Rimondi is correct that Calvino hardly mentions the music in New Orleans, he does intelligently discuss jazz in New York, as the epigraph to this chapter attests). Calvino also collaborated with Luciano Berio on the theatrical and orchestral work *Allez-Hop* for which Calvino penned lyrics to the vocal parts, both of which are in the vocal jazz, torch-song vein of "Misty," both lyrically and musically (not to mention his extensive work on popular music with Cantacronache). And regardless how much Calvino may or may not have loved jazz and music more widely, it is certainly the case that his writing has been quite inspirational for musicians. A number of jazz composers have turned to Calvino's "cosmicomic" stories besides Mezzacappa: Fernando Benadon has a piece titled "Cosmicomics" inspired by "Without Colors" and "The Stone Sky" that moves between jazz and a more classical composition; Tonino Miano has a free jazz improvisation for jazz ensemble based on "The Moon Like a Mushroom"; and Telesmar Sanchez composed and recorded four of the cosmicomic stories as his senior project in jazz composition, later released as an EP entitled *Cosmic Music* (the title is a double gesture to Calvino and to Coltrane). Evan Anthony and Jeremy Abel created *Genesis Noir*, a video game that is deeply inspired by Calvino's *Cosmicomics*, especially "All at One Point."[5] The game largely revolves around jazz, and reimagines the central characters of the *Cosmicomics* as jazz musicians and listeners, albeit at a stellar and galactic scale.

These are hardly the only jazz compositions inspired by Calvino; Claudio Angeleri, for example, has an album of compositions inspired by *The Castle of Crossed Destinies* (the title in English), Andrea De Martini's jazz big band is called Ottimo Massimo (the name of Cosimo's dog in *The Baron in the Trees*); Vito Liturri has a jazz album inspired by *Invisible Cities* (where the title is again given in English); and Giuseppe Romaniello wrote a series of reflections on how Calvino's categories in the *Lezioni americane* might apply to jazz (*Six Memos in Jazz*, 2014)—the title is yet again in English, a play on Calvino's title that only appeared in the English-speaking world, *Six Memos for the Next Millennium*. The *Cosmicomics* have inspired plenty of non-jazz music, too, including the late Luis Vasquez's highly successful industrial rock project, The Soft Moon; "Cosmicomics," by the French pop band Œ; an indie rock meditation on the end of the world by St. Terrible; an ambient sound collage by 4th World

Orchestra; the debut album by the all-female Roman band La distanza della luna (the name of the band is also the title of a cosmicomic story in Italian); experimental Japanese hip-hop from the trio Dos Monos; or *Lunaria* by the Swedish composer Ivo Nilsson, a suite of ten avant-garde classical pieces, each of which is inspired by a cosmicomic tale.

Jazz as Play

Jazz is a musical tradition that emerged in the early twentieth century from African American communities in the US South, coming out of earlier African American musical traditions like blues and ragtime. Its growing popularity throughout the early twentieth century eventually made it into a complex and global musical practice with a huge range of possible styles and forms, from commercial, popular music to extremely artistically complex and technically challenging pieces. Because of its unusually broad range of forms, no single definition can suffice for jazz, and I don't want to essentialize it. One might instead turn to the notion of "family resemblances." It's rarely the case that every member of a given family has the same physical trait or traits (red hair, skinny shoulders, a large nose), but instead family resemblances work through *partial* networks of shared characteristics (one child has the father's eyes, the other has the mother's, both have their grandmother's chin, which strangely skipped a generation, and so on). In the spirit of such family resemblances, then, I might gesture to certain musical practices that characterize many (although not all) forms of jazz, including improvisation, "swung" rhythms, rich and sophisticated harmonies, and complex interactions between different members of the group. I should also specify that I focus in this chapter on instrumental jazz, meaning jazz without vocals, which existed from the start, but which became especially popular after World War II when Calvino started his writing career. I do so not because this is the canonical form of jazz or "the correct jazz," but simply because that is the most relevant frame for both Calvino's interest in cool jazz as well as for Mezzacappa's jazz imagining of the *Cosmicomics*.[6]

Improvisation is when a musician invents their musical part in the moment, rather than reading from a composed musical score. The swung rhythm in jazz follows a regular and steady pulse, but the subdivisions of that pulse are treated more loosely and freely, and can be pushed and pulled to give the music an expressive lightness. Many jazz critics and musicians, however, say that swing can't be defined or explained at all, but is a certain rhythmic feeling. Avril Dankworth calls it something that must be "caught rather than taught" (38), while Richard Lawn (18) quotes from Count Basie, Louis Armstrong, and Duke Ellington, all claiming that it is almost undefinable, before offering an example ("Every Tub" by Count Basie) rather than a definition.[7] Romaniello observes in *Six Memos in Jazz* that "nulla più dello *swing* sfugge alle definizioni" (66, nothing resists definition more than swing). Harmony is the "vertical" dimension of musical expression, what notes of different pitches sound like when they are played on top of each other, as in a chord. Jazz has a preference for chords and harmonies that are more complex than the often more straightforward major/minor chords of much popular music, or the properly "classical" period of classical music. Lastly, all good ensemble musicians listen to each other as they play, but jazz's improvised nature can mean that everyone is "playing off" everyone else, so that a drummer might incorporate a rhythmic figure the saxophonist just used in her solo, which might then be echoed by the guitarist, perhaps with a new twist.

In its most well-known form (say, Horace Silver's "Song for My Father"), an instrumental jazz piece begins with a composed and orchestrated "head," which consists of a melody and its harmonic accompaniment (the chords); subsequently, a given instrument improvises (or solos) while the other instruments provide an improvised harmonic accompaniment ("comping") that follows—or at least gestures at—the chords of the head. After several performers (piano and tenor sax in the Horace Silver piece) have taken solos, the entire ensemble returns to restate the head and bring the piece to an end. This structure is by no means obligatory, however, and is often abridged, extended, complicated or otherwise modified.

Because so much jazz is improvised, the status of a jazz piece is perhaps different from that of its counterparts in classical music: There is no definitive version or performance, not even an imagined ideal one, as is perhaps the case in classical music where there is much discussion and anxiety about faithfully fulfilling "the composer's intention." The musical score, if it exists, is more like a short outline than an essay, or perhaps even more like an essay prompt. Even the composed portions of a piece can easily be seen as merely suggestions. Sometimes jazz musicians might elect to omit or alter portions of the head, or begin soloing right away, for example. Although a jazz band might release a recorded album of songs, those recordings would simply be one interpretation representative of one moment, and indeed, those same pieces might be recorded again and again in totally different versions on later albums, or even two versions of the same piece on one album. In short, even well-known recordings would be understood as reaching toward at least an imagined "live" experience, with an element of contingency (anyone might suddenly try something new or different), the charge of the "now."

Calvino spent a year in the US precisely as "cool jazz" was emerging into prominence (he arrived in New York just weeks after Miles Davis was there to record *Kind of Blue*). Cool jazz was a new form of jazz in the 1950s and '60s that was musically "serious" (interested in formal experimentation), that had slower, more relaxed tempos, and that emphasized a more nuanced, delicate, and melodic exploration of its musical territory. Many of the recordings by the Modern Jazz Quartet, or Miles Davis's *Birth of the Cool*, are notable examples. Cool jazz was contrasted with traditional Dixieland or "hot" jazz on the one hand (seen as more popular and focused on entertainment, music to dance to), and bebop on the other hand (more "serious," but also featuring extremely fast, virtuoso musicianship). All the "serious" forms of jazz (including cool and bebop) were fundamentally improvisational in character, however, always understood as being realized in the moment. I suggested earlier than in some sense, jazz always must be understood as "live," and this liveness is certainly part of why Calvino felt it was more capable of avoiding crystallization into an image.

This improvisational live character also makes jazz fundamentally playful in character, a playfulness which should emphatically *not* be understood as making it in any way less musically serious or important. One of the thrusts of this book is to emphasize that Calvino is both more playful *and* more resonant than we have realized up until now, a playfulness that should make us take him more seriously. A part of the playfulness of jazz is responding with the improviser's infamous "Yes, and . . . ." In comedic improv, you are never allowed to refuse or reject whatever wild suggestion your comic partner gives you. You must go along with it, and perhaps even take it further, which helps produce the proper nervous and delighted laughter in the audience. At any moment a performer might go too far, a performance might go off the rails, your partner might balk at the next suggestion, become offended, go blank and run out of ideas—but that anxiety makes it all the more delightful when your partner, instead of balking or freezing, finds a way to make it work instead.

As long as it lasts, the sense that the performance is on the edge and could go in any direction is precisely what gives improvised performances like stand-up comedy or jazz their special charge and makes them feel like they are happening now, that the work is not composed in advance but is emerging in the present. A jazz soloist might abruptly include a piece of a famous tune from the jazz tradition (a quotation from Miles Davis's "So What?" for example, or "the lick," a frequently repeated seven-note musical phrase that has become a humorous jazz cliché) or from outside that tradition (anything from "Twinkle, Twinkle, Little Star" to a rock song popular on the radio at that moment). The other musicians might laugh or shake their heads, but they will play along, recognizing that fundamentally playful character in the music, and sometimes finding someone's apparently "silly" musical quotation a real springboard for their own creativity, a swerve into new territory.[8]

Jazz, Lucretius, and the Irrational

I use the word "swerve" deliberately, since it's an important part of Calvino's thinking, and it helps explain why a jazz musician might gravitate particularly to the *Cosmicomics* and its playful narratives of the new and unexpected coming into being. Calvino was deeply indebted to and delighted by Lucretius's conception of how the universe might have emerged from its initial state of a cloud of undifferentiated atoms. In Lucretius's early universe, atoms do nothing but fall through the void in a straight line, but every now and then, for no apparent reason, one might swerve and collide with others. That movement in turn creates every form of difference, every kind of material, every event that follows. These straight lines are something like creative ruts, the all-too-concrete and finalized "images" that Calvino found inadequate to the historical moment in the epigraph to this chapter. They need to have some dynamic play that leaves them without a final form. The abstract impressionist painting that Calvino also praises in the epigraph resists condensing into a crystallized image, but jazz goes one step further, by refusing any final, definitive form. Lucretius, whom Calvino cited over and over again as a model for thinking about creativity in art, contends that the universe is *by its very nature* improvisational. It unexpectedly swerves at random: The universe is jazz.[9]

The term Lucretius uses for this phenomenon is *clinamen principiorum*, literally, the swerve of the first things (*clinamen* comes from the same root as "incline," *in+clinare*, to bend). It suggests an impulse, an inclination, to swerve away from the way things have always been. It is, for Lucretius, the motor of all difference and diversity in the universe, which would otherwise consist exclusively of the primary elements, falling endlessly in the void without touching. The clinamen also brings things into contact—without it, no body would ever have come into contact with another body. The clinamen, like the word *inclination*, could also indicate a bias, and it is in this sense that Harold Bloom uses the term in *The Anxiety of Influence*. Artists, plagued by an Oedipal resistance to those who came before them, "naturally" swerve away from them, according to Harold Bloom, in *The Anxiety of Influence* (19–48)—although one could just as easily think of the bias as a positive attraction, and one of the contributions I hope *Transmedial Resonance* makes to our thinking about influence is the way that resonance emphasizes the positive, the new, and the creativity that an impulse *toward* another artist might engender.

As Natalie Berkman has persuasively argued,[10] Calvino very deliberately and openly dramatized Lucretius's clinamen scenario in one of the *Cosmicomics*, a story of anthropomorphized particles that fall endlessly through space waiting for that unexpected swerve or clinamen that will change their existence and create something new. "The Form of Space" effectively retells Lucretius's atomic paths and their potential swerves into new territories and new combinations using Calvino's familiar Qfwfq. The clinamen is nondeterministic, meaning that it can't be predicted on the basis of the atoms' state right before the swerve. It happens for no reason, and hence it is also irrational in some sense, a spontaneous impulse in a random direction. To repeat the argument from chapter 1, Calvino is in fact insistent throughout his writings on the *necessity* of the irrational and the unconscious (they are not merely valuable, but the essential foundation, what turns language into literature),[11] so in what follows I want to try to hear some of Calvino's qualities that are perhaps less accentuated in the criticism in the works that respond to, translate, and reshape his writings.

Calvino's relatively frequent references to Lucretius reflect a deep respect for the Roman author as one of the primary sources of Calvino's thinking about art as a combinatorial procedure. Lucretius is explicit about the ways that the primordial elements could be understood also as letters, combining and recombining to generate text as well as different materials. But Calvino's use of the clinamen as a theoretical concept for thinking about art *also* comes from his engagement with OuLiPo, the Ouvroir de la Littérature Potentielle, or Workshop for Potential Literature, a Paris-based group that had theorized not only the necessity of making rigorous mathematical and logical rules for the creation of literature, but also the need to sometimes playfully break those rules, a rupture they referred to as the clinamen. OuLiPo actually inherited this notion of the clinamen, however (Berkman, 258). OuLiPo was originally founded as a subdivision of the Collège de 'Pataphysique, a humorous and satirical (and initially, entirely fictional) "research institute" created by Alfred Jarry, the forerunner of Dadaism and surrealism and author of the influential and scatological 1896 play *Ubu Roi.*

For 'Pataphysicians, the clinamen was a small change—like the addition of a single letter—that produces a large difference, just as this minimal swerve of elementary atoms brings about the entire universe. The canonical example of the clinamen that OuLiPo inherited from

'Pataphysics is the first word of Jarry's *Ubu Roi*. A character steps on stage and intones the word *"merdre,"* the vulgar French word for excrement, but with an extra letter r added at the end (translated as "pshit" in English). It is important to remember that, for all the serious talk about combinatorics and mathematics, there is a playful, often childish, even vulgar impulse at the core of OuLiPo that has the potential to swerve us into unexpected terrain (just one additional letter unexpectedly transforms OuLiPo into OuLiPoo). Dennis Duncan (105) quite rightly doubts that Calvino's concept of the clinamen came *exclusively* through 'Pataphysics and OuLiPo, but Calvino was certainly familiar with this playful and irreverent—even profane—lineage in addition to its more "noble" source in Lucretius.[12] Here one can begin to see why Calvino would understand the improvisations of cool jazz as a "thinking through" of contemporary anxiety. It offers a complete but nonfinal form of the modern subject's impossible double bind: You must follow the rules and conform, but you must also somehow be an innovator and a rule breaker. Jazz allows one to witness this dialectic playing out in real time, the high-wire act of modernity.

The Form of Space

In *Cosmicomics* (2020), bassist and bandleader Lisa Mezzacappa and her ensemble (the Lisa Mezzacappa Six) offers a jazz suite of Calvino's "cosmicomic" stories, a clear instance of program music—Mezzacappa even offers interpretive ideas in the album's liner notes.[13] The titles either are taken verbatim from Calvino's stories, or are slight modifications. Mezzacappa's sextet has some fairly traditional instruments (bass, drums, guitar, vibraphone, saxophone) and a somewhat less traditional suite of "electronics" played by Tim Perkis, which produce a wide variety of sounds, some tonal and "musical" in character, but more often whirring, scratching, or squeaking noises, animal-like chittering and chirping, or wobbly and comic glissandos. In its most extreme moments ("All at One Point"), it can sound like an aggressively horny R2-D2. Often the pieces begin in a quite recognizable, even traditional, form of jazz (the Latin rhythms at the start of "The Soft Moon," cool jazz in "Solar Storms," the up-tempo swing of "The Form of Space"), but progressively veer into more unexpected territories, as if beginning with a logical premise and then progressively and insistently taking it farther and farther. This can go surprisingly far in some cases, as in "Blood, Sea," when a heavy guitar and drum duet briefly starts to lean into hard rock, or even the plodding gravity of heavy metal.

Mezzacappa's pieces often feature composed sections alternating with improvised sections that generally involve multiple instruments without a predefined harmonic structure. The overall sense is perhaps less of a traditional jazz format (head, solos, head) and more like a constantly repeated oscillation between more organized and structured forms of music, and playful sonic chaos. A perfect example of this oscillation is "The Form of Space," a story about the notion of form itself. Mezzacappa imagined the piece as essentially a trio, with the saxophone, the vibes, and the guitar playing the principal roles, and the bass, electronics, and drums joining in only during the heads and the transitions in and out of the heads. Essentially, the piece has a fast, bebop-like head (from the start to about 0:16), a deliberately awkward improvised duet (0:16–1:14), a second, more bluesy head (1:14–1:33) and a second improvised duet (1:33–2:41), and then a brief return to the original head (2:41–2:48) with a final improv (2:48–4:02) and coda (the band works very slowly into this section, but you can hear it beginning around 4:03).

If a verbal description is perhaps a little difficult to understand, we are fortunate that Mezzacappa makes striking visual diagrams of her pieces in addition to more conventional musical notation. In *The Thought of Music*, Kramer writes that "the history of the [musical] score is a progressive narrowing of latitude" (175), contrasting classical musical scores with their much freer opposites, lead sheets in jazz, which only sketch out the head in traditional notation and a few other phrases. Mezzacappa's diagrams, however, can *enlarge* the performer's interpretive latitude, and this diagram of "The Form of Space" (see fig. 8, a preliminary study she used for the final composition in traditional musical notation) is a good example.

The structure becomes immediately clear, and so do the ways in which it reflects Calvino's story. The A part of the piece is the story's narrator (Qfwfq, aptly described by Mezzacappa as "earnest, insistent, almost aggressive"), the B part the curvaceous Ursula H'x ("dancelike, slippery, lilting"), and the C part Lt. Fenimore ("square, march-like, clunky," and a comical tempo description: "very medium"). Now one begins to understand why the first improvised duet sounds like a train wreck (the two instruments playing in different tempi, totally out of sync), at least initially, and the second is more harmonious, if no less improvised, playful and chaotic—the first duet is between Lt. Fenimore and Ursula H'x, while the second is between Ursula H'x and Qfwfq.

Mezzacappa's musical intervention does not exactly reproduce the structure of Calvino's story, in which the (imagined) union between Ursula H'x and Qfwfq occurs first, following by a paranoid (equally

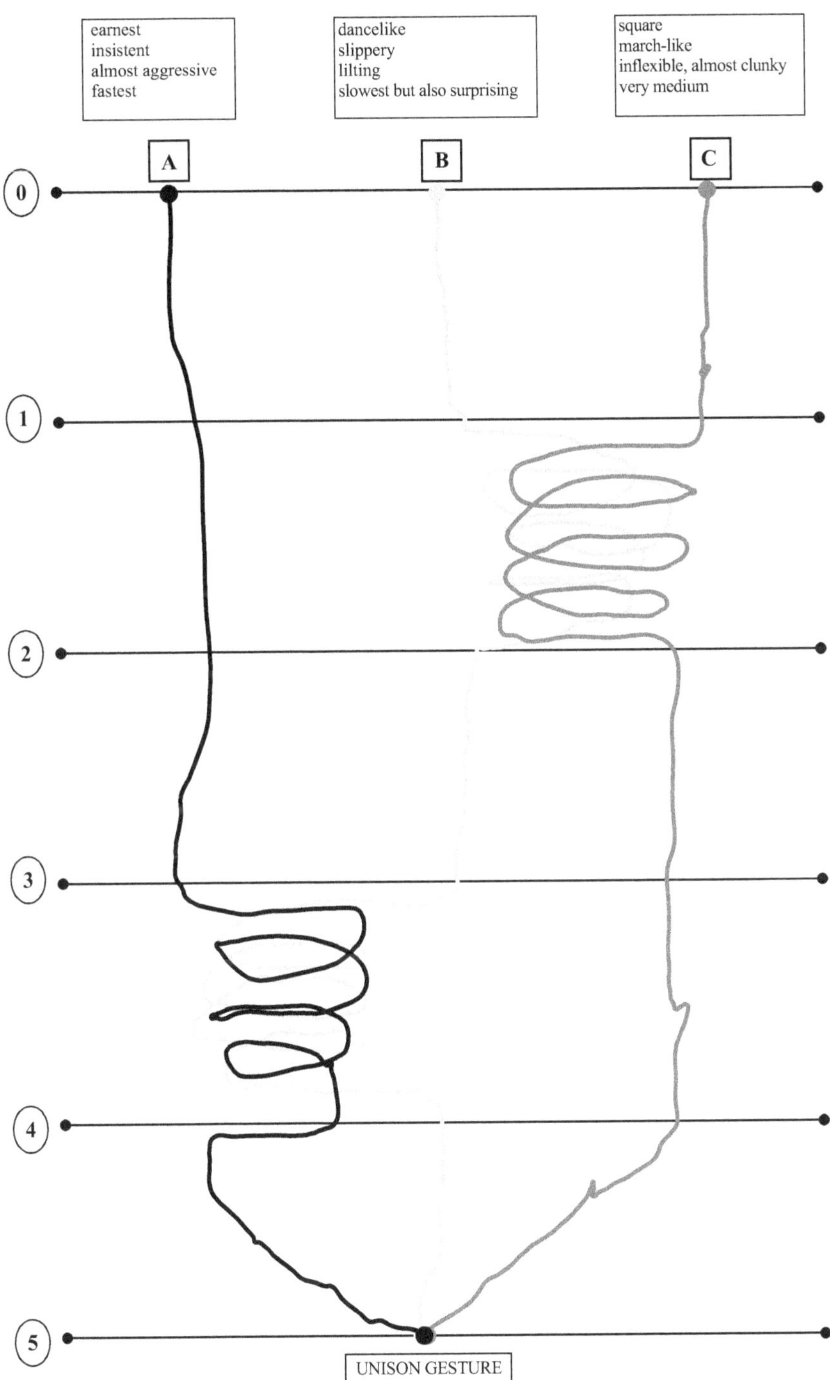

FIGURE 8. "The Form of Space," preliminary study. Courtesy Lisa Mezzacappa

imaginary) union between Ursula H'x and Lt. Fenimore. That in turn is followed by a hostile conflict set in a Wild West desert between Fenimore and Qfwfq, who attempts to flee with Ursula H'x and hide inside the very letters of the story we are reading, specifically the word "parallel," whose vertical letter l's form the three lines of our narrative, two of them together, and one separated.[14] One of the reasons for trying to think through these pieces by way of *resonance*, however, is to help us understand that these homologies should *not* be understood as translations or adaptations, which would be inevitably measured in terms of fidelity to the original. That would be the traditional understanding of the echo as a pale, weaker imitation of the original. Resonance, by contrast, understands that the echo is a *part* of the sound, a part that both enhances and enriches it, but that also tells us something vital about it, namely the space in which it was produced, and hence its acoustic environment (the "echological" reading of the previous chapter).

The salient question then is not how this musical version is different or faithful, but what it tells us that is new, as well as what it can tell us about Calvino's original story and the larger space in which we are now hearing that sound. Looking at Mezzacappa's diagram, its most striking feature is that it is organized *vertically*, three lines in free fall—and any horizontal motion of those lines represents a possible entanglement. This rotates standard musical notation by 90°, so that time is represented by the movement of numbered sequences from top to bottom (since the characters are falling), rather than from left to right; harmony and polyphony, which would normally be sought in the vertical dimension of standard musical notation, here appear as the horizontal entanglement of vertical lines. So far, this follows the Lucretian conceit of Calvino's story: three figures falling along separate but parallel tracks that may or may not converge.

The second distinctive feature of Mezzacappa's diagram is its insistence on the *neurotic* character of the story, a term she also uses in the liner notes: Qfwfq is not an objective witness, but rather is caught up in a scenario of hostility and erotic attraction. He is "earnest, insistent, almost aggressive," while Fenimore is awkward and clumsy. Visually, this is expressed in the way that the various lines interact—they don't simply touch, but frantically and chaotically spiral around each other (literally "screwing"), missing each other as often as they make contact. We might look even more closely at the lines and observe that none of them is perfectly smooth or straight at any point—they're all slightly twitchy, veering sometimes toward and sometimes away from their ostensible object of desire, even occasionally moving briefly backward (Lt. Fenimore in particular shows signs of retrograde movement).

Much has been made of Calvino's love of the geometric and the cerebral, often with the concomitant sense that his love of geometry and abstraction is a deliberate and defensive gesture against the world's complexity, especially sexuality. As Elio Baldi indicates in one of his articles on Calvino's authorial image, Calvino's "racconti e romanzi sono definiti come asessuali" (60, stories and novels are defined as asexual) by critics.[15] This is true both in Italy, where Carla Benedetti contrasted Calvino's escapist "purity" and desire for a permanent "verginità artistica" (85, artistic virginity) against Pier Paolo Pasolini's more laudable "impurity" (13–17), and in the US, where Kathryn Hume equated Calvino's "majestic geometric patterns" with sexual "frigidity" (160).[16] But Mezzacappa's diagram indicates that there is a very antigeometric impulse at work, something that sabotages the neat, orderly straight line in favor of mess and entanglement, the sudden twitch rather than the smooth movement, an anxious and excessive circling around rather than a direct line toward the object of interest.

I would like to argue that Calvino is instead trying to say something surprising about the pretensions of the geometric to be dispassionate, detached and objective—in short, the tradition of the Cartesian thinker who, seated in his armchair, dedicates his mind to a priori mathematical truths. Here is the surprising part: In Calvino's world, geometry is *always* linked to sexuality and hostility. It is *never* neutral, detached or dispassionate. To put it bluntly, Calvino does not believe in objective rationality—in his "cosmicomic" universe, all reasoning is neurotically motivated reasoning. Although some of his characters try to sustain a belief in Enlightenment rationality, the overall effect of the text is always to expose such pretensions to objectivity as absurd; the lines that reason follows are those of desire, fear, and jealousy. The narrator of "The Form of Space" spends a great deal of time pondering parallel lines and non-Euclidean geometry, but only in the hopes that it will get him to the girl, in terms that leave no doubt about the character of that union:

> . . . la linea invisibile che percorrevo io e quella che lei percorreva
> sarebbero diventate una sola linea, occupata da una mescolanza
> di lei e di me dove quanto di lei era morbido e segreto veniva pen-
> etrato, anzi, avvolgeva e quasi direi risucchiava quanto di me con più
> tensione era andato fin lì soffrendo d'essere solo e separato e asciutto.
> (2:184)

> . . . the invisible line that I was running along and the one that she
> was running along would become a single line, occupied by a mix-
> ture of her and me in which that part of her that was soft and secret

was penetrated, no, it enveloped and I would almost say sucked up that part of me that had, up until now, suffered from being alone and separate and dry.

Mezzacappa is exactly correct to refer to this character's slightly desperate and neurotic character—he's not just horny, but almost existentially lonely as well. What he would *like* is this perfect union along a single line, one that in its geometric simplicity would be pure and containable. This is emphatically *not*, however, what happens. There is instead a clinamen, or several of them. To begin with, the formula of the simple, straight line is already troubled, since the story emphasizes again and again that what is sexually appealing about Ursula H'x is that nothing she does follows a straight line: Her wrists twist in "una maniera quasi serpentina" (2:184, an almost serpentine fashion); she turns and twists in "una specie di capriola" (2:186, a kind of somersault); she begins a kind of falling dance by "ondeggiando" (2:187, waving or wiggling her whole body), "un inarcarsi della schiena" (2:188, an arching of her back), "un certo suo andare come volteggiando" (2:189, a certain way of moving like twirling); and so forth. Moreover, the great discovery of the story—and of the scientific premise from which it departs—is that space does not have a simple geometry: Space itself is rough, permeated by densities and empty spaces, not linear. It is textural, tactile. And this is a good thing, because it means that all kinds of sexual adventures are possible in it and with it: The narrator imagines that he and Ursula H'x get sucked onto a kind of "isola subspaziale" (2:190, island of subspace) in which they roll together:

> intrecciandoci in tutte le pose e i capovolgimenti, finché a un tratto le nostre due rette riprendevano la loro distanza sempre uguale e proseguivano ognuna per conto suo come se niente fosse stato. (2:190)

> entwining ourselves into all the different positions and their upside-down versions, until suddenly our two straight lines return to their ever-same distance and follow along each one by themselves as if nothing had ever happened.

Calvino's "pure geometry" turns out to be the Kama Sutra, and maybe more. The simple and abstract geometry of straight lines is repeatedly sabotaged here. Straight lines become braided or entwined (*intrecciarsi*). Geometry is put to use to find all possible sexual positions, and in a delightful (and very Calvinian) gesture, they are then redoubled by the recognition that they can all also be done upside-down. These *capovolgimenti* are literally perverse—the positions fully turned around (*per-versus*). Calvino could also not be clearer that the apparent abstract formalism of the straight line, and of geometry more generally, literally *conceals* these perversions: After they're done, everything returns "as if nothing had happened."

Mezzacappa's diagram and music don't just recognize this—they explicitly encode it at a formal level, both visually and acoustically. Not only does Mezzacappa twist or rotate standard musical notation, but the parallel lines of her piece (which are never smoothly straight in the first place) don't unite in any simple, straightforward way; they too prefer a complex twisting, a messy spiral. Musically, this is clearest in the duet between Lt. Fenimore (guitar) and Ursula H'x (vibraphone). Fenimore plays at a completely different tempo and does not swing the beat. His military background makes him march instead to a rigid tempo of strummed chords, totally out of sync with the rest of the ensemble and with his would-be lover. After a while, he does eventually begin to improvise, to try to find a different musical language, but it is mostly awkward attempts to continue in the same rigid rhythm and with the same chords. Ursula H'x's vibraphone, however, stays within a much more traditional jazz idiom, both rhythmically and harmonically, testing out a series of more sprightly scales and figures (Mezzacappa describes her as "slippery"), even as Fenimore is mostly reduced to silence at the end of the duet, and the drums lead in to a new composed section of the piece at a much slower tempo.

The duet between the narrator (saxophone) and Ursula H'x (vibraphone) seems different, potentially more compatible, as both are fluid, quickly adapting and venturing in new directions. Although they are more compatible stylistically, however, in both duets (especially the first, less successful one), the players play more often *over* each other than they do *with* each other. It may be that our idealized fantasy involves the abstract simplicity of "two becoming one," making a united, harmonious sound (a unison, literally), but the messiness of the real world means that people rarely behave in ways that allow for this. What is clear in Calvino's story, and what Mezzacappa's insistence on Qfwfq as "neurotic" gets so right, is that the failure of interpersonal harmony is usually because people stay trapped in their own heads, as it were, even when they are together (this issue particularly affects Calvino's male protagonists). The musical effect the sextet achieves is delightfully chaotic, but emphasizes the impossibility for the different characters to get out of their established positions. (It is, in the words of the epigraph to this chapter, quite literally a "razionalizzazione del nervosismo attuale," a thinking through of contemporary neuroticism.) Fenimore isn't sexy and he doesn't know how to swing, and our narrator is stuck on his own preoccupations, which are not only about the beautiful if elusive Ursula H'x, but perhaps even more about Lt. Fenimore, his nasty mustache and his habit of soundlessly whistling while he pretends that he and Ursula H'x are dancing together to some unheard music.[17]

Mezzacappa's acoustic chaos helps us understand that Calvino's story is quite a bit more perverse than has been generally understood, not just in the etymological sense of bending straight lines—although we might begin from there, from the apparent deviation from the straight, the *clinamen.* When the narrator first imagines swerving into a union with Ursula H'x and having his "dry, lonely" parts being engulfed by her, he almost immediately imagines something else. If parallel lines come together in space, then not only does his line join with Ursula H'x's, but so does Lt. Fenimore's. Although Calvino's language is "refined" here, it is also clear and follows logically from the scenario he has laid out. It is in fact a "rationalization" (thinking through) of the neuroticism implicit in the clinamen itself. The narrator's encounter with Ursula H'x is described as face to face, but *all three lines converge simultaneously*—so Lt. Fenimore "encounters" her from behind. What is remarkable is that this quite perverted scene seems to have been "scotomized" by the critics, as Freud would say, gone invisible and been instantly forgotten. It is easy to skip over block quotes, but the context is necessary to understand what is happening, so read this one carefully:

> Succede ai sogni più belli di trasformarsi a un tratto in incubi . . . nel momento stesso in cui Ursula H'x avrebbe cessato d'essermi estranea, un estraneo con i suoi sottili baffetti neri si sarebbe trovato a condividere le nostre intimità in modo inestricabile . . . sentivo il grido che il nostro incontro—di me e di lei—ci strappava fondersi in un unisono spasmodicamente gioioso ed ecco che—agghiacciavo al presentimento!—da esso si staccava lancinante il grido di lei violata—così nella mia parzialità immaginavo—alle spalle, e nello stesso tempo il grido di volgare trionfo del Tenente, ma forse—e qui la mia gelosia raggiungeva il delirio—questi loro gridi—di lei e di lui—potevano anche non essere così diversi e dissonanti, potevano raggiungere essi pure un unisono, sommarsi in un unico grido addirittura di piacere. (2:184–85)

> It happens to the loveliest dreams to suddenly change into nightmares . . . in the same moment in which Ursula H'x would cease to be foreign to me, a foreigner with his wispy little black mustache would find himself inextricably sharing our intimacy . . . I heard the cry that our encounter—mine and hers—tore from us meld into a spasmodically joyous unison and then—I froze at the thought

of it coming!—from that unison there broke off her piercing cry, violated—so, in my stubborn prejudice I imagined—from behind, and at the same time the Lieutenant's vulgar cry, but perhaps—and here my jealousy became delirium—these cries of theirs—of her and of him—could even not be so different and dissonant, they could arrive at being a unison too, adding together in a single cry, one even of pleasure.

There is a good deal to unpack in this breathless, fragmented (just look at the number of em dashes!), run-on description, but I will first stop and take some guidance from Mezzacappa's diagram. Although the diagram shows two duets, the more traditional sheet music she wrote out has two duets and a "tutti improv" (everybody improvises) section. The actual recorded performance effectively contains *three* duets, however, not two, since the "tutti improv" section begins with two instruments only, just as the other two improvised duets do. Logically, of course, there *is* a third possibility for the duets: guitar and saxophone. A and B can intertwine, B and C can intertwine, or *A and C could intertwine*, Qfwfq and Lt. Fenimore. In the recorded performance, the rhythm section (the bass and the drums) has that final duet instead, one that is longer, more tightly coordinated, and more harmonious than the other two, and what is perhaps the most erotic portion of the piece (it is perhaps stereotypical for a bass player to celebrate the romance of the rhythm section). As the other instruments join, we hear a great deal of *portamento* from many of the instruments, the smooth slide across a wide range of pitches that tends to sound both comic (it is the "sad trombone" sound effect used for comic effect when someone experiences disappointment) and sexual (it is also the "wolf whistle" of sexual desire). In other words, Mezzacappa's third duet raises precisely the same possibility of this queer entanglement that Calvino's story does, and just like Calvino, while the music does not realize it, it does not fully foreclose on it either—after all, who is to say just what might happen in a "tutti improv" section? Isn't everyone playing with each other? The clinamen cannot be predicted; all we know is that it sometimes swerves unexpectedly from the straight line.

As I argued above, the narrator of the story himself is quite clear that, although his fantasy begins with an imagined union between himself and his female object of desire, his fantasy then expands to also include his male rival, if only in a negative way. When he imagines a second encounter with Ursula H'x later in the story, on an "island of subspace," he describes their coupling as including "all the positions" and—let us try a different translation of "capovolgimenti" that gestures to both yoga and nineteenth-century sexology—their inversions. Calvino describes this pansexual litany of positions as an "intrecciarsi." Unlike the typical English translations of this term (enlacing, entangling, entwining), however, the number three (*tre* in Italian) is visible and audible in the word *intrecciarsi*, which literally means to braid (braids are *trecce* in Italian), a formal pattern that requires *three* formerly straight lines which are then wrapped around each other. Moreover, in the standard braid *every* possible pair of strings (AB, BC, AC) will be together on one side at some point in the process, separated from the third (this is the braiding that grounds the whole scene in the word *parallel*).

If on a Winter's Night a Threesome . . .

This is not the only queer threesome in the supposedly "pure," "frigid," and sexually defensive Calvino, however. Let's take a brief excursus to a third text from some ten years later, a text that is perhaps referring back to "The Form of Space," at least unconsciously. *If on a winter's night a traveler* is Calvino's experimental "hyper-novel," consisting of ten first chapters of ten different novels that the main character tries to finish writing (alas, to no avail). In the "revolutionary" novel, entitled "Without Fear of Wind or Vertigo," the narrator, Lt. Alex Zinnober, and his friend Valeriano walk with a young woman, Irina Piperin, their arms intertwined. Their positioning should be familiar. Irina is naturally in the center, and our narrator to her right, so that the heavy pistol on his right hip will have space, and Valerian on her left (he carries a smaller pistol in his pocket, since he is part of the revolution, but not part of the military). The tone of the chapter is strikingly dark and serious, and the psychosexual elements are clearly present right away: Despite the apparent initial hierarchy of who has the bigger gun, it becomes clear that Irina is a kind of dominatrix ("prendeva veramente possesso di noi," 2:686, she really took possession of us) who imposes a sort of magic circle of submission on the two young men.

The initial scenario is once again acoustic in character: They emerge from an underground club after a night of music and dancing into a grim world of corpses in the streets and revolutionary plots; like Lt. Fenimore, Irina begins to whistle, silently at first, then with sound, and the two young men join in. Later, "il nostro terzetto ormai inseparabile" (2:695, our by now inseparable trio) will meet for "una scena che dev'essere d'intimità ma anche d'esibizione e di sfida, la cerimonia di quel culto segreto e sacrificale di cui Irina è insieme l'officiante e la divinità e la profanatrice e la vittima" (2:695, a scene that should be one of intimacy, but also of exhibition and challenge, the ceremony of that secret, sacrificial cult of which Irina is simultaneously the officiant and the divinity and the profaner and the victim). Abruptly, the three are naked among the "tendaggi a disegni geometrici" (2:695, drapes with geometric designs), and the narrator looks over Irina's body, her skinny thorax and slight breasts, her "pube stretto e acuto a forma di triangolo isoscele (la parola «isoscele» per averla una volta associata al pube d'Irina si carica per me d'una sensualità tale che non posso pronunciarla senza battere i denti)" (2:695–96, narrow, sharp [*acuto*] pubis in the shape of an isosceles triangle [the word "isosceles" now by virtue of once being associated with Irina's pubis is charged for me with such an intense sensuality that I cannot speak it without my teeth chattering]). That isosceles triangle (the triangle in which all three angles are acute) is also the diagram of their relationship in which all three lines represent a sexual relation: AB, BC, *and* AC.

I'm trying to weave together three different strands here as well, so let's return to "The Form of Space" and see something else that is conspicuous but perhaps manages to pass unobserved as well. When the narrator first imagines his sexual union with Ursula H'x, it leads to an acoustic outburst, a cry: "il grido che il nostro incontro—di me e di lei—ci strappava fondersi in un unisono spasmodicamente gioioso" (2:184–85, the cry that our encounter—mine and hers—tore from us melds into a spasmodically joyous unison). What is so conspicuous and yet invisible here is that the narrator feels compelled to *specify the antecedents* for the possessive adjective "our" in "our encounter"—they are "di me e di lei" (mine and hers—AB). With this one phrase, Calvino makes it clear that *he must have considered* the possibility of some other set of antecedents, and there is *only one other possibility* for the adjective *our* in this scene, "di me e di lui" (mine and his—AC). This is a possibility unfulfilled, but not foreclosed, just as Mezzacappa's performance and diagram suggest. It is never articulated directly, but Calvino brings the possibility just to the edge of the reader's consciousness.

This is absolutely true of the revolutionary threesome in *If on a winter's night* as well. The actual sexual acts depicted there are heterosexual, but homoerotic overtones are clearly present as well (even more so than in "The Form of Space," in fact). And once again we see Calvino's penchant for the perversion of geometry, which is never neutral, but indeed so sexually charged that Alex cannot say the word "isosceles" without his teeth chattering. Irina, for her part, is determined to move beyond this world of straight lines (including the lines that make up an isosceles triangle), here associated with the phallic, by perverting (literally) the geometric. She grabs her two lovers' penises:

> Sono due teste di serpente che Irina afferra con ambe le mani, e che reagiscono alla sua stretta esasperando la propria attitudine alla penetrazione rettilinea, mentre lei pretendeva al contrario che il massimo di forza contenuta corrispondesse a una duttilità di rettile che si pieghi a raggiungerla in contorcimenti impossibili. Perché questo era il primo articolo di fede del culto che Irina aveva istituito: che noi abdicassimo al partito preso della verticalità, della linea retta, il superstite malriposto orgoglio maschile che ancora ci aveva seguito pur nell'accettare la nostra condizione di schiavi d'una donna. (2:696–97)

> They are two serpents' heads that Irina seizes with both her hands, and that react to her grasp by increasing their aptitude for rectilinear penetration, while she demands on the contrary the maximum of force contained should correspond to a reptile flexibility that could twist to reach her in impossible contortions. Because this was the first article of faith in the cult that Irina had instituted: that we should abdicate the preconceived notion of verticality, the straight line, the misplaced surviving masculine pride that had still followed us even after we'd accepted our condition as a woman's slaves.

I want to be as clear as possible, because otherwise it's too easy to gloss over it: Irina, Valerian, and Alex are in a threesome that practices bondage and domination, specifically one in which Irina bends the men's erect penises as a marker of their subjection to her in order to deny masculine penetration of the female body. In short, the scene's putatively heterosexual character—which is how Tommasina Gabriele defines all erotic activity in Calvino[18]—is more accurately "technically heterosexual," or "not explicitly non-heterosexual," a characterization that takes us into the territory of the queer. The scene's queer charge emerges more clearly in what follows, however, when Irina stands upright and forces Valeriano to perform oral sex on her while she stares intently into Alex's eyes.

> —Giù,—diceva Irina e la sua mano premeva la testa di Valeriano all'occipite, affondando le dita nei capelli lanosi d'un color rosso stoppa del giovane economista, senza lasciare che sollevasse il viso dall'altezza del suo grembo,—giù ancora!—e intanto guardava me con occhi di diamante, e voleva che io guardassi. (2:697)

> "Down," Irina was saying, and her hand pressed into the back of Valerian's head, sinking her fingers into the young economist's wooly,

red-blonde hair without allowing him to raise his gaze from the height of her lap, "farther down!," and meanwhile was watching me with diamond eyes, wanting me to watch.

One can begin to see why Domenico Scarpa asserts that Calvino "ha invertito il suo *spin* sessuale" (inverted his sexual "spin") if not his actual sex in order to write *If on a winter's night*.[19] Alex's eyes remain locked with Irina until she finally closes her eyes and begins to cry out with pleasure. Again, Calvino, like Mezzacappa, ensures that the woman remains between the two male characters, while simultaneously leaving markers that make it clear that logically there are other sexual possibilities that are inherent to the geometry of the scene. The narrator of the *Cosmicomics* is not running away from sexuality when he turns to geometry. On the contrary, it is geometry itself that sets his teeth chattering with desire. He is running *toward* it, because he has created a universe in which geometry is the sexiest thing there is. This point is actually made repeatedly and explicitly in the cosmicomic stories. In "Crystals," Qfwfq declares that "se io amo l'ordine, non è . . . una repressione degli istinti. In me l'idea d'un mondo assolutamente regolare, simmetrico, metodico, s'associa . . . alla tensione amorosa" (2:250, if I love order, it's not a repression of the instincts. In me the idea of an absolutely regular, symmetrical, methodical world is associated with amorous tension). The geometric is nothing but a series of potential sexual scenarios. Far from a defense mechanism, it is the route to the object of desire.

Let us recall that Mezzacappa does, in fact, bring the three main characters (along with the rest of the band) together at the end. They clumsily try to play in sync and initially fail (what Mezzacappa calls in her notes a "unison gesture," rather than a unison), before finally landing together in perfect unison on that last note, a D coming just after an A (the A to D movement gestures at a strong V–I resolution, typical in both classical and jazz music as the most emphatic and final resolution). They all come together—read that however you like—at the end of the piece, but then something remarkable happens that does not happen anywhere else on the album: That ending of "The Form of Space" becomes the beginning of the next piece. All the instruments land on that final note (vibraphone, bass, saxophone, guitar, and electronics, as well as the drummer striking a cymbal), and as the other sounds decay, the saxophone swells slightly above them, holds the note, and then stops. The saxophone, still on the same D, swells up and stops again, and slowly, over a series of swelling and falling pulses on D, the other instruments come in and gradually begin to complicate the music once more.

All at One Point

Mezzacappa links the ending of "Form of Space" seamlessly to the beginning of "All at One Point." Before we turn to that piece, however, we should recall the Calvino story that serves as the impetus for Mezzacappa's linkage. In this cosmicomic tale, the narrator begins this story by describing the world before the big bang: All the matter in the universe is condensed into a point so small it has no size at all. Within this infinitely small point, however, Calvino describes a world that is remarkably like ours: petty neighbors, secret romances, socioeconomic hierarchies (there is a cleaning woman, despite the impossibility of cleaning an infinitely small point), and even anti-immigrant xenophobia. One family, the Z'zus, is widely disliked: They have too many belongings and children that everyone is always bumping into, they want to stretch a line across the point to dry their laundry, but worst of all, they are immigrants—despite the fact that there is nowhere to emigrate from or immigrate to, and time has not yet begun. Some in the point insist that "il concetto di 'immigrato' poteva esser inteso allo stato puro, cioè indipendentemente dallo spazio e dal tempo" (2:119–20, the concept of "immigrant" could be understood in a pure state, free of space and time). This "narrow-minded" (naturally, in an infinitely small point!) thinking that was so common in the early universe, however, gives way in front of one special individual, a maternal figure who doubles as an object of sexual desire for everyone in the point, Mrs. Ph(i)Nk$_0$. The signora has a lover, Mr. De Xuaeaux, that she goes to bed with, but this provokes no cheap gossip, no denigration, not even any jealousy.

> Ma in un punto, se c'è un letto, occupa tutto il punto, quindi non si tratta di andare a letto ma di esserci, perché chiunque è nel punto è anche nel letto. Di conseguenza, era inevitabile che lei fosse a letto anche con ognuno di noi. Fosse stata un'altra persona, chissà quante cose le si sarebbero dette dietro. (2:121)

> But in a point, if there's a bed, it takes up the whole point, so it's not about going to bed but rather being there, since whoever is in the point is also in the bed. As a result, it was inevitable that she was also in bed with each one of us. If she'd been a different person, who know how much stuff they would have said behind her back?

It is easy for the reader to bracket off this relationship in the warm glow that even the worst persons (such as the irritating Mr. Pber^t Pber^d) who live in the point feel toward Mrs. Ph(i)Nk$_0$. This warm glow of sex and love is expressed, as usual, in geometric terms:

La felicità che mi veniva da lei era insieme quella di celarmi io puntiforme in lei, e quella di proteggere lei puntiforme in me, era contem-
plazione viziosa (data la promiscuità del convergere puntiforme di
tutti in lei) e insieme casta (data l'impenetrabilità puntiforme di lei).
Insomma, cosa potevo chiedere di più? (2:121)

The happiness that came to me from her was that of concealing myself, punctiform, in her, and that of protecting her, punctiform, in me,
both sinful thinking (given the promiscuity of everyone's punctiform
convergence in her) and yet chaste (given her punctiform impenetra-
bility). In short, what more could I ask for?

Calvino makes it clear, however, that with any other figure inside the
pre-universe, this radical "promiscuità del convergere puntiforme" (promiscuity of everyone's punctiform convergence) could only be read
negatively. In particular, the poor family of "immigrants" serve as an
example of this infinite and universal co-penetration: "Degli Z'zu, tanto
per cambiare, le cose orribili che ci toccava sentire: padre figlie fratelli
sorelle madre zie, non ci si fermava davanti a nessuna losca insinuazione"
(2:121, about the Z'zus, as usual, the horrible things that we happened to
hear: father daughters brothers sisters mother aunts, they didn't hesitate
before any lewd insinuation). Calvino uses no punctuation in his incest
list: The family members become a series of elements in an array that can
recombined in any form. If one wanted to, one could follow the same line
I followed in "The Form of Space" and observe that once again, Calvino
has found scenarios that—because of their use of geometry and logic—
require us to think perversely. Pierpaolo Antonello wrote that "le scienze
e le loro strutture razionali hanno rappresentato per Calvino un tenta-
tivo di ridurre le proprie contraddizioni e le proprie ansie" (science and
its rational structures represented for Calvino an attempt to reduce his
own contradictions and anxieties).[20] I agree with matrix of coordinates
in this sentence, but would replace the word "reduce" with "expose"—or
better still, "explore." Calvino consistently works to showcase rationality
as rationalization. Thinking is how we get to anxiety, desire, and contra-
diction, not how we avoid it. Rather than geometry playing the role of
a cerebral distraction from the real world, it *requires* us to think about
prejudice and racism in this story, not to mention erotic possibilities.

Eventually, however, these fantasies about an erotic life with Mrs.
$Ph(i)Nk_0$ come to an end; one day, she says she would like to make everyone some noodles, if only she had some room. And they all begin to
imagine the room she'd need for rolling out the dough, for growing the
grain to make the dough, the solar system needed for the environment

to grow the grain in, and so forth—and as they think it, it happens. The whole universe comes into being, but somehow in the process, Mrs. Ph(i)Nk$_0$ is lost, and they can only dream about being reunited with her.

Mezzacappa links the ending of "Form of Space" to the beginning of "All at One Point" by repeating identically the "swell" or "pulse" in unison that ends "Form of Space" at the very beginning of the subsequent piece. This is unique within her jazz suite—no other pieces are linked in this way (in fact, the piece entitled "Signs" is broken up into three parts and distributed across the album so that no two parts are adjacent). The two stories are not consecutive in the *Cosmicomics*, and while "The Form of Space" deals with the largest expanses of space, "All at One Point" by contrast is set in spaces that are not just microscopically small, but literally *infinitely* small: a singularity, a geometric point with no size whatsoever. Lastly, there is another important divergence. While "The Form of Space" is not set late in the history of the universe or at its end, "All at One Point" is very clearly set at the origin of the universe—indeed, *before* time and space even begin.

Mezzacappa's double "unison gesture" of joining the two pieces, however, is deliberate. All instruments join together in a pulse on the note of D, the final note of "The Form of Space," and then fall silent. About 3 seconds later, they repeat the pulse, but now it is the beginning of "All at One Point." They fall silent again for another 3 seconds or so, then another pulse, another pause, another pulse . . . the effect is to join these pulses together seamlessly, as if it were one continuous composition. The waveform for the whole piece looks like this (see fig. 9), and you can distinctly see the pulses in the introductory section.

Slowly, those pulses add in harmonic complexity and eventually swell in volume as well; after several repetitions of the pulse on D, there is a quick E♭, which hurriedly slides down to D again, almost as if it were a mistake. As the pulses continue, that E♭ returns, more confidently now, and over time, more notes are slowly added in (C, A♭, B, B♭), sometimes returning to D after a moment, sometimes persisting and finding harmonies with other instruments. It would not be out of place to say that Mezzacappa is slowly, subtly—almost undetectably—creating a universe, an acoustic universe that is literally monotonous at the start (a single tone, that of D) before the "accidental" slip of the clinamen to a brief E♭, before it then begins to slowly elaborate an increasingly complex, although still limited, world. While this corresponds to the overall affect Calvino describes—a kind of steady-state of repetition (the narrator uses exclusively the imperfect tense, used for habitual actions in the past)—it is clear already that the jazz piece is nothing like a musical "transcription" of

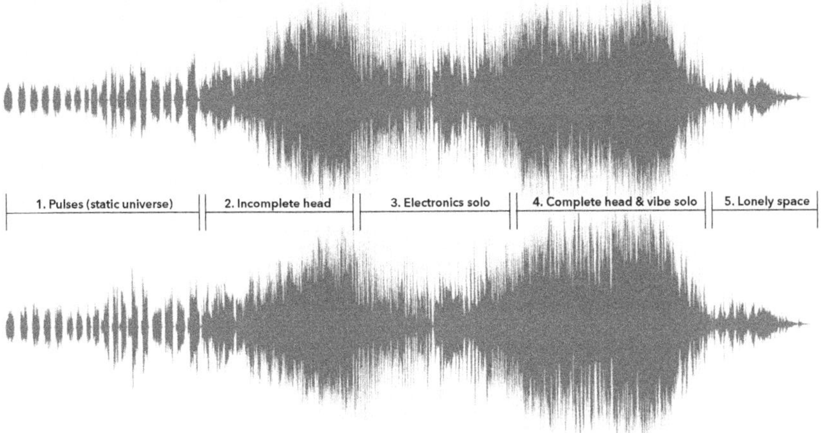

FIGURE 9. The waveform of "All at One Point" (x=time, y=amplitude).

the story. Rather, it is something inspired by the energy of Calvino's ideas to explore an idea we have already encountered in the chapter on Chris Cerrone's opera: How do we make (musical) space expand?

Mezzacappa's universe expands not only in terms of the slowly increasing volume (see Figure 9), and the slowly increasing harmonic complexity, but also through instrumentation (that is, musical timbre). After some initial percussive accents, the drums gradually find a repeating, syncopated rhythm (by 2:30), and eventually the guitar takes the first brave steps along a melodic path (suggesting D Locrian, with its distinctive flat 2, a rather eerie, unsettled sound).[21] The piece quite deliberately fails to find any consistent order or direction—it's neither a complete head nor a clear solo—and that regular, clear rhythm changes around 3:45 as an extended solo from the electronics suite begins, while the rest of the band comps with abrupt (and often unexpected) staccato pulses. This seems to be a way of imagining the (non) space of before the big bang as initially unchanging and invariant (section 1 of fig. 9, the pulses), followed by the slow growth in complexity (section 2 of fig. 9) as Qfwfq describes the petty jealousies and prejudices that characterize the "narrow-minded" inhabitants of this infinitely small point of space. This piece does not assign specific instruments to specific characters or ideas in the stories, but I don't think it is too bold to argue that the electronics suite solo (section 3 of fig. 9, consisting of suggestive moans, groans, and yowls, with lots of large glissandos) represents something like the sexual undercurrent that runs throughout the point before the expansion of the universe. That undercurrent unites all in their desire to be with Mrs. Ph(i)Nk$_0$.

This is a structure we have already seen: an erotic desire that is both engendered by the geometry of space-time, and simultaneously rendered impossible by that same geometry of space-time. Mezzacappa's linkage of these two stories into one continuous sonic experience tells us something that would not be apparent at first glance to the reader of the *Cosmicomics*, where they are not sequential—in fact, I've dedicated my whole professional life to reading, teaching, and thinking about Calvino, and it wasn't until I listened to Mezzacappa that I understood how they are related: They are both stories about the erotic possibilities inherent in the advanced geometries of spacetime. Parallel lines meet at infinity because space itself has a shape that is contorted and bent in the first story, the universe compressed to an infinitely small point in the second. Again, it is not the dirty-minded reader who brings this interpretation to the text; it is unquestionably already there in Calvino, but it is Mezzacappa's formal joining of the pieces that makes it *audible*.

The electronic expression of desire and longing lasts until about 5:15, when a steady rhythm builds into a clear accompaniment on the vibraphone and around 5:34, at last a more traditional, developed "head" arrives (section 4 of fig. 9), a clearly precomposed melodic section that would appear to correspond to Mrs. Ph(i)Nk$_0$'s exclamation: "Ragazzi, avessi un po' di spazio, come mi piacerebbe farvi le tagliatelle!" (2:122, "Guys, if I just had a little space, how I'd like to make you some tagliatelle!"). This in turn is followed by an extended vibraphone solo (the "generous impulse" of Mrs. Ph(i)Nk$_0$) that expands and eventually collapses into the sounds of ambient space. As the inhabitants of the point imagine the space necessary to make the grain, the planets, the universe necessary for making tagliatelle, we hear distant squeaks and noises drenched in reverb (once again, there is a tight correlation between the enormous and lonely space being depicted and the quantity and quality of the reverb, the "echo-logical"). A final coda (the "lonely space" of section 5 of fig. 9) consists of fitful notes, occasional touches on cymbals, musical suggestions that are left undeveloped, drone tones, and a final, quiet, melancholy wail from the electronics, as the inhabitants of the point discover that they possess an entire universe, but one bereft of Mrs. Ph(i)Nk$_0$'s comforting presence, the only thing they ever really wanted.

Conclusions

What does Mezzacappa's composition bring out about Calvino that we might want to pay attention to? Certainly, we can point to what "The Form of Space" taught us before (the neurotic-erotic character of these stories), and the fact that the two pieces form a single sonic unity that underscores how geometry and logic are ways *into* desire in Calvino, embodied and deeply *felt*. This last point is one worth underscoring as well, since it is another category that we do not associate with Calvino but should: feelings. Music is the emotional art par excellence, and Mezzacappa's piece effectively literalizes the destitution that ends "All in One Point," given the impression of directionlessness, meaninglessness, and the destitution of a universe without Mrs. Ph(i)Nk$_0$ that characterizes the finale (and is also a depiction of a universe without music—true destitution indeed!).

But it is perhaps in space itself that we might find the real lesson of Mezzacappa's conjoined stories. Because, in proper cosmicomic fashion, she effectively discovers a wormhole to travel from one story to another, using the closure at the end of one piece (the finalizing "unison gesture") to find a way to make that space expand again. That closing gesture becomes a pulse, a new life that is waiting to emerge. "The Form of Space" and "All at One Point" (both Calvino's stories and Mezzacappa's jazz versions) do precisely what a resonant reading indicates perhaps all art does or at least might potentially do, and what midcentury American jazz was also attempting to do: expand into a cultural space, but more radically, expand the possibilities of space itself. In other words, while we have always understood that Calvino's works open up a space, the space that we imagined they opened (largely literary, centered on the image, dominated by a sense of the author as controlling, rigid, and cerebral) was only a fractional slice of what was actually happening. A significant part of the reason Calvino continues to resonate through much of the Western world and beyond is precisely the jazz-like character that Mezzacappa realizes and makes audible in her album: playful, improvisational, unexpected, and open. For Mezzacappa, Calvino is an invitation to play with ideas, and to play music.

4 /   Desires and Fears: *Silent City*

The most successful theater experiences generate resonance as well as memories. The reverberations engendered in an artistic encounter can have a profound effect on the body, on one's actions in the world and in the world at large.

—ANNE BOGART

The Shame of Italy

The city of Matera is located in the Basilicata region of Italy, the arch at the bottom of the Italian boot. The city is particularly famous for the Sassi, picturesque neighborhoods whose houses are carved out of the rock rather than built on top of it and that date back to prehistoric times. It's hard to go anywhere in Italy and not be reminded of deep historical roots, of course, and Italians take a great deal of pride in pointing out the modern remnants of and connections to ancient Rome, or to the even older Etruscans. Only in Matera, however, was I told that in order to understand the present-day city, I really needed to take a tour of the Park of the Murgia Materana, the local portion of the enormous karst plateau that runs through much of southern Italy. There, Mimma Giovinazza (a "dottore forestale," a kind of park ranger/scientist) gave me the *really* big picture, going back to the Paleolithic and even earlier, the geological and evolutionary background that has shaped the region. By the end of our walk, we had worked our way up to some of the prehistoric remains of human inhabitants in the region, and even (so recent!) early Medieval constructions. Matera is truly ancient, even by Italian standards. It is the third-oldest continually inhabited city on Earth. Only Aleppo and Jericho are older.

In addition to its distinctive and picturesque appearance, Matera also has a remarkably distinctive *acoustic* profile that extends deep into the past. On my tour of the Murgia outside the city, Mimma demonstrated how light and easy the upper layer of rock was to shape, even by hand, while rocks from the lower base are quite hard. She distinguished them not through the visual differences between the two types of rock (in fact, they look almost identical), but through *sound*. The shapable rocks are easily identified by the soft sound they make when tapped, quite unlike the hard, dense base rocks, which make a sharp "clack!" when tapped together.[1] (The two rock strata are in turn formed by quite different geological processes.) In fact, Matera really has three layers: the flat, mesa-like base of hard rock; the layer of soft rock above that was tunneled out into a series of caves; and a layer of built construction above (using, in part, the rock removed during the previous subterranean digs) that takes more conventional forms (houses, churches, campaniles, and the like).

Standing in the Park of the Murgia Materana, you look at the city of Matera across a steep ravine called the Gravina, which literally means ravine, with a river (also called the Gravina) at the bottom, about 100 meters down. From there, you can clearly see a rocky mesa that forms the flat base of the city, and then the city growing up from that base. The Sassi (literally "the Stones") are the oldest part of Matera. They were initially carved out of the rock rather than built on top of the flat base, like a conventional city. Because of this unusual construction, over thousands of years, the Sassi give the impression of a city that is partially built and that partially seems to grow up out of the rocks (see fig. 10 for an example of this half-built, half-organic architecture; it often looks more like the original rock is growing back over the human environment, although in fact it is exactly the reverse). The city is so picturesque that it has often been used in film, in order to indicate Biblical antiquity in historical films (Mel Gibson's *The Passion of the Christ*, Pasolini's *The Gospel According to St. Matthew*) or just to provide a visually astonishing backdrop (the motorcycle chase sequence in the James Bond film *No Time to Die*).

The town has experienced something of a tourist renaissance in recent decades, with a vibrant arts scene, and is one of the fastest-growing cities in Italy's largely poor south. It is also one of the only growing cities in the South, a region Italians mostly have moved away from, historically. The Sassi are now home to luxury hotels, chic restaurants, and cute shops (as well as some private homes), and contemporary Italians may know it primarily through tourist visits, its film appearances, or perhaps its setting for the popular comedy-murder mystery series (based on Mariolina Venezia's novels), *Imma Tataranni: Sostituto procuratore* (Imma Tataranni, Deputy Prosecutor). The oldest inhabitants of Matera, however, still vividly recall when the Sassi *were* Matera, and were branded the "vergogna nazionale" (national shame) of Italy. Before World War II

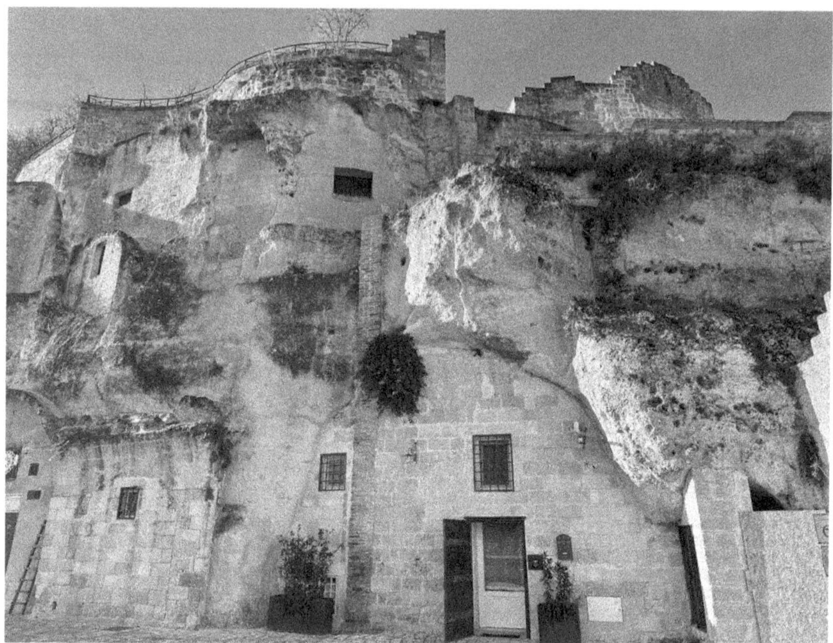

FIGURE 10. The city carved out of rock. Photo by author

they were overpopulated, with rampant disease and unimaginably high levels of infant mortality, over 40 percent at the beginning of the twentieth century. Starting in 1953, almost the entire population of the Sassi was removed and placed in public housing (construction largely financed by the Marshall Plan). The modern rebirth of the Sassi is largely due to their being declared a UNESCO heritage site in 1993, and their subsequent restoration led to the area being reborn less as a residential area than as a cultural destination. This process culminated when Matera was formally declared a "European Capital of Culture" by the EU for 2019.

It is worth recalling that Italians conceptualize identity much less along national lines than Americans do; the primary way of understanding someone's identity is through their city.[2] An inhabitant of Milan is a Milanese first, and an Italian a distant second. (Indeed, many Italians think of themselves first according to their city, second as Europeans, and third as Italians.) In the case of Matera, the city's dedication—in the midst of one of Italy's poorest and most conservative regions—to being a cosmopolitan arts community and a capital of European culture gave it a particular impetus toward this kind of postnational self-conceptualization. While Europe recognized it as a "capital of culture," the Italian state, after all, had branded it as a "national disgrace." The Italian national project, that is, the project of Italy as a nation, has been notoriously fraught for Southern Italians—rather dramatically, as we will see. All this is a way of saying why the question of a city's historical and cultural identity might matter so much to Materans, and why, more specifically, having a coherent urban identity might be both unusually pressing and problematic for them. As I'll go on to show, while Materans have very much embraced their modern and cosmopolitan European identity, they have also conceptualized the forced modernization resettlement of the 1950s as a historical trauma that still needs working through.

The need to work through that trauma was so profound, in fact, that Matera made use of its designation as a European capital of culture in 2019 to also create a collective musical work that would directly address the experience. A women's theater group from the city, L'Albero (The Tree), decided that a work that would address the community's traumatic past would need to be a collective effort, one that would privilege those who directly remembered the forced resettlement (the elderly) as well as those who were so young as to have lost any sense of the historical event (the children), a transmission of cultural heritage that is typical of what Marianne Hirsch calls "postmemory." In "Hearing Postmemory," Spitzer describes it thus: "Postmemory considers the impact of history upon people who were born too late to have direct recollection of its events," although rather than attempting a historical reconstruction, postmemory tends to make use of "creative imagination."[3] These works of creative imagination, Hirsch argues, are particularly likely to "enact a fantasy of rescuing at least one child" (163) who was a witness to the traumatic historical events, and who will serve as a bridge to the younger generation who has no primary recollection of what happened.[4] As we will see, this is precisely what happens in the work that L'Albero and the community of Matera created, *Silent City*. The title, *Silent City* (in English), already references Calvino's novel as a way of thinking about cities and the multitudes of communities they contain that go unseen. While Calvino's *Invisible Cities* is about communities that are real and present but that do not appear on the map, *Silent City* is about a community whose history has gone unheard, but can now take resonant form in a collective *musical* celebration.

Silent City is unlike the other works that I examine in this book in a number of ways, the most obvious being that, while Calvino's role here is still resonant, it is unquestionably much less one-to-one than in the other works I look at. It is not an adaptation or transmedial retelling in operatic or theatrical form of *Invisible Cities* or any other work by Calvino, and the sources that inspired it were numerous, both local (Matera's annual celebration of the Madonna della Bruna) and European (Walter Benjamin, Guy Debord, Georges Perec). The resonant, reverberant space surrounding Calvino is still expanding, but the normal path of echoes is to journey away from their source (Italy, in this case) and then back to it, to grow fainter, more diffuse and more mingled over time, until they are simply an indistinguishable part of the sonic background. *Silent City* helps to show that Calvino has become a deep and hence inextricable part of the way that we think about cities and the cultural memory of the people who live in them. It also helps to show the vital importance—including political importance—of form, as well as the importance of the "acoustic turn" when thinking about how to express Calvino's thinking about cities, memories, and communities forced into invisibility—and silence.

Word and Music

Structurally, *Silent City* perhaps resembles a "sung-through" musical— a musical with no spoken dialogue, like *Les Misérables* or *Hamilton*— more than an opera. The distinction is not always clear, and *Silent City* is somewhere in between the two: Its reliance on popular singing styles and dance indicate musical theater (*commedia musicale* in Italy, a form that is seen as fundamentally American in origin), while its serious political-historical origin and music that ventures into more avant-garde territory suggests opera (with its long Italian history).[5] The creators of *Silent City* elected to call it a "community opera" in English translation, perhaps to indicate that it lies somewhere at the intersection of musical theater, community theater, and opera—but also (and more importantly) because the opera was also designed by and for the community, and was intended to be an expression of the community and a collective act of remembering.

Silent City tells the story of a band of three children from Matera today who descend deep into the Gravina and enter into ancient caverns below. There they find a lost boy described only as the *fanciullo*, a literary term for a boy or young man. He wears ragged clothing and a homemade scarf, and remains mysterious and mute throughout the opera: He dances, but he does not speak or sing. Other scenes in the opera make it clear that he is from the time just before the forced relocation, the early 1950s; the caverns are a kind of magical, atemporal space where the past can touch the present. The three children join up with him, and together they overcome several obstacles to return to the surface—but the fanciullo vanishes along the way. It is like a folktale, the narrative and symbolic expression of a community, but more directly and literally so: The story was collectively written by the children and the elderly of Matera (again, those too young to remember the expulsion from the Sassi even secondhand, and those old enough to remember the events directly).

The libretto does not have formal divisions into acts, and there are no pauses in the action, but there are roughly nine major scenes that structure the opera:

1. The fanciullo dances alone as we hear a variety of sounds (dripping water, songs of the 1950s on the radio), increasingly marked by orchestral dissonance and cacophony, as well as sounds of construction.

2. The fanciullo's mother sings a lullaby to her son as she finishes knitting him a scarf, then he departs for school.

3. The "Faceless Futures"—developers and builders eager to build a new city—appear and sing a song ("Senti il rombo atroce?" [Do You Hear the Terrible Roar?]) that emphasizes the environmental destruction their building will entail. The mother repeats her song, and then transforms into an old woman with a cane. We have arrived in . . .

4. . . . the present day—modern Matera, where we meet the three modern children, Domenico, Caterina, and Rocco, each with his or her own song.

5. The trio descends into the ravine and discovers the fanciullo, who leads them into underground tunnels and caves; they labor to return to the surface, crossing an underground lake on a homemade raft.

6. The "Faceless Futures" (also called "the faceless men" and "builders") return to offer the children a life of modernity and light (they unfurl maps of present-day Matera).

7. An "electroacoustic interlude" follows, in which, as the libretto specifies, "i bambini tentano di attraversare le barriere traumatiche del tempo e del passato per ritornare al mondo presente" (the children try to cross the traumatic barriers of time and the past to return to the world of the present). This interlude consists solely of instrumental and electronic music (extremely dissonant, largely electronically generated noise) and abstract dance—there is no voice.

8. The modern-day children climb back up into the present, but the only remaining trace of the fanciullo is his scarf, which they return to his aged mother.

9. In a choral celebration of the city of Matera, first the modern-day children with the mother, then the entire cast and crew, join.

Although the story itself was a collective effort, the libretto was written by Ubah Cristina Ali Farah, contributing to the cosmopolitan character of the opera. She is a Black Italian poet born in Verona who has led an extremely itinerant, multilingual life: She currently lives in Belgium, but grew up in Mogadishu, before leaving during the Somali civil war, first for Hungary and then for Rome. For *Silent City* she drew on a number of poetic sources, including the poet Rocco Scotellaro, well known in Italy as a "poeta contadino" (peasant or farmer poet) and Socialist politician from Tricario (part of Matera county), who extensively thematized childhood and early adolescence and the intense bond between mother and son,[6] as well as the chronically poor and underprivileged condition of the region. Ali Farah remarked on how rhythmically marked the poetry needed to be—some of the songs (especially those of the children and the "faceless men") are sung to an emphatic rhythm, more typical of popular styles.[7]

The music in *Silent City* is surprisingly varied, but falls into perhaps four primary styles: traditional tonal music in the sweeping, emotional, late-Romantic register (such as the song of the mother) that is typical of canonical opera; the rhythmic chants of the "men without faces" (still tonal, but always in a minor key and sung to a moderately slow march tempo); more dissonant pieces that accompany wordless action, such as the more symbolic dance music—these are sometimes dissonant and without a definable tonal center because they are cacophonous, with many melodies and sounds playing simultaneously; and finally, a handful of pieces that sound like traditional songs from musical theater—jaunty show tunes, midcentury in style (as when the three children introduce themselves). Of particular importance is the "electroacoustic interlude" (scene 7 above), because it is explicitly marked in the libretto as both the final struggle between past and present as well as the climactic symbolic resolution. Not only is that sequence largely musically based on noise, but it is also entirely wordless.

The composer, Nigel Osborne, is a well-established Scottish musical figure whose 1987 opera *The Electrification of the Soviet Union* (based on autobiographical works by Boris Pasternak) is probably his best-known work, and choosing him (along with Ali Farah) contributes to the sense that *Silent City* should be understood as a cosmopolitan work rooted in local traditions, but with an eye toward a larger European context befitting Matera's selection as a capital of culture. Musically, Osborne's work is mostly modernist, in line with the more relaxed versions of serialism and atonality, but not so radical as, say, Stockhausen. Osborne is also, however, fairly eclectic, and can shift styles easily even within the same piece. In *Botanical Studies*, for example, the first four movements are all in a broadly atonal, experimental style, while the last—"Galanthus nivalis"—is fully tonal with a bittersweet melody that would be right at home in a film like *Cinema paradiso*. What he has been most famous for since the mid 1990s, however, is his work in musical therapy with children, particularly traumatized children "in zones of conflict and postconflict," including Bosnia-Herzegovina, Lebanon and Syria, North Uganda, Palestine, Thailand, and most recently, Ukraine.[8]

Music therapy is a well-established field with considerable evidence showing that it has therapeutic value, largely because of a feature that I have tried to stress at several points throughout this book. We listen with our bodies—not just the ears, but also the skull, the abdomen, and the feet all play a role in our acoustic life. We hear with our whole body, but the effects of music are also felt throughout that same body. Music doesn't just influence our minds, but also our breathing and our heart rate, and is capable of stirring subjects who may otherwise be mobility impaired—either physically or psychically—to clap, step, and dance. Entrainment is in fact remarkably hard to resist, especially when it is as part of a large group. As a result, music presents a kind of unconscious aperture into a traumatized subject who might otherwise refuse or resist engagement, an engagement that not only stirs the body into mobility, but also back into community. Like the other aspects of the production, Osborne's aimed at making the audience *feel* a sense of community. *Silent City* understands the historical background to its story to be *traumatic* in character, a point that I will also return to later, but for now one of the most important things to understand about trauma is that it is precisely what we cannot spontaneously put into words—it resists signification (which is why this city is silent). As a result, however, it can be addressed through music and its capacity to precipitate the traumatized subject into movement, song, dance, and ultimately feeling part of a coherent group.

In Form, Not in Content

When we spoke in Matera, Vania Cauzillo (who was co-responsible for *Silent City*'s artistic direction along with Alessandra Maltempo) was notably enthusiastic about the process of *Silent City*'s creation.[9] I was already familiar with some of it, because they had chronicled some of the workshops, especially with the children, on YouTube and on the various websites associated with the project, but in fact the process took over a year and was incredibly involved. Participants did worksheets, wrote stories, kept diary entries, did group work, and much more. Andrea Ciommiento, who served as the official playwright, had a fourteen-page (single-spaced) artistic itinerary for those who were collaborating, with programs designed for children and teens, adults, and seniors, which included children role-playing Romeo and Juliet playing tag; all ages creating a "life-map" around them while seated on the floor; an orienteering exercise for adults that explored the city through all five senses; and much more. Brainstorming sessions involved small cards for story ideas that could be arranged and rearranged into almost any combinatorial pattern: The community becomes a combinatorial story machine (a very Calvinian idea). In terms of process, Ciommiento was responsible not only for eliciting this mass of ideas from the people of Matera, but also for extracting and refining a stageable story from those materials, a process that was also subjected to a long, rigorous, and collaborative process.

Every aspect of *Silent City*'s creation that Cauzillo discussed was like this—a careful, recursive, and insistently collaborative process that was meticulously delineated in advance. Most crucial was the funding, and it was one of the very first things that Cauzillo said, emphatically and proudly: "we spent two-thirds of the funding on process, and only one-third on production." This led to some issues, including the fact that they still had no venue forty-eight hours before the premiere, but it was clear that, for Cauzillo, the goal in many ways was the *process*, not the opera. That is perhaps less surprising when we recall that *Silent City* was undertaken as a form of therapy, the working out of a historical trauma that the community had not yet come to terms with, and the voicing of a shared memory that had fallen silent. The opera does indeed stage a symbolic voyage into the past, a fantastic and symbolic working through of that historical trauma, and lastly a very real, even literal, transformation of silence into sound, the sound of voices singing solo and together about precisely what was once kept in silence.

The process that Cauzillo, Ciommiento, and their collaborators created and implemented had, in some sense, already accomplished all that before the opera even began, in ways that were practical, ordinary, and everyday rather than symbolic, epic, and artistic. Young and old had already shared memories and their ideas about the city, learned to *hear* the city as much as see it, and so on. A sense of community had already been created and rebuilt precisely through orienteering and role-playing exercises, and an image or idea of the community was also created and projected, not only for the world looking at Matera, but perhaps most crucially for Matera looking at itself. I know, of course, that some of that process also created (and revealed) dissensions and rivalries, as every collective art project probably does. Ethan Philbrick, in *Group Works*, is very attentive to the ways in which collaborative and group processes can be "an ambivalent relational form" (21); the group can be, in his acoustic terminology that recurs in every chapter, "cacophonous"—but it can also "resonate" (20).

At one point in our conversation, I asked Cauzillo if *Silent City* was political, something I asked almost all of the artists I talked to for this book. She did not hesitate: "non è politico nel contenuto, è politico nella forma" (it's not political in its content—it's political in its form). This statement needs some unpacking, not least because the actual content of the opera is, albeit in a symbolic and fantastic key, about how a paternalistic act by the state should be understood as a historical trauma to the community, which seems pretty political. For an older generation of Italian cultural critics trained to think that only socially committed Lukacsian realism was acceptable, Cauzillo's reply would be surprising, however, since—for them—attention to form is politically regressive. When I claimed at the start of this chapter that the resonance of Calvino in *Silent City* was more diffuse, a part of the atmosphere, this is precisely what I meant, however: Even in conservative Italy there is now a recognition that *form itself* can have a positive political value, something embraced by most or perhaps even all of the resonant art I look at in this volume.

The formal apparatus surrounding *Silent City* (part of its "politics through form") is almost radically inclusive and collaborative, particularly with regard to sound. Not only were the "least heard" members of the community foregrounded (the very young and the very old), but the process and the performance included those with mobility restrictions and cognitive disabilities, as well as people with hearing and vision loss, who not only attended, but also participated in the performance. This aspect was highlighted not only in the video documentation, but also in all of the written materials, including the program for the performance—all materials were provided in Braille and LSI, Italian sign language.[10] A striking feature of the program/libretto is that it doesn't just emphasize inclusion but also foregrounds collaboration and process as key to a sense of community. After the final chorus of the libretto, the program includes an additional dozen pages, and—in a radical departure—only one of them lists the corporate sponsors of the event. The rest are activities for the spectators, including writing their own music and a sound walk in which they walk away from the Church of Santa Maria de Armenis and try to find a silent location, documenting all of the sounds they hear. The final two pages list all of the collaborators who worked on the opera—about three hundred of them. But that list ends with a reminder in the voice of the spectator: "questa storia è anche mia" (this story is also mine).

According to its promotional booklet, the creation of *Silent City* had a nine-step timeline in which Step 8 was the premiere (held on November 29, 2019). The performance, however, was not the end goal of the process. It was to have been followed by Step 9, a report of the social impact of the opera (Step 9 never took place because of the COVID-19 pandemic). Even Step 9 was not conceived as the end of the process, however—two more steps, left unnumbered, were imagined for the future of the opera, which would have continued in an extremely Calvinian way (reminiscent of the city of Ersilia, which the inhabitants constantly abandon and rebuild elsewhere). *Silent City* would move to a new city and be performed there, where the entire collaborative, inclusive, artistic process would be repeated, leading to the creation of an entirely new opera based on the new city and its relationship with silence. In short, *Silent City* was envisioned from the beginning as a dynamic and evolving work, a title whose content was provisional and whose meaning was found in its formal process.

City Thinking

On January 8, 2024, I talked with Andrea Ciommiento, who was responsible for the "theatrical research" for *Silent City*, the bulk of that formal process of collaborative composition. The highly collaborative, distributed, and community-based process behind *Silent City* meant that the opera did not have an "author" in the conventional sense. In the heyday of Italian opera (the nineteenth century), most operas were based on a preexisting novel, play, or musical work, almost invariably French, and then the librettist would work with the composer to create a poetic text that would work with the music. In the case of *Silent City*, that original story was generated by the entire community before librettist Ali Farah worked with composer Nigel Osborne to create the text that would eventually be sung. Ciommiento's role, then, was to invent and manage a process that would allow the community to produce a story: workshopping it, collecting it, collating it, and giving it its final form before Ali Farah would take over. Originally from Gorizia, now living in Torino, Ciommiento does theater and anthropology, and is the founder of Invasioni Creative, a "fabbrica di narrazione multimediale" (multimedia narrative factory), which does extensive work with schools and young people.

Ciommiento explained to me that he started off trying to think about ways to "scrivere la città" (write the city), and his first thoughts were of three authors and their texts: Calvino's *Invisible Cities*, Georges Perec's polemic on the "infra-ordinary" (about which more in a moment), and Walter Benjamin's *Arcades Project*. Looking at Ciommiento's detailed booklet of exercises for jump-starting the community into thinking about how to "write the city," one can also spot a number of traces of a fourth thinker and text, namely Guy Debord and his idea of the *dérive* or "drift," a city walk that violates ordinary thinking about routes. A *dérive* prompt might say something like "Go to the Beverly Hills sign, and then follow any red vehicle," an idea codified in the 1956 "Theory of the Dérive." In his exercises with the community, Ciommiento also drew on other writers and texts (Gianni Rodari, Shakespeare's *Romeo and Juliet*, one of Calvino's Italian folktales, Rossini's *William Tell*, and more), but the two writers he explicitly mentions in his program of writing exercises are Calvino and Perec.

The constellation of writers and thinkers Ciommiento mentioned and referenced (Calvino, Perec, Debord, Benjamin) are all part of what we might call "city thinking." City thinking is basically a toolbox of ideas and concepts that have become standard, almost automatic, for thinking about cities and our relationship to them. Unsurprisingly, they form part of the core of the urban humanities, but here I am interested in the ways that they have had a larger resonance across national and disciplinary borders, making them available to artists, geographers, city designers, academics of all stripes, and more. To be clear, Calvino has had a much larger resonance than just "city thinking," but it is a particularly important part of the resonance of *Invisible Cities*—almost any serious attempt to think about cities and how we live in and navigate them will almost invariably make use (perhaps even unconsciously) of this toolbox. Linder's volume on *Invisible Cities* and thinking about cities is a case in point.[11] In fact, within that volume, Ana Ivasiuc's chapter is organized around precisely the same quote that Ciommiento used to organize *Silent City*: "Cities, like dreams, are made of desires and fears."

Looking at Ciommiento's "city thinking" toolbox for constructing *Silent City*, however, I'll begin with Perec, whose contribution to city thinking is perhaps the least known. Perec was a French writer (best known for his novel *Life: A User's Manual*, which won the Prix Médicis in 1978) who was part of the same experimental writing group OuLiPo (see chapter 3) that also included Calvino (the two were also good friends). Ciommiento was particularly interested in a piece by Perec, however, a short essay called "Approaches to What?" where he develops his notion of the "infra-ordinary."[12] In this essay, Perec calls for thinking about what falls below the threshold of the ordinary (like infrared light), what is so ordinary and mundane within the city that it isn't even seen at all. We need to discover and see these elements with the same wonder "that Jules Verne or his readers may have felt faced with an apparatus capable of reproducing and transporting sounds" (210), he writes. At the end of the essay, he moves from the speculative to the imperative, and what emerges is a program for perceiving urban life quite differently, with precise and meticulous attention to what we haven't even noticed yet:

> What we need to question is bricks, concrete, glass, our table manners, our utensils, our tools, the way we spend our time, our rhythms. To question that which seems to have ceased forever to astonish us. We live, true, we breathe, true; we walk, we open doors, we go down staircases, we sit at a table in order to eat, we lie down on a bed in order to sleep. How? Where? When? Why?
>
> Describe your street. Describe another street. Compare.
>
> Make an inventory of your pockets, of your bag. Ask yourself about the provenance, the use, what will become of each of the objects you take out.
>
> Question your tea spoons. (210)

Intriguingly, we would find something not really very different if we looked at Guy Debord's notion of the *dérive*, which he defines as "a technique of rapid passage through varied ambiances."[13] In many respects, the *dérive* functions as an intensification of Flaubert's *flânerie*, the idle stroll through the city in which one peers into shop windows and stops to admire some notable architecture or perhaps a nice park. Unlike *flânerie*, however, the *dérive* is a deliberate attempt to undo the sorts of logic that would unconsciously guide the *flâneur*, such as a long boulevard lined with shop windows—no longer an idle stroll, the infra-ordinary and the *dérive* aim to destabilize the city's explicit and ordinary logic. In fact, Ciommiento includes precisely these kinds of exercises in his *Silent City* writing program, and they are even included in the official program for the opera as activities for children ("follow the street that least inspires you!").

Similarly, Walter Benjamin in the *Arcades Project* assembled a vast archive of fragmentary materials, organized into folders called convolutes (etymologically "folded together") about turn-of-the-century Paris, without any clear, overarching system of classification, literally convoluted. Each convolute once again becomes something like a *dérive*, a random walk through the city that is intended, in Benjamin's terms, to turn the "merely" legible aspects of the city—the aspects whose meaning we are sure in advance that we know without thinking of them (Perec's teaspoons)—into the "readable": what is unknown, open to interpretation, even storytelling. It's clear that the infra-ordinary, the *dérive* and

Benjamin's "readable" are all different concepts, but all of them attempt to make the parts of urban life that are trite and unremarkable suddenly visible and new, and all of them do so through the assembly of fragmentary and partial perspectives. Benjamin and Debord's models both implicitly model new knowledge about the city emerging from juxtaposition, one thing next to another, and a break from the linear. The notion of the *dérive* is perhaps the most explicit in this regard: In French, it literally means drift, and its original meaning is nautical, such as a ship sailing due North that drifts off to the West, for example.[14] For Perec and Calvino, as we will see, the model is one of depth, however. What surprises Perec and Calvino is not off to the side—it is underneath us, a model that is particularly appropriate to the Sassi of Matera and their completely vertical organization that stretches back into prehistory, but is also appropriate to a depth model of psychology. What surprises us from beneath may be a truth we knew, but did not want to know.

Desires and Fears

In our conversation, Ciommiento said that it is not possible to think about a city, its history, and its politics without thinking of Calvino's *Invisible Cities*. He was attracted above all to the idea that "cities, like dreams, are made of desires and fears." This is one of the most frequently cited lines from the novel, and it is a frequent "pull quote" from the novel in reviews. I'm going to put a lot of weight on this phrase in the argument that follows, so it's worth recognizing that it has had a certain resonance before we start to ask why it has been so compelling. To begin with, the quote appears in such a variety of places as to make one curious about its plasticity. It shows up on "inspirational quotes" websites, or you can buy a poster for your dorm room on Amazon featuring the quote underneath an image of the London Underground (the vendor describes it as "indie room decor," a kind of "live, laugh, love" poster for the young bohemian intellectual). But it is also clearly resonant in the sense that I mean in this book: It is widely repeated, but has also expanded across space and media into what I am calling "city thinking" here. When New York's Mayor Bill de Blasio spoke in 2014 to the Regional Plan Association, a group of mayors and city planners, he cited precisely this line from *Invisible Cities*, noting that "every one of us, every one of the mayors in the room, immediately understands what that means. I think planners do, too." The political and architectural sense of Calvino's book has in some way become *obvious*, part of the toolbox of city thinking, even in the halls of US city and regional government.

It might be a little too obvious, in fact, because a quick look at the source immediately indicates that it's actually a rather strange quote for dorm posters or regional planning meetings. Marco Polo offers up this pithy phrase in one of the novel's philosophical dialogues, one in which he and Kublai Khan—as they frequently do—struggle for control of the narrative. Khan gets bored listening to Polo's city descriptions and abruptly declares that he is reversing their roles: Henceforth, *he* will describe the cities and Polo will tell him if they exist or not. He begins describing a very plausible "invisible" city, but Polo interrupts and takes back the upper hand: This is the very city that he was describing for the Khan, he says, when he was interrupted. Moreover, this city cannot exist—it has no secret "connecting thread" or "inner rule." He explains:

> —È delle città come dei sogni: tutto l'immaginabile può essere
> sognato ma anche il sogno più inatteso è un rebus che nasconde un
> desiderio, oppure il suo rovescio, una paura. Le città come i sogni
> sono costruite di desideri e di paure, anche se il filo del loro discorso
> è segreto, le loro regole assurde, le prospettive ingannevoli, e ogni
> cosa ne nasconde un'altra. . . . D'una città non godi le sette o le settan-
> tasette meraviglie, ma la risposta che dà a una tua domanda.
> —O la domanda che ti pone obbligandoti a rispondere, come Tebe
> per bocca della Sfinge. (2:391–92)

> "It is with cities as with dreams: Everything imaginable can be
> dreamed, but even the most unexpected dream is a rebus that con-
> ceals a desire or its reverse, a fear. Cities, like dreams, are made of
> desires and fears, even if the thread of their discourse is secret, their
> rules absurd, their perspectives deceitful, and each thing conceals
> something else. . . . What you enjoy in a city is not its seven or sev-
> enty-seven wonders, but the answer it gives to a question of yours."
> "Or the question it asks you, forcing you to answer, like Thebes
> through the mouth of the Sphinx."

As I have observed at several points throughout this book, we have consistently underappreciated Calvino as a reader of Freud, perhaps because he generally does not refer to him by name, although he does refer to very specific works and passages that demonstrate a careful reading and a sharp memory. Here he is referring to Freud's *Interpretation of Dreams* (specifically chapter 6), where Freud says that the meaning of a dream (the dream-thought) is effectively expressed in a different language (the dream-content). He specifically states that dreams are organized like a rebus, using pictures not as a visual image, but in order to convey individual letters, sounds, and words (277–78). There is a "secret thread" that organizes the apparently impossible or fantastic elements of a dream (perhaps, say, children wandering into magical underground caverns that travel through time), and that thread represents a repressed—which means, for Freud, literally unspeakable—desire or fear. For Ciommiento and many others, this piece of *Invisible Cities* is perhaps the key contribution by Calvino to city thinking because Calvino is saying that *cities have an unconscious.* Moreover, he is saying here that cities have a *Freudian* unconscious. When they are silent, it is because they are structured by a desire or wish that they cannot articulate, something that functions as an unspeakable trauma. Our encounter with the city, or the dream, involves in some crucial way a demand or a question. We ask the city-dream something, or perhaps—in the final, somewhat ominous line of this dialogue between Marco Polo and Kublai Khan—it asks something of us. Something that we may not be prepared to answer, since the dialogue ends at this point.

In what follows, I will argue that there are several questions we might ask of *Silent City* as we probe its unconscious: Why are there *three* children from modern-day Matera and not simply the emblematic duo of boy and girl, Domenico and Caterina? Both Domenico and Rocco are boys of the same age—so why are they assigned to sing in different registers (Domenico is a baritone, while Rocco is a tenor)? Why is Rocco disabled when none of the other characters have anything remarkable or different about them? (Domenico and Caterina are in fact curiously banal.) Why are the crucial moments of struggle in *Silent City* wordless? Why did the organizers choose Nigel Osborne, a composer best known for using music therapy to treat traumatized children? Finally, we must turn to the last and most obvious part of the quote from Calvino, the part that suggests why everyone everywhere, from indie-chic dorm posters to the former mayor of New York, quotes only the one line from this passage and does not continue to the end, since it raises what Freud argues is one of the most central repressions for the modern Western psyche, namely the story of Oedipus. Calvino ends by referencing a specific city, Thebes, that poses a specific demand, and that is structured by a very specific desire and fear: to have sex with the mother and murder the father.

In *Relating Narratives*, Adriana Cavarero argues that autobiography as such is impossible. We cannot ever tell our own stories without relying on someone else because parts of our own stories are occluded to us, particularly the story of our own birth. Oedipus, unsurprisingly, is one of her crucial examples. He may walk upright as a man, but he limps because his parents—in an attempt to avoid the terrible prophecy that he would grow up to kill his father and marry his mother, abandoned him on the hillside with a spike driven through his foot. (Oedipus literally means "swollen foot" in Greek.) A full accounting of Oedipus's life, then, requires the family story, what Freud calls the "family romance." That said, we can actually take Cavarero's critique a little further: It would be a mistake to think that the memory is even simply *familial.* Reconstructing the truth about Oedipus will require the work of the whole city, and the King commands them *all* to investigate and all to punish the killer of Laius once he is found. This all takes place in front of the chorus, symbolically representing the community, but crucially, it also all occurs at court. Memory, even my own memory of my own life, is not individual, and it is not just collective: It is political. To say it with Calvino, my desires and fears both construct the city, and are created by it.

What is traumatic is also what we can't speak of, our unspeakable desires and our shameful fears—all the more so when the stage for such desires and fears is political, which is to say, in a city. Oedipus in front of his court, or the city of Matera on the international stage being called a "capital of culture" or the "shame of the nation." It is precisely *music* that has the capacity to express a thought and a feeling (especially the *intensity* of a feeling), but without giving it a fixed and determinate content. In psychoanalytic terms, music is ideally suited to express the *symptom*—like the body, it can speak what cannot be said. In *Silent City*, our three modern-day children return to the surface having had a direct contact with the past, and it is clear that a kind of symbolic reconciliation is understood to have taken place. We return from "electroacoustic" noise to conventional late-Romantic melody (the mother's song) and eventually a celebratory chorus, but we have never said just what it is that is being reconciled. Like Freud's famously third-person "a child is being beaten" (which child? by whom?), there is a struggle and a resolution, but the terms of both are articulated only through the wordless energy of *noise*—it is as if the repressed (unconscious) content is too threatening to even take on a melody. *Silent City* has precisely such an agency-free, "passive voice" event at its core, leaving much unspoken. The fanciullo is wordless throughout: Is he traumatized into silence? Does he harbor desires and fears that he cannot speak? His mother sings him a love song at the beginning of the opera, when she is still young ("Vieni anima mia bella / fior di giacinto e rosa," Come my beautiful soul, hyacinth and rose flower), and his father is entirely absent, never mentioned. Is she in mourning for the father (already lost) or the son (about to be lost)—or why not both, since the unconscious never has to choose between possibilities? She can be a "mater dolorosa" for all (see fig. 11 later). Moreover, like *Oedipus Rex*, in a curiously occluded and indirect fashion (precisely what marks the censorship of the unconscious), we could say that a murder takes place: A child disappears. At the beginning of the opera, there is a young boy who is alive and present; at the end, he is no longer alive or on stage. Whatever happens in between, it is so traumatic that it can only be said through pure inarticulate noise.

Perhaps we should demand, in the name of the Italian state, then, that the citizens of Matera should bring us the killer! Perhaps before we did so, however, we should recall that same demand did not turn out so well for Oedipus. After all, *Oedipus Rex* is the first real murder mystery: Oedipus demands that the citizens of Thebes "bring [him] the killer of Laius," only to slowly realize, as he accumulates evidence and testimonies, that he himself is the killer, and that Laius was his father. As Cavarero says, Oedipus's problem is precisely that he does not know his own story; it is not that the story he does know about himself is wrong precisely—it's that there is another story, obscure to him, that alters the meaning of the story that he does know.

This is Calvino's "secret thread" that organizes the dream or the city: another drama happening somewhere else that we cannot directly see. Freud—tellingly—drew on theatrical language repeatedly when he discussed psychoanalytic fantasy (often spelled "phantasy"), and this other drama is no exception. Freud called this the "other scene," but *andere Schauplatz* is better translated as "other stage" (literally "other show-place"). For a dream, this is the unconscious, the dreamer's unspeakable desires and fears that can be expressed only through a bizarre rebus, or an apparently innocuous fantasy about time-traveling children. Freud's "primal scene" (*Urszene*, the ur-Scene) is the fantasy of a traumatic childhood encounter with adult sexuality as the child accidentally stumbles upon their parents having sex, in another instance of Freud's deeply theatrical understanding of the psyche. A neglected feature of these theatrical scenes that run through Freud's work, however, is that they are fundamentally *acoustic* in nature. The primal scene does not begin with the child witnessing a sexual encounter—it begins when they hear "something" from the parents' bedroom. Mladen Dolar has an extensive account of the fundamentally acoustic nature of psychoanalytic fantasy (see his reading of "the click" that initiates the paranoid fantasy of one of Freud's patients).[15] As I indicated earlier, this emerges from the way that sound models the unconscious in its enigmatic nature and location—it is present to me but without being visible, and it is somewhere near me but without having a definable location. Michel Chion maintains that we only ever ask two questions about sound (the mode that he calls "causal listening"): What is it? Where is it coming from?[16] These same uneasy questions are also why horror as a genre depends so crucially on sound (the phone call coming from inside the house). Moreover, this link between sound, paranoia, and the psychoanalytic is foundational for an article that had a huge influence on Calvino, Barthes's entry for "ascolto" (listening) in the *Encyclopedia Einaudi* (available in English as "Listening"), which was the original inspiration for Calvino's "A King Listens." There, Barthes argues that psychoanalytic listening is listening *par excellence*, and that modern listening is always both paranoid and psychoanalytic.

Silent City applies the logic of Calvino's "secret thread" (unconscious desires and fears) not only to its own fantastic story line, but to the real city of Matera. The architectural and structural features of cities may *seem* to be the work of either logical deliberation or random chance—"cities believe they are the work of the mind or of chance," Polo advises—but in reality they are built out of histories that conceal unspeakable desires and fears. Virtually every major city in the US, for example, is fundamentally structured and ordered by "redlining" (the systematic denial of credit and financial services to areas with large proportions of racial minorities). The apparently random variations in the cityscape ("why did they put the freeway *here*?") turn out to be motivated by an unspeakable (racist) fear, buried because it is both unacceptable and concealed in the past. The city's scenes of daily life are always conditioned by a drama played out on an "other stage," out of sight—but all the more potent for that.

It is time to answer the questions I posed at the start of this section. Let's begin, then, with the apparently trivial questions that revolve around the figure of Rocco: Why are there *three* children from modern-day Matera and not simply the emblematic duo of boy and girl, Domenico and Caterina? Both Domenico and Rocco are boys of the same age—so why are they assigned to sing in different registers (Domenico is a baritone, while Rocco is a tenor)? Why is Rocco disabled when none of the other characters have anything remarkable or different about them (indeed, Domenico and Caterina are curiously banal)?

The character of Rocco is something of an extra, a third wheel positioned off to the side of Domenico and Caterina, supplemental to their budding romance (see fig. 11—the libretto informs us that Domenico is in love with Caterina, but gives no sense of whether those feelings are returned). My initial suspicion was that Rocco was perhaps being subtly coded as gay: In the performance I saw, he carries an umbrella that he refers to as his "spada d'orpello," a "sword of tinsel." *Orpello* is a term used to describe fake gold (it is pinchbeck, a copper-zinc alloy), but metaphorically any sort of useless, flashy ornamentation (tinsel, frippery, glitter), as well as excessive rhetorical artifice. Perhaps a sword of glitter, then. That said, Rocco is also marked as belonging to a world before sexual difference: Domenico is a baritone (his voice has broken), but Rocco is a tenor. Even so, Rocco is marked by a singular sign of adult sexuality from another drama, *eine andere Schauplatz*, one that should be familiar to us now. Like Oedipus, he carries his umbrella because he walks with a pronounced limp; he uses it as a cane (again, see fig. 11). Rocco's voice has not broken yet, and I know why, even if the audience of *Silent City* did not. This drama answers a question that is asked somewhere else, on the *andere Schauplatz*, the other stage of memory and actual history that is shameful, out of sight. As Cauzillo informed me, Rocco was based on a real child, but a child of Matera before the forced relocation, a boy with an injured foot and a pronounced limp, one who, like so many other children of his generation in the Sassi, did not survive to adulthood, which is why Rocco is both too innocent (he never knew adult sexuality) and too knowing (he knew mortality).[17] The *mater dolorosa* remains at the center of the scene, but can only bestow her blessing on the couple that remains.

I suggest earlier that *Silent City*, like *Oedipus Rex*, is a murder mystery, with the quote from Calvino providing the crucial clue. Who killed the fanciullo, and why is the answer to this question unspeakable? The question itself is unspeakable, as it is never asked openly, and the fanciullo's

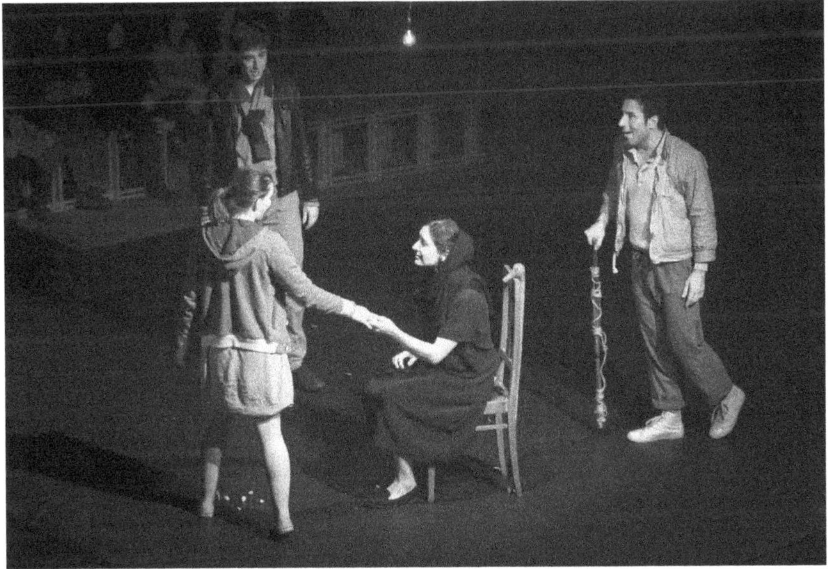

FIGURE 11. *Mater dolorosa* and the three children. Photo by G. Marino, courtesy of Compagnia Teatrale L'Albero

"disappearance" is not narrated or even accompanied by a musical melody. There is clearly a traumatic rupture here in the text, both musical and lyrical, and we might find a clue in the identity of the composer. Nigel Osborne is best known for his work as a music therapist treating traumatized children, but more specifically, he works primarily with children traumatized by war and other forms of *state-sponsored violence.* The Italian state killed the fanciullo. Indeed, I am tempted to say that the state kills the fanciullo twice, once historically and once symbolically, the first time by allowing the conditions of poverty and neglect in the South of Italy and Matera in particular that led to an astonishing 40 percent childhood mortality rate. This is the historical death: the real child Rocco was based on who did not live to see the forced relocation. The second killing, however, is a symbolic one that suggests that the relocation itself was a kind of fatal blow, truncating a city that could have been, the original Matera that could have flourished. This is the child of the past, the fanciullo who could have grown up in a safe, hygienic, modernized city, unusual only for its being carved out of the rock, its spectacular views, and its exceptional olive oil: what the Sassi would have been if they had been made residential and not commercial. As the 1990s proved, rectifying the infrastructure of the Sassi was neither difficult nor even especially expensive, and—in a story all too common—it took "worthless" land from the poor that turned out to be exceedingly valuable once it was privatized and commercialized.

Conclusions

Calvino's role in *Silent City* is certainly more diffuse, even more nebulous than in the "resonant" chapters of American artists who form much of the content of *Transmedial Resonance.* As I've already argued, however, this is fitting for an acoustic model in which Calvino's writings become more and more assimilated when we think about form, about cities, about urban design and communities—the echoes grow gradually fainter as the energy of the original sound simply becomes part of the air, part of the background hum of the world. I don't for a moment think that we're done with remarkable examples of resonant art inspired by Calvino, but I do think that in some fields Calvino's thinking really has become simply part of the atmosphere. (Recall the anecdote that opens this book, and the Vellum/LA art show about imaginary architecture, named after a quotation from *Invisible Cities,* but that never mentions Calvino at all.) That said, Calvino's influence on the project is evident, not only in the attention to the political value of form, but also in understanding the city as a theater of desires and fears. Equally important is that, although the toolkit of "city thinking" is largely dominated by philosophers and other theoreticians, *Invisible Cities* transcends its "fictional" status to become an indispensable part of that kit. It was as natural for Ciommiento to reach for Calvino as it was to think of Benjamin's *Arcades Project* or Georges Perec's infra-ordinary. It is as much a theoretical tool as it is a strangely beautiful experimental novel.

Finally, as I have argued about all the musical works I examine, *Silent City* has also understood some things about this resonant Calvino that we have not always noticed: Calvino is rigorously insistent that apparently rationalist discourses such as city planning are always underpinned by something "inatteso" (unexpected), something that slides into our thinking from some place deep below. In the case of *Silent City*, the opera could not be clearer that the city's desires and fears are not found on the surface, but in the form of a journey to the underworld, a confrontation and reckoning with an unspeakable memory. The "vergogna nazionale" (the national shame) wasn't Matera after all, but state-sponsored neglect and underinvestment that led to the deaths of enormous numbers of children that were "solved" by forcing Materans out of their traditional homes (rather than, say, improving their infrastructure) and into modernity. I argue here that this unspeakable trauma and fear can be expressed only in pure noise-music, not even in singing—noise-music appropriately written by a composer who specializes in music as a therapy for children of state-sponsored violence. Lastly, Calvino's argument from *Invisible Cities* that was so instrumental to Ciommiento's compositional process, the city as a kind of psyche structured by a rebus of desires and fears, draws on a theatrical logic from Freud that may very well help explain why Calvino has been so resonant with the performing arts (and why *Invisible Cities* in particular has leant itself to large-scale theatrical works like operas, music festivals, and dance). What these works have understood is how much Calvino's writing is structured by the *scene*, both the Freudian acoustic scene of the strange sounds coming from the parents' bedroom and the theatrical scene more broadly. Far from a static image or emblem, however, these scenes are tableaux, actors frozen in a moment of dramatic tension that is about to explode, often in a scenario that appears absurd but that nonetheless is shot through with the possibility of sexual desire ("The Form of Space" in chapter 3) or the menace of mortality (the story "t zero"). There is, in other words, always a drama that is happening in front of us, but the power of literature is that there is always another drama happening elsewhere, on that "other stage," one that gives the story unfolding in front of us its strange fascination and power.

5 /   Dancing About Architecture

Writing about music is like dancing about architecture.

—UNKNOWN[1]

Calvino refers to dance throughout his writings, from the autobiographical (he laments the lack of floor space for dancing at a disappointing beatnik party in San Francisco in 1960 in his American diary), to the theoretical (Mercutio's dancing gait in the essay on "Lightness"). Also, the fictional: the silver-scaled aquatic dancers in the city of Moriana, the dancing maidens who entertain Gurdulù in *The Nonexistent Knight*, or Verbena and Mirtillo dancing through the branches of the forest in the screenplay "La foresta-radice-labirinto" (Forest-root-labyrinth), from a RAI children's television series that almost happened. One doesn't get the impression that dance holds an exceptionally important place in the Calvinian imaginary, but even so, some do think of Calvino when they think about dance, and more broadly, the body and its potentials for movement. Edward Tufte, for example, probably the best-known authority on the presentation of graphical information, chose two ways to illustrate the section on dance notation in his landmark 1990 *Envisioning Information*: images from an eighteenth-century Neapolitan dance manual, and a citation from Calvino's *Cosmicomics*.

Numerous dancers and choreographers have found in Calvino's writings a resonant source of inspiration. In 2014 the Austin, Texas–based theater director Rudy Ramirez worked with a troupe of aerialists called Sky Candy to stage a danced version of *Cosmicomics* that took place as much above the stage as on it.[2] Joanna Wright, one of the core members of that troupe, noted that the show drew on the "the aesthetics of silent film, *commedia dell'arte* and turn-of-the-century circus arts," and emphasized—like Mezzacappa—the playful dimension ("clowning") of Calvino's stories.[3] Whether they realize it or not, aerialists are also certainly putting into practice the Calvinian ideal of "lightness" from *Six Memos for the Next Millennium*, so it is perhaps unsurprising that in that same year stage director Ildiko Nemeth did a completely different theatrical version of the *Cosmicomics* in New York, also with an aerialist.

But it is not just the *Cosmicomics* that have served as resonant inspiration for dance. The aptly named French choreographer Louise Lecavalier was inspired by *The Nonexistent Knight* (*Il cavaliere inesistente*) in 2017 to create the dance work *Mille batailles* (A thousand battles) for two dancers. In 2023, the New Grounds company in Rotterdam continued the aerialist circus theme with a production of *The Baron in the Trees* that combined "circus, dance, music, spoken word and visual arts," and the Lost in Translation Circus in Norwich, founded by an Italian expat, also did an outdoor aerialist version of *The Baron in the Trees*, entitled *Above*, in 2021.[4] This combination of storytelling and coordinated and choreographed movement in space, much of it literally in the trees, is an ideal example of Calvino moving transnationally and transmedially, but in a way that is fully resonant with both the original story as well as Calvino's theoretical ideal of lightness.

As we've already seen, much of the artistic activity that resonates to Calvino is focused on *Invisible Cities*, and that is also true of dance. Back in 1985, the year of Calvino's death, Bay Area composer Michael McNabb, known for pioneering work in electronic music, debuted a ballet of *Invisible Cities* that was billed as "the first full-length ballet to feature a choreographed robotic dancer."[5] More recently, starting in 2013 and continuing at least through 2021, British filmmaker Jevan Chowdhury has made a series of prize-winning dance films inspired by *Invisible Cities*, entitled *Moving Cities*, in which dancers appear in surreal juxtapositions against panoramas of the city Chowdhury has chosen.[6] Leo Warner's *Invisible Cities* of 2019, a major work, was produced for the Manchester International Festival; it combined digital animation, theater, and dance (Sidi Larbi Cherkaoui was the choreographer) with music by Adam Bryanbaum Wiltzie and Dustin O'Halloran, also known as the ambient music duo A Winged Victory for the Sullen.[7] In late 2021, Belgian director Nicolas Musin debuted *Archipelago* at the Théâtre National Populaire in Villeurbanne, a "dramatic dance work" that combined readings of *Invisible Cities* with quintessentially urban forms of movement: skateboarding and parkour. In 2022–23, the Shanghai International Dance Center staged *Invisible Cities 2.022*, a dance work of "retro sci-fi surrealism,"[8] and no doubt the Calvino-inspired dance continues. The focus of this chapter, however, is from early 2023, Ashwini Ramaswamy's large-scale multimedia dance performance of *Invisible Cities*.

Why Dance?

Throughout this book, I have restricted myself to primarily acoustic forms of Calvino's transmedial and transnational resonance, both for reasons of scope (to cover everything, from music and painting to urban planning and architecture, would be impossible) but also because I think that my underlying acoustic metaphor, resonance, gives the best model for understanding Calvino's afterlife as an expanding *space* that other artists found inspirational. Dance is deeply and intimately connected to the exploration of acoustic space, primarily through its connection to rhythm. Although dance without music is possible, it is quite rare, and generally still relies on a rhythm (which may come only from the vibration of feet on the floorboards). Group dance without a rhythm to coordinate the movements of the dancers is almost impossible. Dance is paired with music in a way that is perhaps unique among the arts: Dance is a natural (often spontaneous, even instinctive) reaction to music, a model for how the artistic energy in one medium might be spontaneously transferred to a different form of art. In short, dance has a *resonant* relationship to music insofar as music calls on us to dance. In fact, as Jerome Lewis observes, some languages don't have separate words for dancing and making music at all, since they are perceived as the same act.[9] Lastly, I have emphasized in several chapters (especially 2 and 3) that part of what makes Calvino resonant for other artists is that he himself was trying to expand the space of literature and art, and even to make cultural and cognitive space itself expand. I would almost be remiss if I did not seek to expand the space of the acoustic in this book, and to help its readers understand what dance has to tell us about sound and space.

Dance is also very directly about the body, its capacities, its shortcomings, its positions, feelings, and a great deal more. But it would be a crucial mistake to think that music and sound are any less corporeal, a point emphasized in chapters 1 and 2. We feel bass notes through our feet and abdomen as well as through our ears; underwater, almost all of the sound we hear is conducted through the skull, and doesn't pass through the ears at all. This book has certainly aimed to reevaluate the role of the body in Calvino, arguing that the notion of Calvino as cerebral, dispassionate, and disconnected is profoundly misguided; dance, then, is the ideal space in which to observe how the acoustic and the corporeal elements of his fictions are dramatized and emphasized in resonant art.

Lastly, dance is expressive, but also communicative and relational, situating figures onstage in relation to each other and in relation to an audience. In this respect, all art is expressive, communicative, and relational, but one of the ways in which dance is unique is in its *pure* relationality of human bodies in space: Stripped of costumes and sets, it is the figures and movements of human bodies, situated in relation to each other in space, structured by rhythm in time. Moreover, it dramatizes, performs, and embodies these forms of relation, and—as Dana Mills, Erin Manning, and others have argued—it is inherently *political* as a result, in precisely the same way I have argued Calvino's *Invisible Cities* is. At a fundamental level, dance deals directly and inherently with the problems and potentials of people being together in the same space, the *polis*. In his chapter on dance in *Group Works*, Ethan Philbrick looks to "the resonance between theories of mobilization in dance and politics." He goes on to contrast smaller, collaborative dance to the monumental figure at the start of Hobbes's *Leviathan*, finding that dance can be "a figure for small group political practices . . . an alternative figure through which to imagine what might constitute a body politic"[10]—a different way of thinking about politics, a micropolitics for an age in which grand narratives are viewed with considerable suspicion.

Any populated setting in an urban space makes clear the connection between dance and politics, in terms that a dancer or even an ordinary spectator immediately understands, and that are repeatedly dramatized onstage. How to hold and move your body when surrounded by other bodies? How to accommodate bodies that are different, that move differently than you move, bodies that feel somehow "out of sync"? How to hold yourself and move around someone in obvious distress? Grief? Rage? In a group of people who are withdrawn, unaware? Do I extend toward the other, pull away, or situate my body in a way that is ambivalent or indecisive? If "hell is other people," as Sartre says, then one can begin to understand why the city becomes the focal point of Calvino's inferno, but also how dance might help us to analyze that hell, even "seek and find" what is not hell about being with other people. The different forms of relationality posited by dancers onstage function effectively as a choreographic repertoire of possible modes of relation to other people in a densely packed space, and the inevitable negotiations with those bodies that result—and hence of possible politics. Crucially, this "political repertoire" of stances and relations and movements is *embodied* in dance, and evokes in the audience what John Martin back in the 1930s called "kinesthetic sympathy,"[11] often referred to as "kinesthetic empathy." Spectators, however fleetingly and unconsciously, imagine their own bodies in those same stances and movements. There is no speech involved here; it is enough to show me bodies in relation to each other for me to know that such a relation is possible (see, for example, Karen Barbour and Alexandra Hitchmough), and the context, progression, and movement of the dance will help me decide if that relation is perhaps desirable, if it *feels* right in an imagined projection of my own body in those same relations.[12]

This claim might have been subject to debate some years ago, but research on "mirror neurons" since the 1990s indicates that humans (as well as other primates and birds, and perhaps other species) have a well-formed system of neurons that fire when we perform a specific movement, but also when we *see someone else* perform the same movement. Many researchers have argued that this system not only helps us predict how other people will act in social settings (a clear evolutionary advantage), but is probably foundational in creating sympathy and empathy: Not only *can* we imagine ourselves in someone else's position, we *automatically* and unconsciously do so.[13]

Kinesthetic sympathy is also literally realized, dramatized, and performed on the dance stage, in at least two ways. First, sometimes dancing bodies move in sync, demonstrating that such movement is possible, even natural (naturally, dance *also* dramatizes the failures and refusals to move in synchrony and harmony, which is part of the way it tells stories of conflict). Second, dancing to music also makes use of another specific mental capacity: *entrainment*. Almost everyone capable of moving has an innate capacity to synchronize their bodily movements to an external rhythmic pulse. While some individual animals can do this, humans are the only species that, as a species, can dance *together*. This fact is quite suggestive: Collective dance emerges from a common humanity, and also (potentially) dramatizes that same commonality. This capacity for entrainment emerges, crucially, where dance's kinesthetic and proprioceptional character touches the realm of the acoustic. To dance together we need rhythm. When we "attend to music, our bodies prepare to dance," as Lewis says (48).

All of this indicates again that dance is political in its very nature, in a way that is perhaps unique among the arts (all of which are expressive and relational, but do not *necessarily* dramatize both our shared capacity to be in sync with each other as well as the many different ways we have of relating to each other). Not every individual dance is political in its content, but what is fascinating here is the immense value (and specifically political value) of form. That said, there is also another reason to look at dance and Calvino. As I argue throughout this book, a certain stereotype of Calvino subtends much of his critical reception: He is geometric, cerebral, abstract, and apolitical. Dance, however, in fact combines the bodily experience and abstract form in ways that make the two much less independent from each other than one might expect at first glance, and that is very consonant with Calvino's constant insistence (see chapters 1 and 3) that abstract geometric form is always saturated and supported by the corporeal. And while dance certainly can be an exuberant celebration of an individual body's capacities and energies, it also poses—in an explicitly formal way—the problem of how bodies interact and move in and out of synchrony with each other, a "purely formal" question that is inherently political, and that characterizes much of Calvino's literary imagination after he stepped away from more obviously militant forms of thinking about politics toward the end of the 1950s.

Toward the *Invisible Cities*

Although Ashwini Ramaswamy was trained in Indian Bharatanatyam dance, her interests are much broader, and her own work combines Bharatanatyam with other forms of modern dance, a path also explored by her mother Ranee and her sister Aparna.[14] In *Let the Crows Come* (2019), for example, Ramaswamy brought together three dancers from three different traditions: her own Bharatanatyam training, Gaga dance (from Israel), and modern dance combined with African diasporic dance forms. The dancers each performed an extended solo in their own dance tradition, as well as joining the other dancers for a number of sequences in which all three performed together at the beginning and end of each solo sequence. The source material is stories from the *Ramayana* (crows play a role in a number of episodes in the epic), and a folk tradition: Rice is offered to crows at a funeral, and if they come to eat, it is a sign that the dead are ready to move on. Crucially for her later work on Calvino, Ramaswamy's choreography does not gesture to any form of avian mimicry (no bird-like movements onstage); in fact, it does not *represent* in any way the stories that stand behind it, which is not the same thing as saying there is no relationship between the dance and the stories. Instead, text for Ramaswamy is the crucial first step in choreographic composition; when I asked her what came first—word, music, or movement—she instantly responded that the text comes first.[15] Both for herself and for her collaborators, however, the next step is to find a way that the original text speaks to their own personal experiences (with, say, loss and grief), and the dance emerges from that. So, when each dancer dances, it is in response to their own personal and cultural frame of reference, one that is in resonance with the source material.

As remarkable as the extended solo dance portions of *Let the Crows Come* are, perhaps even more remarkable are the sequences that link them, sequences in which all three dancers appear onstage together. Not only do these sequences formally unify the work by "braiding" the three solos together, but they have an even more important purpose. The dancers remain "in character," as it were, each dancing in their unique style of dance, but performing moves that are homologous although not identical. Although Bharatanatyam, Gaga, and modern dance are all very different dance styles, the repertoire of typical and possible movements in each—expanding the body in space or contracting it, for example—have equivalents in the others.[16] On a formal level, they are the same (in that they represent the same bodily impulse within a given dance style), even as the actual expression is different. In this way, dance is like language, with grammatical structures that represent similar impulses (talking about the past, designating different actions, designating different people), but whose individual expressions and meaning are quite different in each idiom. This isn't merely theoretical or academic: As Gia Kourlas observed in a glowing review of *Let the Crows Come* in *The New York Times*, "even as the dancers matched and echoed one another's arms and feet, their interpretations were, at times, wildly—and certainly stylistically—different. Yet they were all capable of holding the stage with a similar intensity."

Even as the dance is programmatically about death, loss, acceptance, and renewal, Ramaswamy's play with formal equivalences that are also different has a clear political valence: The three bodies moving in space demonstrate the basic principle that equivalence is not sameness. (Equivalence is to be understood here in its etymological sense: not "being identical," but having an equal value.) All languages have the same level of complexity and cover the same range of meanings, and yet each is precious and distinct, has its own unique "flavor" and character. This is once again Martin's kinesthetic sympathy, now enlarged, however. No longer is it "merely" a sympathy between the dancer and the audience, but the dance itself becomes a demonstration of kinesthetic sympathy between different forms of dance—the formal equivalence of formal equivalence, as it were. This understanding of dance as a gesture to the universal is fairly widespread in theories of dance, particularly the phenomenological approach (Sondra Fraleigh calls it the "universalizing impulse" of phenomenology[17]) that tends to underpin the notion of a shared kinesthetic empathy.

Ramaswamy's casting decisions are not referred to explicitly in the program to *Let the Crows Come*, but it is probably not an accident that the specific equivalences being demonstrated in *Let the Crows Come* are those between the movements of Black, brown, and white bodies, bodies that have different gestural and postural idioms that can nonetheless speak to each other, that exist both separately and together onstage in formal equivalence. I will return again to one of the ideas that I think is at the core of the political value of *Invisible Cities* for so many artists: Politics is how we address the problem of people being in the same space, and Ramaswamy is pretty clearly using dance to demonstrate one possible way that bodies could share the same space; they could be different, with very different histories, and yet understand each other. Those bodies could maintain their unique modes of embodiment, and also live and move together. What the dance demonstrates is the simultaneous difference and yet equality of those forms of embodiment.

This idea—establishing formal equivalence while still recognizing difference as the grounds for political life—is also the basis for Ramaswamy's *Invisible Cities*. It expands the idea in a number of ways, both with the number of dancers and dance styles (which I'll discuss in detail in the next section), and with the media at play during the performance. Where *Let the Crows Come* had a minimalist staging (a section reserved for the musicians on one side of the stage, the dancers and a single large bowl of rice illuminated by a spotlight), Ramaswamy's staging of *Invisible Cities* is elaborate and complex, principally through her extensive collaborations with the digital artist Kevork Mourad, who provides not only animated and layered imagery projected as a backdrop but also live drawings projected onto a special screen (essentially transparent to the audience) in *front* of the dancers, allowing dancers to interact not only with each other, but with the imagery that appears to surround them. As Kerry Francksen indicates, many of the conversations about the use of technology in dance center on the "apparent tension between the seemingly separated worlds of the live and the mediated,"[18] but in the case of Mourad and Ramaswamy's work, the "mediated" is as live as the dancers' movements.

I first became aware of Ramaswamy's *Invisible Cities* project when she was still developing it. She posted a number of "proof-of-concept" videos on the project's website showing how an individual dancer might "dance a city" from the novel while interacting with Mourad's artwork, such as Gaga dancer Berit Ahlgren performing Euphemia (the city in which not only goods but also memories are traded), or breaker Joseph "MN Joe" Tran interpreting Ersilia (the city in which social relationships are marked by different strings that eventually overwhelm the inhabitants and force them to move). As she explained to me later, however, this approach proved artistically frustrating and eventually felt like a dead end to her and her collaborators, since it led to something like a charade or "acting out" of the description of a given city. Each city became a crystallized *image*, precisely in Calvino's negative sense of something frozen, static, and inadequate that I discuss in the chapter on jazz. While such images (the city of Octavia suspended on ropes above a chasm) might be evocative and then productive for visual artists, it should be evident why a form of art based on movement would find the still image unproductive. In *Dance and Politics*, Mills refers to the attempt to render narrative *content* in dance as a "weak political reading," which is "the representation through moving bodies of ideas previously articulated in words."[19] Ramaswamy eventually rejected this approach to the text, as she had rejected it in *Let the Crows Come*.

Instead, Ramaswamy hit on an approach to the project that is, to the best of my knowledge, unique among the adaptations of *Invisible Cities* I am familiar with: At the suggestion of her artistic collaborator Mourad, they turned almost exclusively to the philosophical dialogues between Marco Polo and Kublai Khan, and left (with one exception) the cities to the side.[20] Each portion of the performance takes a short quotation from the dialogues and uses that as a springboard for an exploration of the ideas, movements, sounds, and feelings it might elicit. This is precisely the "strong political reading" of dance that Mills counterposes to the "weak political reading." The strong reading instead creates "a phenomenologically independent world which includes its own system of inscription and world of reception" (3). That is, the dancing is not to be understood (or is not reducible at least) to a representation of the actions in Calvino's novel; it has to be understood in its own terms, as a dance that creates a world. Crucially, this is something like an embodied description of what I am calling resonance here: It is not about fidelity to a source of origin, but rather about the energy that is created in the new reading and the world that *it* creates.

Crucially, finding that "phenomenologically independent world," one that does not remain trapped in the content of Calvino's text ("ideas previously articulated in words"), happened because of a turn to the formal *frame* of the novel instead. Calvino was always attracted to the idea of a frame narrative that would structure smaller pieces of content (cosmicomic stories, fantastic cities, opening chapters of novels, minute observations of everyday life) into larger narratives, sometimes using quite elaborate forms. Of all his texts, *Invisible Cities* has the most complex formal structure, however (see fig. 12). The structure is so elaborate, in fact, that—unlike *If on a winter's night a traveler* or *Mr. Palomar*, which display their formal structure in the table of contents—Calvino did not go out of

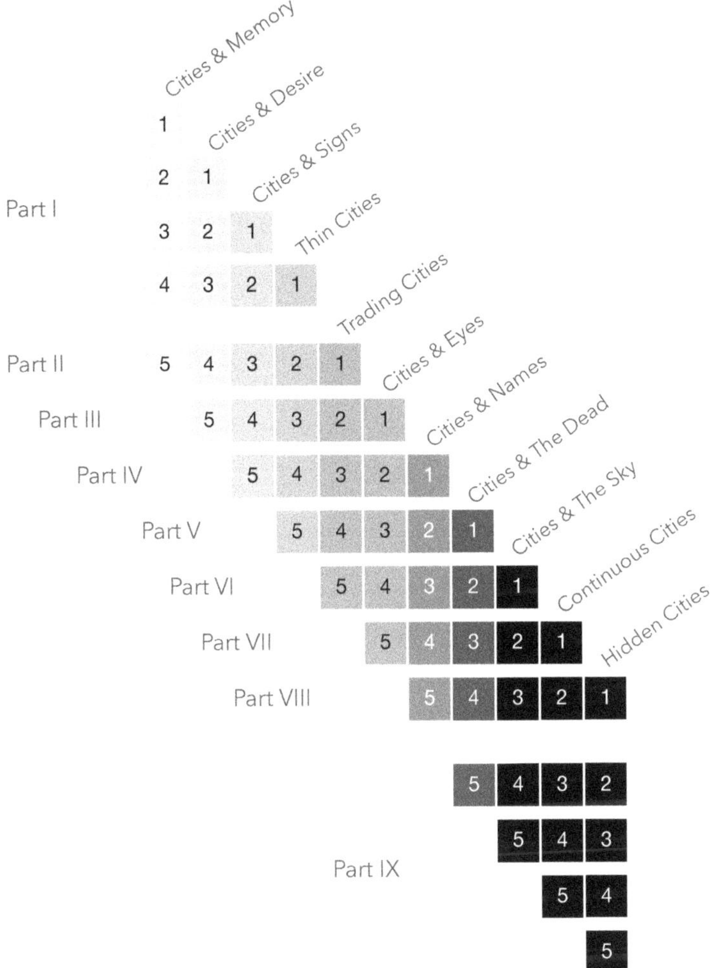

FIGURE 12. The complex form of *Invisible Cities*.

his way to explain it.[21] When editor Mario Barenghi describes the structure in Calvino's collected works, he is very aware that the scheme sounds cumbersome and deliberately complicated, "artificioso" (2:1360, artificial, affected), with parts, cities, categories, and a complicated numbering system for each city. Barenghi feels that a visual representation simplifies the "affected" character of Calvino's form, however; the version I offer here is similar, although not identical, to the one compiled by Claudio Milanini in *L'utopia discontinua* (114, The scattered utopia) in 1990.

With the aid of this chart, the reader can now understand why the first city, Diomira, is the first of the "cities and memory," and why it is followed by the second "memory" city (Isidora) and then the first city of "desire" (Dorotea) and so on. Even if it explains things, the complexity of this diagram speaks to precisely why so many professional readers of Calvino have found these later works to be politically disengaged, trapped in sterile games and esoteric problems of geometry, a suspicion only barely allayed by the occasional city that speaks to real-world problems like pollution or overpopulation. In 1999, Alessia Ricciardi, for example, described Calvino as "a solipsistic thinker removed from the exigencies of history [with] an idea of literature as a formalist game that avoids any costly or serious 'human' association."[22] The philosophical dialogues that open and close each part (not pictured in this chart), dialogues that form the frame story, in many ways work to reinforce this concern, with Kublai Khan and Marco Polo playing charades, inventing theoretical models for generating new cities, or, at one point, getting high and wondering if they are really even having a conversation or just dreaming the whole thing. Calvino's attention to form can be labored, even irritating: Chiara De Caprio, discussing *Marcovaldo*, calls this problem "ostinazione formale" (formal obstinacy).[23] Like a musical *ostinato*, a figure that stubbornly repeats, however, there is also something of value, even political and ethical value, in this repeated and insistent return to form.

Ramaswamy's central insight is that the political value of *Invisible Cities* is to be found *precisely* in its obstinate attention to form—not, mind you, to any specific form the novel might take, whether parallelogram, circle, or zigzag, but to *form itself*. It is only in the space of formal equivalence that something like Martin's kinesthetic sympathy can emerge: My legs are not the same as the dancer's legs, but they have a certain formal equivalence when they are abstracted that allows me to see possible forms of bodily relation I *could* have.[24] As important as this might be for the potential political value of dance, it is equally key for thinking about how a work of art might give rise to another work of art (in another language, in another medium, in another culture): The *content* will be different, even radically so—music or dance instead of words, for example—but in form something of the first may also be present in the second, as with Lisa Mezzacappa's improvised duets in "The Form of Space" that mirror Qfwfq's imagined encounters between himself, Ursula H'x, and Lieutenant Fenimore. Eugenie Brinkema argues in the brilliant *Life-Destroying Diagrams* that form is always in some sense the absolute limit of the work of art, the invisible ground that gives the work's content meaning; form in this view is predicated on the finitude of our mortality, the end of the story or the symphony, the edge of the painting or the boundary of the sculpture.[25] At the same time, however, form also conceals a resonant potential that is not just intellectual, orienting itself toward a future that goes beyond individual human finitude: "This formal logic [of the work of art] is also an ethical and political claim, and suggests a radically antimemorial, antimelancholic quality to design. The diagram commits entirely to the *It is still possible*" (66). Perhaps Calvino's hyperformalism in *Invisible Cities* is neither a defect nor a crystallizing immobilization, but an opening to, in De Caprio's words, "riflettere sul valore di una forma" (23, reflect on the value of a form), as well as an invitation to movement and response. In *Invisible Cities*, it is certainly the hope of Kublai Khan, who is searching for a form that will transcend his melancholy and go beyond his historical existence. This possibility is implicit in the novel's structure and in its title, which both gesture to the possibility of continuing the work endlessly: more cities, more categories, more parts, an ever-larger parallelogram—and perhaps a dance or two.

Invisible Cities: A Dance Suite

Ramaswamy's *Invisible Cities* involves not only Mourad's double projection screens and interactive digital art, but a capacious stage that can hold about a dozen dancers at the same time.[26] It is similarly ambitious in its length: Organized into ten different sections, the run time of the debut performances (January 27 and 28, 2023) at the Cowles Center in Minneapolis was about 75 minutes, without intermission. The different sections are set to different pieces of music, sometimes more than one piece per section. In addition to the South Indian music that might typically accompany Bharatanatyam dance, Ramaswamy makes use of compositions by the Grammy-winning Iranian composer Kayhan Kalhor and the classically trained Chilean Canadian composer Cristobal Tapia de Veer, best known for the music from the television series *Utopia* and *White Lotus*. As with *Let the Crows Come*, one can see Ramaswamy and her collaborators articulating a global vision for the work, a point I'll return to shortly. Each individual section also features shifting groups and ensembles of dancers, rather than a single or primary soloist.

Each section of the dance, with the one exception I've mentioned, takes its inspiration from one of the dialogues between Marco Polo and Kublai Khan, proceeding in a roughly linear way through the material from the book. The program given to the audience provides the specific lines from Calvino that served as inspiration for the dancers. Although the citations are linear, they are not rigidly structured: While the first four sections of Ramaswamy's dance suite take their quotations from the dialogues of sections 1–4 of the novel, the dialogues from sections 5 and 7 are skipped, and three of the dance segments take their quotations from the dialogues in section 9 of the novel.

Here is the overview that was given in the Cowles Center program:

> In this adaptation, the bulk of the choreographic ideas come from imagined conversations between the explorer Marco Polo and the emperor Kublai Khan, resulting in 10 "sections" that are woven together with visual storytelling and music:

Section 1: The Tracery of a Pattern
In the lives of emperors there is a moment which follows pride in the boundless extension of the territories we have conquered, and the melancholy and relief of knowing we shall soon give up any thought of knowing and understanding them.

Section 2: A Negative Mirror
Arriving at each new city, the traveler finds again a past of his that he did not know he had: the foreignness of what you no longer are or no longer possess lies in wait for you in foreign, unpossessed places.

Section 3: A New Dialogue
Cities, like dreams, are made of desires and fears, even if the thread of their discourse is secret, their rules are absurd, their perspectives deceitful, and everything conceals something else. You take delight not in a city's seven or seventy wonders, but in the answer it gives to a question of yours.

Section 4: The Surge of Elements
Your cities do not exist. Perhaps they have never existed. It is sure they will never exist again.

Section 5: Andria
Andria was built so artfully that its every street follows a planet's orbit, and the buildings and the places of community life repeat the order of the constellations and the position of the most luminous stars.

Section 6: Mists of Memory
Memory's images, once they are fixed in words, are erased. The cloud dissolved at times in a wisp of wind, or else remained suspended in mid-air; and the answer was in that cloud.

Section 7: Recreated Perspectives
If each city is like a game of chess, the day when I have learned the rules, I shall finally possess my empire, even if I shall never succeed in knowing all the cities it contains.

Section 8: The Quantity of Things
The atlas has these qualities: it reveals the form of cities that do not yet have a form or a name.

Section 9: Promised Lands
You, who go about exploring and who see signs, can tell me toward which of these futures the favoring winds are driving us.

Section 10: Making Space
The inferno of the living is not something that will be; if there is one, it is what is already here, the inferno where we live every day, that we form by being together. There are two ways to escape suffering it. The first is easy for many: accept the inferno and become such a part of it that you can no longer see it. The second is risky and demands constant vigilance and apprehension: seek and learn to recognize who and what, in the midst of the inferno, are not inferno, then make them endure, give them space.

Procedurally, Ramaswamy asked the dancers in each segment to reflect on the lines from Calvino, and find a narrative of their own that the lines might connect to—a source of resonant energy that the original text produced, and that could lead the artist to produce something new. That is, while the choreography work was collective (Ramaswamy credits all the dancers as choreographers), the affect informing and animating each dancer's work was personal and individual. (This is broadly in line with the practice that Barbour advocates for in *Dancing Across the Page*, in which dancers and audience members connect to each other through kinesthetic empathy, and each connects to the material of the dance by elaborating personal narratives to make sense of it.)

The program for Ramaswamy's *Invisible Cities* begins with a quotation from journalist Eric Weiner on Calvino, one that frames the author in terms that are philosophical, but also ethical and political: "The question that Calvino seems to be asking is a big one: How should we live?" Ramaswamy amplifies this approach even further in her own prefatory note in which she emphasizes the "interwoven cultural perspectives" of *Invisible Cities*, and again insists on the novel's political resonance: "This book deals with matters that are as prescient today as they were when it was published . . . the potential for artistic and ethical dialogues about built environments, natural environments, and how humanity can share this world." The action that unfolds strongly conveys affect and often suggests ideas, but it is not precisely narrative: It *embodies* rather than "acting out" the dialogues that it depicts.

The citation from Calvino that marks the beginning of the dance (here entitled "The Tracery of a Pattern") is from the novel's opening: "In the lives of emperors there is a moment which follows pride in the boundless extension of the territories we have conquered, and the melancholy and relief of knowing we shall soon give up any thought of knowing and understanding them." The action begins in darkness with the opening strains of Kayhan Kalhor's "Where Are You?," a slow, plaintive and throbbing melody on the *kamancheh* (a bowed stringed instrument), accompanied by a hammered dulcimer (the *santur*). Abstract blue lines of light cross the base of the stage from left to right: a river? Are those rocks on each side of the stage? As the dancers, ten of them, barely visible at first, rise up, so too does a cityscape rise up from the river, courtesy of the magic of Mourad's projected and animated images. The dancers form a curve that rises from left to right, each dancer increasingly outstretched with arms held upright: a human flying buttress that seems to support this ethereal city. As the dancers shift their balance from the right to the left, the city falls, to be replaced by another that rises in response to their movements, a process repeated several times before the dancers collapse and the cities with them, indicating a cyclical progression (fig. 13, empires rise and fall).

The front curtain rises and a new cityscape appears, now in the background. The music becomes more intense, more rhythmically marked,

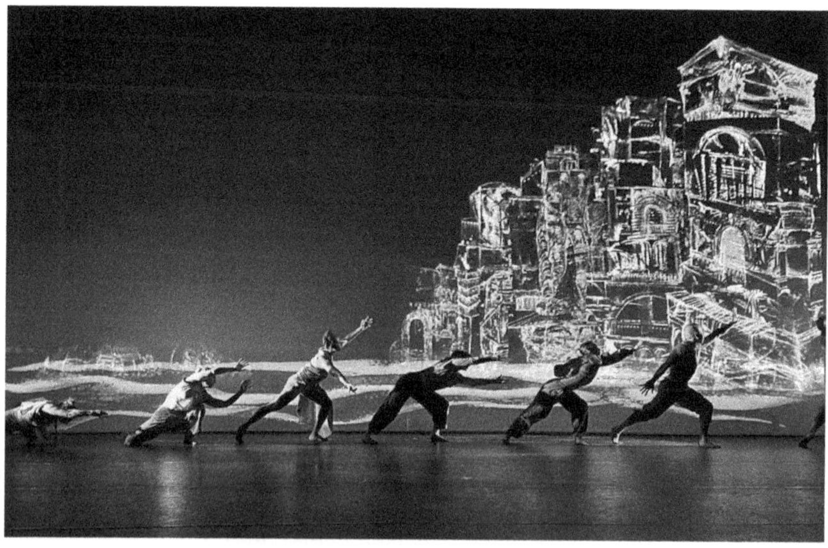

FIGURE 13. The empire rises. Photo by author

and an *ostinato* melody and chord progression takes over that will last for the remainder of the introduction. As is typical of much of the piece, different groups of dancers form, dissolve, and reform over the course of the action onstage, ending with Ramaswamy and her sister dancing in front of an open gate in the city—but rather than passing through it, the entire cityscape splits in half to reveal an image of pure texture, melting, animated, and dripping down the rear screen. Without words, and in a quite different world, what we see here clearly makes the same point as the opening of Calvino's *Invisible Cities*: an anxiety about the maps and shapes that we use to understand the world dissolving into "a formless ruin." It also makes a crucial political point much more clearly than Calvino (although he certainly makes it, too): All those cities of Khan's empire exist as meaningful entities only when they are supported by the bodies that inhabit them, bodies in motion.

Breaking and Affect

Ramaswamy's artistic procedure was to use citations from Calvino, but individual dancers would find a personal resonance, their own story that would inform the dance. To take one concrete example, the second section of Ramaswamy's work is titled "A Negative Mirror," and gives the following citation from the dialogue that opens part 2 of Calvino's *Invisible Cities*: "*Arriving at each new city, the traveler finds again a past of his that he did not know he had: the foreignness of what you no longer are or no longer possess lies in wait for you in foreign, unpossessed places.*" Joe Tran, one of the breakers in the ensemble, dances to two pieces by Cristobal Tapia de Veer in this segment, while two other dancers play a background role. The first musical piece is "Always On, Always Suffering" (from de Veer's work on the television series *Black Mirror*, the episode titled "Black Museum"), and the second is "Jessica Gets Off" (from de Veer's score for *Utopia*; the title is a reference to one of the show's main characters, Jessica Hayes). The music in both pieces is slow, although with a clear rhythmic pulse, especially the first piece, which is also staged more darkly. The front screen is down for the "Always On, Always Suffering" portion of the dance, which significantly cuts the amount of light the audience can see, and Mourad's light drawings in this section are clouds of dark smoke that surround and trail Tran as he moves haltingly across the stage, as if slowing him down, tripping him up. As is typical of de Veer's compositions, the music is "ambient"—it evokes a mood more through tone, timbre, atmosphere, and texture than through melody. The music shifts from slow and haunting in "Always On, Always Suffering," to dramatic and somber in "Jessica Gets Off," although the differences are fairly subtle. The tempo of "Always On" is 60 beats per minute, and "Jessica Gets Off" is only slightly faster at around 64 bpm, both hovering on the border of lento and larghetto. Both pieces are unsurprisingly in a minor key, traditionally associated in the West with the serious, the dramatic, and the tragic. De Veer is well known for an ability to compose scores that also evince an underlying sense of dread and anxiety. He jokingly referred to the music he composed for the first season of *White Lotus* as "Hawaiian Hitchcock."[27] This music is particularly effective for Tran's dance performance, whose "secret story" will in fact turn out to be one of isolation, work, and sacrifice (always on, always suffering).

In Ramaswamy's *Invisible Cities*, this segment is one of the few that is primarily focused on an individual dancer (it is not a solo, however). Although the popular image of breaking associates it primarily with a showy and competitive athleticism (erroneously called "breakdancing"), especially rapid spinning, Tran's performance is first and foremost *emotional* in its character, and the performance depicts depression—when he moves quickly, his movements express someone desperate, frenetic, even trapped. For almost the entirety of the first four minutes of this section, Tran remains either doubled over, bent at the waist, or on the ground, either in apparent despondence, or struggling to get to his feet. Two other dancers are onstage, but standing far away in the back, motionless, even when Tran briefly finally stands upright. (Eventually, hundreds of indifferent figures are added behind them by Mourad in the rear projection; see fig. 14). The effect produced not only by the dancing, but equally by the staging and the distance of the other dancers, is of a depressing isolation.

Tran's movements evoke struggle throughout, but also indicate an adversarial relationship with his surroundings, and he adopts defensive poses (see fig. 14) that suggest his experiences are painful. The movements are intense but sporadic, and generally indicate failure: He unleashes a terrific spin at one point (known as a "flare") that looks like it will get him upright—but he ends up in another crouch. Shortly after, a head spin brings him to his feet, fully upright at last. A tower appears behind the mass of indifferent observers, reminiscent of Bruegel's famous Tower of Babel, and Tran faces it as he gasps for breath (the long dance in a hunched-over posture is physically very demanding). The tower flares into brightness, and Tran defiantly gestures to the right, as if commanding the other dancers to move. They do not, and after a moment, Tran's wrist suddenly, almost robotically, twists so that he is instead pointing to the ground, and he abruptly drops back into a hunched-over crouch once more. The only command he can give is to himself, and it is to return

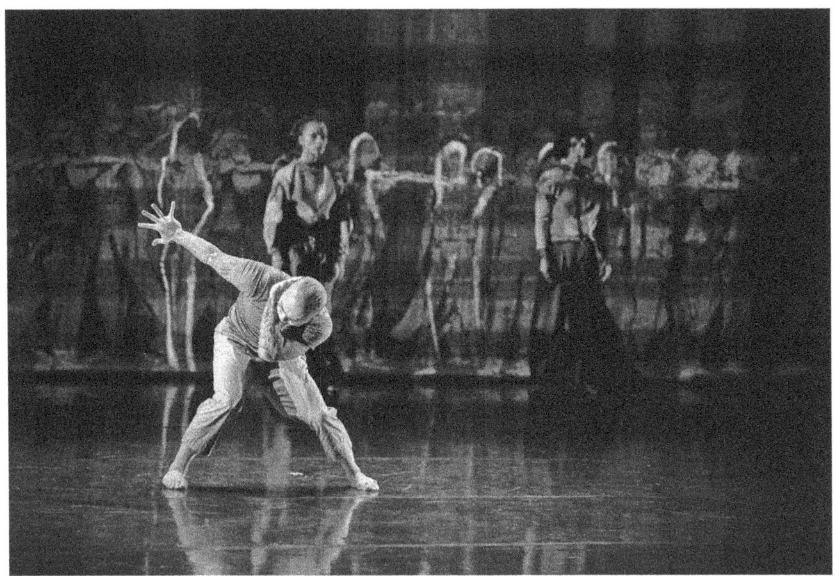

FIGURE 14. Defensive pose, indifferent observers. Courtesy Jayme Halbritte

to a position of abjection. As the sequence comes to an end, the tower dims and Tran shuffles offstage, fully hunched over once again. He moves in the direction he had previously indicated, following his own orders, while the other two dancers stride confidently offstage in the opposite direction. In a painful irony, Tran genuinely embodies "breaking" in a literal sense, the bodily experience of being broken in dance. (Indeed, when Tran first started working on the dance, he was injured, which led to some of the specific forms and movements he developed.)

It isn't hard to understand some of this choreography in relation to the citation from Calvino: In the search for "foreign lands," the traveler inevitably discovers alterity, but on the inside. You are no longer a native, no longer in command of custom or language; *you* are the foreigner in this new place. The traveler-cum-foreigner is isolated, cut off from domestic support networks. In this new place, you are no longer an airplane pilot or a systems administrator or a professor—you are a tourist, an intruder, a foreigner. This is a typically Calvinian "inversion," the dialectical flipping of frames in search of the truth, from the individual stones to the archway that they make up and back again. Travel (at least potentially) functions as a negative mirror of your usual self-image. That image is foreign, not because of some kind of existential alienation ("I don't recognize myself now that I've aged!") but because the frame surrounding it has changed; you are the foreigner.

This reading of Tran's dance is fully compatible with such an understanding of Calvino, but we might also notice a dimension that this reading does not fully account for, which is affect. Tran's performance conveys an emotion felt and expressed at the level of the body that is well in excess of experiencing "mere" foreignness. It conveys anguish, miserable isolation, even desperation. Moreover, there are numerous indications that Tran's movements convey something more specifically *political*. It is not "simply" loneliness, but isolation from a group; not "merely" a personal or individual depression, but something more like oppression; and his (repeatedly failed) attempts to literally stand up for himself are indications that *power* is a key factor in how Calvino resonated with him. I've argued before that the key feature of the transnational frame of analysis is that it pays attention not just to cultural differences, but also to differentials of power between nations and cultures. Tran's performance, then, indicates that he and Ramaswamy understand Calvino to be talking about *transnational* movement, a movement from a place of relative plenitude to a place of dispossession and disempowerment, one that configures you as a certain kind of subject, the foreigner. In other words, the traveler is an immigrant.

During our conversation, Ramaswamy explained what the specific point of resonance for Tran had been: Calvino's "negative mirror" of foreignness that is produced by dislocation was for Tran his father's immigration to the US from Vietnam, and the immense sacrifices his father had made for his family, sacrifices that Tran attempts to embody in his dance performance and that in turn produce an empathetic response in the spectator. The immigrant body labors ceaselessly, "breaking" itself, and surrounded largely by indifference, and this compulsive labor is fully internalized, as the dancer's body gives commands—to himself. Tran understood the tower that appears near the end of the dance sequence as something like an architectural embodiment of the American dream, a seductive lure that, like the Tower of Babel, doesn't quite lead to where it promised. The audience's understanding of this narrative is at the pre-cognitive and bodily level of affect, however: I know that I am feeling something (rejection, isolation, suffering) without consciously knowing *why* I am feeling it. This is yet again a perfect example of Martin's "kinesthetic empathy," in which the spectator *feels* the meaning of the dance at the level of their body more than their brain. The narrative is there, structuring my feeling as a spectator, but without my knowing it fully or consciously.

Ramaswamy said that she had always understood Calvino's *Invisible Cities* as a political text, and her method of moving from text to dance (finding a personal point of resonance) serves to effectively activate the political material that is there, not in a didactic way, but in a way that allows the dancer to develop a response to Calvino's material that emerges from their lived experience. On some level, this is once again a form of resonance—finding the ways that a work of art speaks to us, but in a way that is also about others, which means that the history it emerges from is never "simply personal" (as if the personal were ever simple!), but also collective.

Cosmopolitan Space

In Calvino's novel, the city of Andria comes toward the end (it is in the last section, and is the last of the "Cities and the Sky" category), but it occupies a central position in Ramaswamy's dance, both because it is the only city taken from Calvino's novel and because it is literally at the center of the performance. The specific quote in the program that the dancers worked with is "Andria was built so artfully that its every street follows a planet's orbit, and the buildings and the places of community life repeat the order of the constellations and the position of the most luminous stars." Like all of the cities Polo describes, Andria is structured by a dialectal reversal, but it is unusual in that the thesis and the antithesis are both positive in character; generally, a city that presents an appealing or positive character to the traveler at first later reveals its dark or monstrous side (see Anastasia or Olivia, for instance), and most cities that block or frustrate the traveler's expectations later show a more welcoming side (Hypatia or Octavia, for example).

Andria is initially presented by Polo as a city of serenity and calm, because it is constructed in harmony and synchrony with the movements of the stars, but then Polo attempts to guess the city's dark secret: The inhabitants, chained to celestial clockwork, must keep everything forever the same, forever frozen and static. The inhabitants of Andria, however, are surprised by his conclusion that the city never changes, and use the occasion to show off their most recent constructions, which include "un porto fluviale, una statua di Talete, un toboga" (2:485, a river port, a statue of Thales, a toboggan slide). The reference to Thales, the pre-Socratic philosopher who famously opined that "everything is water" (i.e., in a state of constant change and flow—and all of the new construction in Andria is water-related), makes clear Calvino's continuing opposition to the "crystallized" image, the structure of thought that can't change and adapt. The twist is that every change in Andria is also reflected in the heavens—say, a supernova or new comet. Thales is the right philosopher to cite, since in truth, "la città e il cielo non restano mai uguali" (2:486, the city and the sky never remain the same). As a result, the citizens of Andria behave with confidence (their actions are in sync with the movements of the heavens, after all) and prudence (their actions could have cosmic repercussions). It is a rare city in the collection that leaves the reader with a sense of how cities might be better, even utopian, spaces.

This section in Ramaswamy's *Invisible Cities* begins with one dancer upright and facing the audience, and six dancers squatting or seated, facing her, as if they were students. Behind this teacher there is a door, set in an archway, projected on the rearmost screen. The seated dancers slowly uncurl and spiral to their feet in unison, and the three non-Bharatanatyam dancers slowly exit to both sides of the stage. That one upright dancer is Ranee Ramaswamy, Ashwini's mother and the founder of the Ragamala Dance Company, which trains dancers in Bharatanatyam dance. The remaining two dancers are Ashwini and her sister, Aparna, who are also part of the company; it is, in other words, a family affair at this point, and the entirety of the dance is in the Bharatanatyam style. The archway behind the trio gradually moves into the distance, and as they dance, faint bands of light move upward on the front screen. Eventually that front screen rises up and the door opens, and small objects appear in the sky behind the dancers and the doorway, objects that gradually grow closer until it becomes clear that they are little planets or moons. The doorway fades away: Have we passed through it? Has the outer space that was behind it come through it? Regardless, as the dance continues, three of these celestial spheres come to dominate, and they are also dancing, spinning around their axes and each other (fig. 15). The abstract, kaleidoscopic surface and the absence of any architecture here give the impression that the dancers are now also in space, perhaps on a little planet of their own.

The music for the opening section is South Indian (Carnatic), and makes extensive use of *konnakol*, a spoken rhythm technique. Here, over a sitar's drone, the vocal percussionist (CK Vasudevan) sings the relevant subdivisions of the beat, matching what is being played on the *mridangam*, the principal drum used in Carnatic music, which, unlike most Western drums, also expresses a wide variety of pitches. While Western musicians associate certain syllables with subdivisions, such as "one-ta-da, two-ta-da," in order to count triplet subdivisions, or "one-and-two-and" in order to count a subdivision into two, konnakol is much more elaborate, and makes extensive use of many possible subdivisions that are less common in Western music, such as five, seven, nine, and ten. And while Western music students use syllables as a vocal mnemonic to guide their performance, they recite it silently (if at all) when they play, whereas konnakol is a major component of the vocal performance. A female vocalist also sings wordless melodic accompaniment during the konnakol section, which abruptly ends as the front screen rises; the sitar drone continues, however, and a more lyrical vocal line begins (also by Vasudevan), forming a kind of duet with the violin, but still accompanied by the mridangam, that continues to the end of the piece.

In the closing portion of the dance, a new frame appears around the image on the rear screen, an iris that surrounds the celestial space as the trio of planets so markedly in sync with the dancers begins to recede into the distance. Iris after iris emerges from the sides, providing a multitude of frames as the dancers turn to face the heavens in what is a clear moment of celestial celebration and harmony (see fig. 15). As with the earlier question of framing and space involving the door, what emerges is evocative without being reducible to a simple denotation: Are we looking through the oculus of a temple's rotunda, the perspective of the citizens of Andria? Perhaps instead we are seeing a literal anatomical eye, with its multiple layers (the pupillary frill, the stroma, the collarette, and so on), or perhaps we are seeing a figuration of the very play between frame and content that animates so much of Calvino's work, particularly *Invisible Cities*.

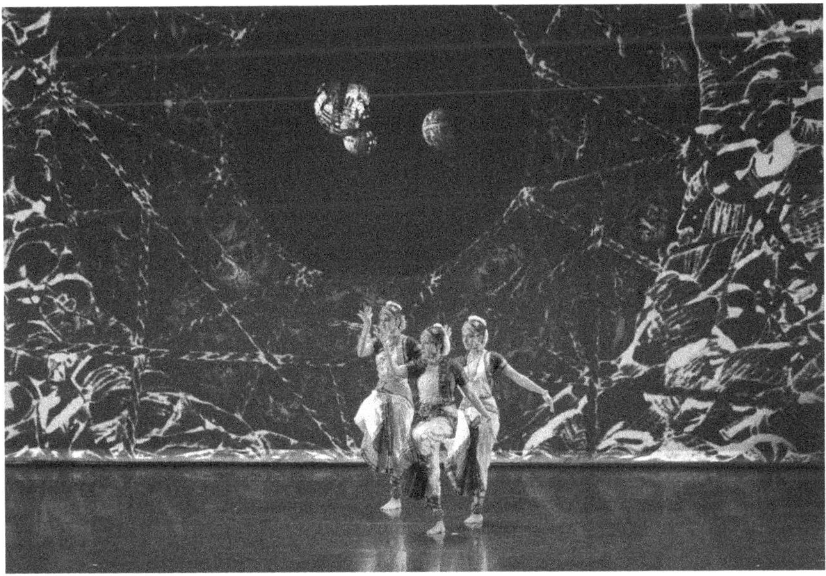

FIGURE 15. A celebration of celestial harmony. Photo by Ying Diao, courtesy of Ragamala Dance Company

What is clear, however, is that this dance is telling a story about harmony and synchrony in complex systems, quite literally the three-body problem of planetary motion: Once you have three celestial bodies, there is no general mathematical solution to how they will move around each other, and their behavior will be chaotic. The three dancers' bodies do, however, find ways of being with each other that are not chaotic, as do the three celestial spheres—it is their dance that brings order to what could have been chaos. We might also return again to the notion of kinesthetic sympathy; the dancers in this sequence are literally modeling it for the audience as they learn to move in synchrony with other bodies and establish a kind of bodily resonance. The bodies that they are establishing this sympathy with are both celestial (the orbs in space above, now seen and celebrated through the eye's iris or the temple's oculus, as if they were on their own stage) and human (the other dancers).

This synchrony between the human and the heavenly is precisely what Calvino depicts in the city of Andria, but I would also suggest that the "three-body problem" here is a way of delineating a space that is both cosmic (the sky) and political (cities). Domenico Scarpa nods toward this dimension in Calvino's writings when he points to a powerful bond between "la cosmologia e la politica" (cosmology and politics).[28] That connection is essentially *cosmopolitan*, in both this unusual Calvinian sense (space + the city, cosmos + politics) and the ordinary sense in which we use it (a dynamic and productive mixture of different peoples).[29] Insofar as the dancers represent a harmonious coexistence of difference (between the earth and the heavens, between each other), they model the cosmopolitan, here at the level of content. Ramaswamy's *Invisible Cities*, which brings together Indian dance, Israeli dance, African diasporic dance, and urban breaking, also highlights precisely the cosmopolitan at the level of form. There is no doubt that this segment of the dance, like Calvino's original city, expresses something positive and hopeful—even the colors are bright and warm (gold and white), and the lighting is brighter.

This cosmopolitan character appears not only on earth, as the dancers model how to be and move in the same limited but shared space of the stage, but also in the heavens. The three spheres are not simple, but have texture and volume, an internal space of their own. In fact, on closer examination, the celestial spheres turn out to be architectural themselves (see fig. 15)—they too are little city-spheres (the *polis*) floating in space (the *cosmos*). One is led to wonder which space represents the heavens here—the stage or the screen? In fact, the whole sequence of Andria in Ramaswamy's *Invisible Cities* is characterized by a curious rupture between the normally distinct spaces of inside and outside, as markers of liminal spaces multiply—the threshold, the oculus, the archways in the spheres—but without ever resolving for the audience which is which. Every space seems to be simultaneously inside (if we are in the city, we are inside a temple) and outside (we are inside a great god's eye in space, watching the city below).

We've already seen the ways in which this dance expresses ideas about harmony (between citizens, between the city and the heavens), but during our conversations, Ramaswamy explained the source of resonance that she found with her family. They saw in the city of Andria's harmonious relationship with the heavens a kind of temple at the center of the dance, sheltered on all sides, that called out for a sacred story. Hence, they chose the story of Brahma's creation of the world. Ramaswamy observed that what Brahma initially creates, however, is chaos, and so the creation myth that they dance here is less about Brahma's creation and more about Saraswati, Brahma's female partner who gives form and order to the nascent universe, and as such is an ideal way to express the way that form can create harmony.[30] Hence, the dance is almost entirely Bharatanatyam, which allows the dancers to tell a story in ways that are both expressive but also partially semantic. I have already "read" their dance as a form of expression (movements in synchrony, expressions of adulation, interplay between the dancers and Mourad's visual art, staging, and so on), but for an audience versed in Bharatanatyam, the dance would communicate the story of Brahma's creation and Saraswati's ordering of the universe more directly (Bharatanatyam dance generally expresses Hindu stories and themes). Importantly, however, the larger form of both Ramaswamy's dance suite and Calvino's *Invisible Cities* means that the audience does not need to be steeped in the Bharatanatyam tradition to understand that this is a story about celestial harmony, or to appreciate the kinesthetic sympathy evoked by bodies in energetic motion moving together that embody that harmony, although no doubt an audience steeped in the Bharatanatyam tradition might derive more enjoyment and understanding from this segment. For Ramaswamy, the personal points of resonance that they found did not replace the stories in Calvino, or treat Calvino's novel as an empty vessel that could be filled. This was instead about the transmedial and transcultural space that opens up when an artist encounters another artist.

Lest this all appear a little too utopian or idealistic, it's worth noting that part of the reason that Ramaswamy gravitated to Calvino's novel was precisely because she understood it on her first reading as political, and political in ways that spoke to her experience as someone raised both in India and in the American Midwest, and with a strong awareness of the multiple legacies she inherited. Early in our conversation, Ramaswamy remarked, "There was no moment in which I thought of the novel as not political—that was right away." Calvino's novel dramatizes an important moment of contact between Europe and what is present-day China, and it's worth underlining that the novel's Marco Polo and Kublai Khan are locked in a struggle that deploys familiar terms, even if it reverses many of the elements that Western readers might be familiar with: a sprawling Asian empire that dominates many different peoples and cultures, and a solitary European "native informant" who serves as a guide for the exploration of the locales that imperial power is not (yet) familiar with.

The Cosmopolitan and the Global

Kublai Khan's empire—at least in Calvino's version—is, in at least one important respect, unlike the imperial powers we might think of today (say, Victorian Britain): It is cosmopolitan without being metropolitan. That is, Khan's empire might nominally have a capital, but Polo's cities and even the dialogues don't usually have a relationship to a capital (only one of the dialogues is set explicitly in the imperial capital of Kambalu). This absence of any political center de-territorializes the space in which the novel takes place—none of the cities is situated in any discernible fashion with respect to any of the others, as the opening sentence of the first city, Diomira, makes abundantly clear: "Partendosi di là e andando tre giornate verso levante, l'uomo si trova a Diomira" (2:362, Leaving there, and traveling eastward for three days, you find yourself in Diomira). The initial "there" from which the traveler departed to head east is never specified, and "eastward" will remain a meaningless term, since it is impossible to situate any of the cities Marco Polo describes with respect to any of the others (or the real cities that are mentioned from time to time). This de-territorializing effect also de-nationalizes the frame of the novel's reception (the city's names are neither Chinese nor Italian for the most part), which may be one of the crucial factors behind its global resonance.

Calvino's *Invisible Cities* doesn't just eschew the frame of the national but takes the city-state as its fundamental political unit. This is, as I noted in chapter 4, a common Italian inclination, the preference for the local rather than the national frame of reference. Italians generally root their identity in their city of origin, and not in the nation, a model that again moves away from the notion of a single dominant metropole (Paris or London) in favor of a diffuse network of similarly important major cities, although important in very different ways (Turin, Milan, Bologna, Venice, Florence, Rome, Naples, Palermo, etc.).[31] The space of Khan's empire (its *cosmos*) is structured entirely by the polis, and while there are larger structures at play (Khan's empire; the city categories, like "cities and the sky"; the numbering system for the cities within their categories; or the nine sections that divide the novel), they are divorced both from any sense of the national and from any spatial orientation, such as the kind of centering that an imperial capital might provide.[32]

In short, part of what makes *Invisible Cities* so resonant is that it is *political without specificity.* It recognizes power, even imperial power, struggle, the citizen (from the word for city), cultural differences, and much more, but all within a frame that floats free of any specific empire or political history. No doubt for some readers (especially those who are attached to, say, a politically engaged Lukacsian historical realism), this is precisely what makes this novel, and Calvino more broadly, politically problematic. This disagreement goes back at least as far as Calvino and Pasolini's debate about the proper use of the Italian language in the mid-1960s.[33] Both authors were concerned that there really was an emerging national language that was spoken, not literary, and that it was terrible. Consumerist commercial language was Pasolini's fear; deliberately obfuscatory bureaucratic language was Calvino's. Each saw a different remedy, however, with Pasolini pointing to local and historical dialects, and Calvino pointing to a guiding principle of international cosmopolitanism, specifically the need for writers to develop a reflexive self-awareness of how *translatable* their writings were, precisely because of the need to develop a *global* understanding of apparently local issues. As Calvino writes, "oggi ogni questione culturale è subito internazionale, ha bisogno di essere verificata su scala mondiale" (*Saggi*, 149, today every cultural question is immediately international, and needs to be validated on a global scale).

What I am arguing here is not that Calvino's approach is better, or that politically committed realist works are deficient in some way (Pasolini himself adored *Invisible Cities*, calling it "bello in assoluto," or "categorically beautiful"), but that scholarship on Calvino has missed the degree to which his formalism and cosmopolitanism have resonated globally, in ways that are often explicitly political, and which are absolutely rooted in local and completely specific histories and places. In short, Calvino's critics might be right that there is no (specific) political content to the novel, but this is precisely what allowed it to speak to a multitude of political issues afterward. Tran found a text that spoke to his family's history, and what emerged was a dance performance that is only fully comprehensible in the light of the Cold War and US imperialism in South Asia, including the war in Vietnam and the immigration policies that decided to settle a large number of Vietnamese refugees in Minneapolis—all performed in a dance language that emerged from African American and Puerto Rican dance performance practices on the streets of New York and cities in California, which in turn emerged from different (and longer) histories of slavery, racism, and imperial power. This is also another example of the *andere Schauplatz* (the "other stage") of the previous chapter: An apparently abstract and formal dance about an alienated traveler is in fact entirely conditioned by and responding to another drama taking place offstage. Indeed, there are at least two such dramas: Tran's personal history, and the larger global history in which that personal history is embedded. Writing in 1990, Claudio Milanini understood *Invisible Cities* as an "utopia discontinua" (scattered utopia), arguing that the fifty-five cities are "le tessere di un mosaico particolarissimo" (114, tiles of a most peculiar mosaic), tiles that trace out a cognitive map that leads us on to "traiettorie sempre mobili" (123, ever-shifting trajectories). In 2025, it's clear that the trajectories engendered by that scattered utopia are more capacious and global than anyone could have imagined.

For Ramaswamy, Calvino's novel led not only to thinking about her cultural roots (Hindu mythology), but to a specifically woman-centered version of it through the story of Saraswati and the Tridevi. What results is a kind of doubled resonance: Calvino's deliberately international and cosmopolitan energy charges an Indian American artist to reflect on her own cosmopolitan and international inheritances—once again, a drama "other" to the one taking place onstage, although linked through a formal resonance. Bharatanatyam is a surprisingly logical choice for a danced response to Calvino's reflection on imperial knowledge and power: An ancient tradition, the dance form was ridiculed and discouraged by British colonizers (repeatedly linked to accusations of prostitution), and eventually banned, before it was revived and popularized by figures like Rukmini Arundale and Esther "Ragini Devi" Sherman in the 1930s and '40s, who both very self-consciously (and successfully) wished to shape Bharatanatyam into an international dance form, rooted in South India but practiced and performed around the world.[34]

Beyond the Planetary

Calvino writes that the inhabitants of Andria are "convinti che ogni innovazione nella città influisca sul disegno del cielo, prima d'ogni decisione calcolano i rischi e i vantaggi per loro e per l'insieme delle città e dei mondi" (2:486, convinced that every innovation in the city could influence the design of the heavens, before every decision they calculate the risks and advantages for them, and for all cities and worlds). In this moment, Calvino once again unites the *polis* (*le città*, the cities) and a *cosmos* (*i mondi*, the worlds) that ranges from the city to the globe to the universe, indicating an intertwined destiny that takes corporeal form onstage in Ramaswamy's *Invisible Cities*. Calvino offers us a surprise plural (worlds) for a vision that goes beyond even the global or the planetary, one that opens up space once again.

This is the final lesson that Calvino's *Invisible Cities* leaves us with, the imperative to give space, leave room, let grow. In the final segments of Ramaswamy's *Invisible Cities* (the last two sections flow together without interruption), four of the modern dancers are in front of a small tree surrounded by a monumental city. The music is a piece by Kayhan Kalhor that builds to a somewhat frenetic and anxious climax. The tree is stylized at first, without leaf or flower. As the dance moves into the very final segment, however, the tree grows a few new branches, and a new piece of music begins that calls all the dancers slowly onstage, each dancing alone, isolated, in his or her unique style. The final piece of music is another work by de Veer, "Leave Osea" (originally from the television series *The Third Day*). As is typical for him, it is slow (adagio) and in a minor key (F♯). There is a rhythmically *ostinato* figure on an acoustic guitar at its core, a simple four-note arpeggio, accompanied by a vocal chant of nonsense syllables, and both are punctuated by a piercing two-note descending figure on strings, a figure developed into a full melody that is half mournful, half haunting. Each of those musical lines, however, takes place in an audibly different space: The guitar is close miked and dry (without reverb), as if the listener were in the studio with the player, but not loud; the vocal chant is muffled, as if distantly heard through the wall; and the strings are Hollywood—bright, lush, forceful, and with an absolutely huge reverb, more like a cathedral than a concert hall.

De Veer's final piece in Ramaswamy's *Invisible Cities* is a great example of what modern recording techniques can do with reverb, and hence, how it can also play with space. It is not at all unusual to hear multiple spaces in a single recording in the digital era, but this does not eliminate the sense of place associated with sound—rather, it multiplies it. This is effectively what Eidsheim describes happening in the performance of Chris Cerrone's "headphone opera" of *Invisible Cities* in chapter 2: incompatible sonic registers that make the listener fully aware of the materiality of their sonic world. Moreover, it is part of a larger play with space that happens at the end of the dance—just as all of the dancers at the start of the piece occupy separate spaces (each dancing independently), we have a musical composition that produces the same kind of spaces in sound:

independent, isolated, initially incompatible (while still forming an aesthetic whole).

But there are signs in the staging and the dancing that things are beginning to change. The tree in the background grows leaves, swells, and becomes gradually infused with a kind of rainbow aura, layers of pink and orange and blue and green. The city that surrounds it grows progressively harder to make out. Whatever is happening, we are definitely seeing something that is *not* "part of the inferno that surrounds us," but rather a little piece of the non-inferno that has been given space, and is growing. Is the city even visible anymore?[35]

Something similar is at work in the music, as well. The guitar becomes more and more prominent at the end of "Leave Osea," and it moves through a series of simple arpeggiated chords, almost like an exercise or study, an insistent rhythm of simple eighth notes accompanied by the sounds of nature (birds, crickets, rain). Popular music tends to be organized by relatively simple chord progressions that form short loops of tension and release. The loops typically start on the root, the chord that feels most like home, and work their way toward a chord that emphasizes a tense distance from that tonal center, that wants to return to it. If a song is in C major, then, it might have a chord progression that starts with C major (the I chord) and ends with G major (the V chord that most strongly wants to return to the I), before restarting the loop. "Leave Osea" is in F♯ minor (see fig. 16), and it follows this pattern pretty closely, moving from the home (F♯ minor, in measure 1) to that V chord (C♯ in measures 4–5, here as a dominant seventh chord for extra tension) before returning home in measure 6 to start a new loop with some additional variations. That new progression once again leads us to the V chord at the end of measure 9. We expect to resolve from the V down to the I, especially since that's what the chord loop has already prepared us for, but instead the C♯ chord goes *up* to a D (this is about 2:09 into the piece), and stays there fairly persistently. This is called a "deceptive cadence" (going from the V to any chord other than the I, but the most common form is the one we see here, a move from the V to the VI), a cadence that typically delays a return home and leaves the listener "hanging" with an unsatisfied expectation of full resolution.

In the same way that the recording deploys multiple acoustic spaces with different kinds of reverb, de Veer is offering the listener another kind of musical choice as well. "Leave Osea" is in a minor key, but the sustained shift to a D major chord seems to be asking the question: Is it really? After all, the title is already an imperative to travel (Osea is an English island and the setting for *The Third Day*, the television miniseries that originally featured the piece). Are we leaving? What are we leaving behind, and where are we going? Have we found a new home? These are particularly pertinent questions at the end of both Calvino's and Ramaswamy's *Invisible Cities*, of course—de Veer, for his part, provides here an opening to something else (a different tonality), but in a carefully ambiguous way.

The listener can hear this final passage in two ways, which is perhaps what generates that "hanging," unsatisfied feeling. The first is that when the C♯ chord in measure 9 moves up to D in measure 10 (fig. 16), we have moved to a new tonal focus, D major, an idea reinforced when we linger on that D chord while fading out. This way of hearing the ending is somewhat dissatisfying, however, since the piece ends on a low F♯ (measure 12), not D. F♯ is part of a D major chord, but, if D is our new tonal center, the listener expects to hear the F♯ *above* and *with* the note of D. The second way of hearing it—and this is how I have written out the score—is that we stay in F♯ minor, with that deceptive cadence going from VI to i, a resolution without a strong sense of tension and release. In short, the final F♯, in this position and in this octave (and rather abruptly cut off), belongs to two "sound spaces" simultaneously, and remains suspended or "hanging" between them. De Veer opens up a potential within the music to hear another space, but without foreclosing on either of them.

There is one last sense of spatial opening in the music, one that is doubled in the dance. Throughout the ending of "Leave Osea," the music fades away, layer by layer: the strings, a second guitar, some faint bells. Even the primary guitar gets quieter and quieter, leaving more and more space for the nature sounds that we hear. After the guitar arrives at that last note, it leaves only that natural sound space; at the same time, almost without the spectator realizing it, the apparently chaotically moving dancers have moved into a circle and come to rest, each facing outward, an even, open space onstage created by their presence. Each layer of this composition (visual, musical, kinetic) has performed the same formal gesture, each in its own way: the movement from multiple spaces (spaces that, if not in conflict, are certainly not communicating) to the creation of a single

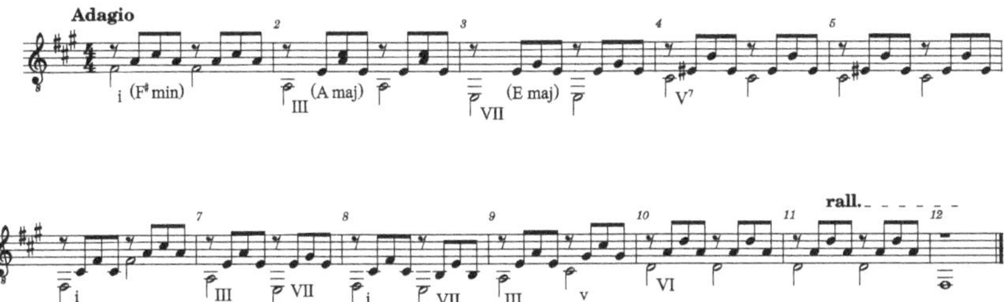

FIGURE 16. The ending of "Leave Osea" (guitar only).

space of the non-infernal, but a space that is open. Form expresses the content, sometimes better than the content ever could.

Of course, de Veer didn't write this composition while thinking about Calvino. His gestures to different kinds of space would have had a quite different aim when he composed "Leave Osea" (although, as I just indicated, his interests were thematically related, since "Leave Osea" is very much about the ambivalence of travel). But Ramaswamy found this music evocative and apt for the ending of *Invisible Cities* for a reason: its musical journey would have felt like the emergence from a kind of infernal anxiety to a *potential* space something that was non-hell, a hope that such a space could endure or even flourish. There is something like a precarious or fleeting happiness that emerges at the end of the piece, one that I think is remarkably resonant with the ending of Calvino's novel. We can't have utopia, but perhaps—with constant attention and vigilance—we can have something that is not hell.

Conclusions

The end result of the "Leave Osea" finale is that Ramaswamy brings the dancers into a formal unity, but one that also aligns three different sensory registers: sight, sound, and body. Ramaswamy's dance leaves the spectator with two lessons that emerge from Calvino's *Invisible Cities*, even if they are not said quite out loud. Calvino says explicitly that the only way to live with the hell of other people, the hell of the modern city, is to find those things that are not hell, and let them endure, give them space. He does not say anything about the nature of these potential pieces of non-hell, but so many modern readers have heard the same two ideas there that I must conclude that they are part of the novel's resonant space, just below the limits of our hearing, perhaps. The first of Ramaswamy's two lessons is that this space of the non-infernal will have something to do with community. That community will probably be imperfect, but it will certainly consist of a group united by difference (we all dance to the beat of our own drummer in this politics) in a kind of formal equivalence (bodies creating a space together, the circle, merely by being there). The second of the two lessons is that the space of the non-infernal will have something to do with nature, with the human city finding a non-infernal relation to the natural world. Has a seed been planted in that open space on Ramaswamy's stage? Perhaps it has: a seed that might grow into Mourad's tree, and then de Veer's forest. Perhaps one day we might climb into those trees and live there, next to the Baron in the trees. Perhaps, as Calvino suggested with a laugh at the end of chapter 1, we already do.

Coda: Invisible Dialogues

I'd like to end by talking about my own experience performing and recording one of these Calvino-inspired acoustic works of art, the Welsh composer Stephen Goss's "Dialogues from *Invisible Cities*," and what I learned about Calvino, resonance, and transmediality from it. In 2017, Goss premiered a concerto of *Invisible Cities* for guitar, violin, strings, and percussion, and a recording of the full work is available at SoundCloud. Goss used a reduced structure similar to that employed by Cerrone in his opera based on the novel, showcasing five cities interleaved with three dialogues between Marco Polo (the violin) and Kublai Khan (the guitar). He also published the "Dialogues" from the concerto as a stand-alone duet for guitar and violin in 2022. It is technically challenging on guitar—with passages of tremolo played very high up on the neck, for example—but is musically quite beautiful. I have played and recorded classical guitar for almost forty years now, so I was pretty sure that I was up to the technical challenge, but it also seemed like something that might provide some insight into thinking about Calvino through music.

Every musician follows more or less the same process when engaging with a piece. First, you struggle with the mechanics of playing the piece at all, however badly. It might present unusual technical challenges (there were several in Goss's "Dialogues," which I'll discuss in more detail below), or perhaps the score presents unusual difficulties (unfamiliar notation or directions, for example). Then you work to understand what the composer might have wanted, how to interpret the piece—in short, how to make it musical and not simply "correct." I went through that same process and eventually recorded the three dialogues in November

2023, and uploaded them to my SoundCloud. According to the site's statistics, "Dialogue 2" was the most listened to of the three, and listeners for all three pieces included traffic from the US, Japan, Iran, Russia, France, Latvia, Egypt, Indonesia, Norway, and elsewhere (although much of the traffic on SoundCloud is actually automated bots, so you cannot really tell if a "listen" is authentic or not).

The individual dialogues are all written without key signature, time signature (there are occasional tempo indications, however), or measure divisions, but they still evoke a warm lyricism rather than an alienating atonality. Rather than an absent tonal center, they suggest a center that is fleeting, constantly changing. Goss, like the other artistic figures I look at in *Transmedial Resonance* (Cerrone, Mezzacappa, and Ramaswamy), is of a decidedly literary bent (Eco, Calvino, Borges, Shakespeare, Chaucer, Claude Lévi-Strauss, art historian Simon Schama, and many others make appearances in his music). His music is deeply serious but also playful, with compositions that are often marked by sudden stylistic and technical shifts, particularly noticeable in the three "Dialogues," which really do sound like a series of statements and responses. Goss's *Invisible Cities* is a clear example of program music (discussed in chapter 3), with specific characters assigned to specific instruments, and Goss gives a detailed account of both his musical ideas and the original novel in the program note that accompanies the sheet music (and that accompanied the original performance): "*Invisible Cities* has no plot or character development. It is a meticulously structured collection of 55 prose-poem descriptions of cities, framed by dialogues between the Venetian explorer Marco Polo and the Mogul emperor Kublai Khan" (1).

Goss uses this description as a springboard for his musical response to Calvino, which emphasizes the extreme difficulty of communication across languages. It is also clear that one of Goss's central interests as a composer is precisely the problem of translating between different forms of expression. This is particularly true, in Goss's works, of the shift between visual and musical languages (compositions that render paintings or even pure colors into music), but also true of the movement between verbal language and music. Calvino's *Invisible Cities* is an emblematic text for him because of the dialogues that emphasize the richness of nonverbal language (Marco Polo's games of charades, for example, using objects to speak) as well as the poverty and deceptiveness of speech itself. Musically, Goss expresses this in "Dialogues" by assigning very different stylistic qualities to each instrument, what is, in effect, a voice: "The two speak completely different languages and frequently interrupt one another. Marco's music is wild, gestural, and varied, the Khan's more statesmanlike" (1). Moreover, Goss asks for the guitar (Khan) to "interpret" (1) the descriptions offered by the violin (Polo). That is, "Dialogues" is itself a musical interpretation of a verbal work—a verbal work that already includes within it characters who also attempt to translate between verbal and nonverbal languages. Tellingly, what appeals to Goss in this is that the characters in the novel, as well as the instruments in his work, frequently fall silent, as "the shift from gesture to words is seen as a loss."

That loss, however, is Goss's gain, since this is precisely the scenario that leads to his composition. In short, Calvino's literary description of the failures of verbal language leads to Goss's musical creation, a clear example of the movement of resonant energy, but also gesturing to the way that all language, of every variety, calls out for yet more language. Goss's musical language—his musical drama of the failure of musical communication, based on a literary text about the failure of verbal communication—produces this coda to my book, yet more verbal language. Peter Szendy persuasively argues that music always inspires language in response, and even a lot of it ("parole, parole"),[1] but in fact, what we are seeing throughout this book is a kind of ceaseless shuttling between verbal language and nonverbal language, words and music, words and images, words and dance. Each one calls out the other, over and over again. (What do we do in response to art, music, and dance except to talk about them?) This is true, perhaps exceptionally true, of the dialogue between the verbal and the nonverbal, but of course, the image also inspires music, music inspires dance, an object inspires a poem, and so on. We have always treated the "transmedial" as a special or separate category, as if it were something exceptional, but in fact, it is simply the other side of a ceaseless conversation.

The individual pieces in Goss's "Dialogues" also underscore the ceaseless flow of the verbal into the nonverbal and back again. Goss specifies in the performance note that "the performers should be oblivious of one another, as if they are playing different pieces" (2) and that they should feel free to interrupt each other, as well as to improvise. Some of the technical hurdles the player has to overcome also speak to the difficulty of communication as well. For example, near the start of "Dialogue 1," Goss calls for the guitar to play a note that is "pre-bent." Guitarists in a variety of styles bend notes, but it is a technique that popular audiences perhaps particularly associate with the blues, or blues-inflected rock music. Regardless of style, the guitarist strikes the note and then bends the string perpendicularly across the fretboard, increasing the tension and thus smoothly raising the pitch of the note just played. With a "pre-bend," however, the player silently bends the string with the left hand first (assuming a right-handed player), and then plucks with the right hand. Then the bent string is smoothly returned back to its normal position. What the listener hears, then, is not a note being bent upward, but a note being bent *down* in pitch. Bending notes at all is very unusual in classical guitar (their nylon strings are too low in tension for it to be a practical technique most of the time), but it makes a lot of sense here given that Goss is seeking to replicate voices; note bending gives an expressive, vocal-like quality to a melody, making the guitar "sing" or "cry" or "wail"—or in this case, speak.

Goss combines this "pre-bent" note with a *harmonic* at the same pitch, however. Harmonics are the chime-like notes on a guitar that keep ringing without the player needing to press the string down. The harmonic will not necessarily be the same note as the string, either: an E string touched at the twelfth fret will change to an E an octave higher, but touched at the seventh fret will change to a B, or at the ninth fret a G♯.[2] Goss challenges the player by combining the harmonic on one string and the pre-bent note on a different string at the same time. This, in turn, catches the ear of the listener with something they have probably not heard before (I had never come across this technique before). When done properly, it simply sounds like one note at first. The result is quite eerie, however, as the player relaxes the pre-bent note (this is about 35 seconds into my recording of "Dialogue 1" and about 30 seconds into the version hosted on Goss's SoundCloud): The G♯ floats in the air for a moment and then *seems to split in two*. The harmonic G♯ remains, but the pre-bent note falls out of it down to a G, a disquieting minor second. Hopefully after this somewhat technical explanation, the reader can understand the larger point that Goss is making here: Unity and harmony, *even within the same voice*, let alone between two voices, are remarkably difficult to maintain. And as "Dialogue 1" continues, there is little indication that the two instruments find any way to really communicate. They never "play together" in any meaningful way at all; it's more a question of overlapping, two speakers who aren't really listening to each other, and one of them isn't even in tune with himself. Moreover, the problems in communication grow worse over time, not better. By "Dialogue 3," the instruments don't overlap at all, and Goss uses precisely the same device that Chris Cerrone does at the end of his *Invisible Cities*: there are fermatas over the rest marks rather than over the notes, emphasizing the turn away from speech and into silence.

As a performer, the difficulty in maintaining a conversation (although also the necessity of doing so) was driven home by the most obvious challenge I faced in playing "Invisible Dialogues"—it is a piece written for two instruments, and I am just one person. (A person who, apart from a very brief period in childhood that my parents no doubt deeply regret, does not play violin.) I used the open-source MuseScore software to synthesize the violin part, recorded my own parts and then combined them in a digital audio editing program. On the one hand, this is the perfect embodiment of Goss's instructions: musicians who really are *literally* "oblivious of one another, as if they are playing different pieces." My recording of "Dialogues" makes use of one performer, and one synthesized instrument, playing in different spaces, at different times, and later stitched together. On the other hand, it clearly defeats the purpose of the piece that Goss discovered in Calvino's novel, which is to *dramatize interpersonal dialogue itself*. While technically proficient, faithful to the score, and perhaps even musical in execution, my performance necessarily missed the larger aim of Goss's work, which tries to create a musical conversation of push and pull, glimpses of insight, and much miscommunication.

One of the principal signs of this failure is that I discovered that it was impossible to improvise when playing to a prerecorded partner. That is, I can improvise, but Goss's piece demands precisely a conversational give and take that was impossible when playing along to a recording made not even by a real instrument, but by a program reading the score. I tried to make that version as expressive as possible, but again, the lesson I learned by playing Goss's "Dialogues" was that technical proficiency, fidelity, and even musicality are not the only elements necessary for the music to work. Specifically, they were insufficient for the *interpersonal dimension* of the scenario. Goss's "Dialogues" may be dramatizing a failed dialogue, but it is still a *dialogue*.

There is (at least) one more important lesson that Goss's "Dialogues" has to teach us, one that emerges from this last point. *Transmedial Resonance* is pretty unashamedly utopian in its approach to and evaluation of Calvino and the artists inspired by his resonant energy. I argue throughout the introduction that resonance is a better metaphor for thinking about artistic influence, or at least for thinking about some examples of artistic influence, especially transmedial. The chapters that follow the introduction offer a very rosy view of that resonance as well, works of art that are aesthetically beautiful but that also make us think more creatively and capaciously about sound and the environment, about sexuality, about politics and space. I could say all the same things about Goss's *Invisible Cities* and "Dialogues," as well (and they would be true), but Goss highlights to an exceptional degree something about Calvino that Cerrone, Mezzacappa, *Silent City*, and Ramaswamy all also acknowledge in their own ways: Calvino is not utopian about any form of human relations.

Conversation is fraught, enormously difficult, and rarely successful. Any successful encounter, moreover, is no guarantee of another in the future. Cerrone's *Invisible Cities* ends with Marco Polo and Kublai Khan passing each other by on parallel paths, never looking back at what a fuller encounter between them might have brought; Mezzacappa's "The Form of Space" dramatizes the apparent impossibility of such parallel lines ever meeting through a series of "near miss" duets, ending in a "unison gesture" rather than a real unison; *Silent City* ends up being a drama about the desires and fears that you cannot speak out loud (even to yourself), but can only articulate in pure noise rather than music; and while Ramaswamy ends with a space of possibility, even subtle hope, her dance is also replete with movements articulated in rhythmic space that signify failure, disconnection, indifference, and separation.

Goss's "Dialogues," then, are actually structured by the most important lesson Calvino had to offer in *Invisible Cities*, certainly the most important lesson in our fraught, unhappy political age that always seems to be teetering on the verge of dystopia. There is no utopia—but there might be something out there that is not a dystopia. To find that non-dystopian political space will be, to quote Calvino one last time, "rischioso ed esige attenzione e apprendimento continui" (2:498, risky and demand constant attention and learning). It can only ever be found for a moment, and the next moment of the non-infernal will require different tactics, different approaches and new knowledge. It will certainly require, as Goss's "Dialogues" teach us, a constant, risky dialogue (between people, between arts, between languages of all kinds), but I am convinced that the works that I explore in this book are a step in the right direction.

Acknowledgments

Acknowledgments play a particularly important and inescapable role in this book, precisely because it is a book about influence and inspiration. Indeed, it is a book that attempts to transcend (or at least move away from) the language of influence in favor of a metaphor that is more about spaces, communities, networks, and future directions, namely resonance. So rather than reciting names, however important it is to do so, I want to instead mention a number of networks that are also (mostly) linked to physical spaces (sometimes overlapping, of course) as part of the expanding reverberation of voices that helped shape this book.

Let me start at UCLA, where I've been able to share many of these ideas and also gain some insight from graduate students (Bella Dante, Miranda Heaner, Joia Duskic) and from my fellow faculty, particularly Todd Presner, Tom Harrison, Kalani Michell, Cara Tovey, Raphaëlle Burns, Dominic Thomas, and Maite Zubiaurre, just to name some of the important interlocutors I've had in European Languages and Transcultural Studies. Emanuele Amendola and the IIC (Istituto Italiano di Cultura), Los Angeles, which he directs, helped to bring both Ashwini Ramaswamy and Lisa Mezzacappa to campus for conversations that they also helped to advertise, and provided moral support for this project from when I first arrived on campus. Still close to home, Claudio Fogu of UC Santa Barbara, Rhiannon Welch of UC Berkeley (working on her own reverberation project, as it turned out!), as well as the entire CICIS (California Interdisciplinary Consortium of Italian Studies) community provided deeply helpful feedback on *Silent City* and more. One of my "mantras" in this book was "going out, coming back," and perhaps the most important expression of that movement of sound has been the reestablishment of the group chat/lunch/dinner/intellectual debate group of Comp Lit Picnic (originally founded at the University of Illinois), namely Michael Rothberg, Yasemin Yildiz, and Lilya Kaganovsky.

I'm no longer at the University of Illinois, but graduate students there (Alice, Debayudh, Brian, Sarah, Cassie, Soraya, Sharayah, Meredith, Aidan) were amazing sound students as I was working out the first ideas for this book, and I'd like to particularly thank Nobuto Sato for introducing me to the study of stutter in his remarkable work on modernism, sound, and dysphonia, which obviously bore fruit in chapter 1 of the present volume. I left behind many wonderful colleagues and friends, and although they already know who they are, I'll mention Brett, Phillip (with his booming bass), Nancy and Gillen, Jim and Renée (now at Toronto), Gabe Solis (now at Washington), Manuel and Nora, Eric and Jaimie, Justine and John and many more—but I wanted to particularly recall here two voices that were hugely important in shaping me as a person and a professional who have, alas, fallen silent: Dara Goldman and Elena Delgado.

While people at your home institution often have an outsized role, I'm very happy to enjoy a widespread network of friends and colleagues who have made contributions of all kinds, large and small, to this project: Elena Past, Ellen Nerenberg, Jackie Reich, Ramsey McGlazer, Serena Bassi, Serenella Iovino, Alessandro Giammei, Dana Renga, Jonathan Combs-Schilling, Lucia Re, Erika Nadir, Timothy Campbell, Laura Di Bianco, and many others introduced me to other "Calvino artists," gave advice, debated, or just generally sharpened my thinking. Two outside readers for Fordham University Press fall into that category as well, and engaged deeply with the material in this book. The sound studies seminar organized by Julie Napolin and Sara Marcus organized an incredible sound studies seminar that I was part of for the Chicago ACLA conference in 2020, a conference that was cancelled after the arrival of the pandemic. In a testament to the zeal of sound studies, however, we held our panel online regardless.

Finally, this book crucially depended on an entire network of people (many now friends) that was entirely new to me: the artists whose works I examine here and many of whom I mention even if I didn't end up dedicating an entire chapter to them. All of them were generously willing to talk to a self-described "Calvino nerd," to share photos, scores, videos, and other materials, and even to come and talk to the students and faculty here at UCLA. In particular, I want to mention Ashwini, Aparna, and Ranee Ramaswamy, as well as Ashwini's entire *Invisible Cities* dance troupe, especially Joe Tran, who made extra time to talk to me about his performance, and Kevork Mourad, whose artwork for the dance performance deserves a whole book of its own; Lisa Mezzacappa and her ensemble; Chris Cerrone (whose *Pieces That Fall to Earth*, even more than *Invisible Cities*, is on regular rotation in my headphones); everyone in and around *Silent City* I spoke to, but especially Vania Cauzilla, Andrea Ciommiento, and Mimma Giovinazza; and finally composer Stephen Goss. Thanks also to filmmaker Duccio Chiarini, playwright John Capecci, and video game designer Evan Anthony and the rest of the programmers who worked on *Genesis Noir*. All of them were generous in talking about their works and Calvino with me.

Fordham University Press has been a delight to work with, and I'd like to extend a particular thanks to Nancy Basmajian, my copyeditor, who provided some very helpful (and thought-provoking) observations as well as much-needed corrections.

Lastly, thanks to my whole family for their help, support, presence, and love, especially Lilya and Sasha.

Chapter 2 is derived in part from an article published in *Italian Culture* on 07 December 2021, © 2021 American Association for Italian Studies. It is available online at www.tandfonline.com/10.1080/01614622.2021.1976972. Chapter 3 is derived in part from an article that previously appeared in *California Italian Studies* 12.1 (2023). Both journals not only found insightful reviewers for those articles, but graciously granted permission for that material to reappear here.

I generally refer to Calvino's works by their English titles, unless the work has not been translated (so *Invisible Cities*, but *Un ottimista in America*). Translations to English from Calvino and Calvino criticism in Italian are mine unless otherwise stated (the one real exception is William Weaver's translation of *Invisible Cities*, because that is the source of Chris Cerrone's libretto for the opera of the same title). In the case of works in French, I have consulted the original, but quoted the published English translation.

References in Italian to Calvino's novels and stories are (with a few exceptions) from the Meridiani edition of *Romanzi e racconti*, Calvino's "opera omnia" in Italian. After each citation I give in parentheses the volume number followed by the page number, such as (2:163), which is page 163 of volume 2 of *Romanzi e racconti*. For Calvino's essays, references are to the Meridiani *Saggi*, and are given as *Saggi* followed by the page number, such as (*Saggi*, 1103). For Calvino's letters, references are to the Meridiani *Lettere*, and are given as *Lettere* followed by the page number, such as (*Lettere*, 201).

Introduction: Writing About Music

1. Elio Baldi and Cecilia Schwartz, introduction to *Circulation, Translation and Reception Across Borders: Italo Calvino's "Invisible Cities" Around the World*, ed. Baldi and Schwartz (Routledge, 2023), 7.

2. Francesca Rubini, "Italo Calvino in Other Languages—Part Three," *New Italian Books*, December 12, 2023, www.newitalianbooks.it/italo-calvino-in-translation-part -three/.

3. Lorenzo Sabatino, "Centenary Calvino, *Here and Elsewhere*," *Textual Cultures* 16, no. 2 (2023): 284.

4. I am aware that Google shows search results tailored not only to your exact location (a computer on a college campus in Los Angeles), but also to your browsing history as an individual (an unrepentant Calvino nerd, in my case). That said, I think these results do tell us something useful and important, both about Calvino's global resonance and about the specifically *acoustic* character of that resonance.

5. It is ultimately a mistake to separate the everyday life and the lofty ambitions of major artists: Ashwini Ramaswamy, whose dance project of *Invisible Cities* is the subject of chapter 5, is an avid reader with sophisticated literary tastes (she was an English major in college). Her first encounter with Calvino's *Invisible Cities*, however, was not in a class or a book club, but when she bought some jewelry inspired by the novel, and found the title so evocative that she decided to read it.

6. That said, writing a history of the present is always a risky proposition; I would suggest that, while Cerrone's opera *might* be a turning point, perhaps the turning point might be better located elsewhere, or perhaps even the notion of a turning point is mistaken.

7. Franco Fortini, *L'ospite ingrato* (Marietti, 1985), 55.

8. Marzia Beltrami, *Spatial Plots: Virtuality and the Embodied Mind in Baricco, Camilleri and Calvino* (Legenda, 2021), 13. See also Anna Botta, "Calvino and the Oulipo: An Italian Ghost in the Combinatory Machine?," *MLN* 112, no. 1 (1997): 81–89, and

Lucia Re, "Pasolini vs. Calvino, One More Time: The Debate on the Role of Intellectuals and Postmodernism in Italy Today," *MLN* 129, no. 1 (2014): 99–117.

9. Iovino previously released a much shorter version of this book in English (2021), but the Italian version (2023) is much more detailed and effectively a different book. A massive number of books about Calvino were published in 2023, the centenary of his birth, an occasion much celebrated in Italy.

10. Jhumpa Lahiri, *Translating Myself and Others* (Princeton University Press, 2022), 142.

11. See https://forbes.it/2024/06/25/futuro-business-lezioni-americane-calvino/.

12. Richard Lord, "Hong Kong Architect William Lim and the Italo Calvino Novel That Changed His Life, *Invisible Cities*," *South China Morning Post*, August 4, 2018, www.scmp.com/magazines/post-magazine/books/article/2158081/hong-kong-architect -william-lim-and-italo-calvino.

13. Daniele Del Giudice, "L'occhio che scrive," in *Italo Calvino: Enciclopedia: arte, scienza e letteratura*, ed. Marco Belpoliti (Marcos y Marcos, 1995), 176–79; Domenico Scarpa, *Calvino fa la conchiglia: La costruzione di uno scrittore* (Hoepli, 2023), 379.

14. Since I was in graduate school, I have heard perennial rumors of a film adaptation of *The Baron in the Trees*, most recently as a limited series from producer Lorenzo Mieli (also responsible for the HBO adaptation of Ferrante's *My Brilliant Friend*). There have been a few adaptations of shorter works, such as a partial (and unsatisfying) adaptation of *Marcovaldo* for television, but they are rare and almost never released commercially. A number of American films have directly referenced Calvino as inspirational, however (more outside than inside), such as *Palookaville* (Taylor, 1995) and *Stranger Than Fiction* (Forster, 2006).

15. Like any good echo, Lightman's novel went on to spawn additional reverberations: a stage adaptation in 1996, and a musical version in 2005 that eventually landed an off-Broadway premiere in the unfortunate moment of November 2019, shortly before the pandemic closed theaters everywhere.

16. James W. Fernandez, *Persuasions and Performances: The Play of Tropes in Culture* (Indiana University Press, 1986), 8–25.

17. Normal human listeners can generally hear differences as small as about 10 milliseconds, and many musicians are bothered by latencies (time lags) that are even shorter.

18. Many of our metaphors for thinking about cultural influence and transmission are based on the movement of water, but almost all of them, from "influence" and "derivative" (both coming from Latin words for river), to the "pebble in a pond" or the New Wave, assert a decisive and singular figure of importance (the river, the pebble), whether it is at the end or the beginning of the chain.

19. Karmen MacKendrick, *The Matter of Voice: Sensual Soundings* (Fordham University Press, 2016), 24.

20. Musical instruments can actually make themselves resonate; plucking or bowing a string at the right pitch, for example, can make other strings vibrate, sometimes quite audibly. The echoes and reverberations of the space they are played in can also make them resonate. A piano, with its eighty-eight keys (most of which have multiple corresponding strings), normally has felt dampers resting on the strings not being hammered to prevent excessive resonance that could be musically unpleasant.

21. Some objects will resonate at just one frequency, other objects (like my guitar) at a variety of frequencies, some more strongly than others.

22. Anne Bogart, *The Art of Resonance* (Methuen Drama [Bloomsbury], 2021), 14.

23. Not only can you tune your instrument *to* a tuning fork, but playing or singing the proper note *at* the tuning fork will also make it hum back at you.

24. Naomi Waltham-Smith, *Shattering Biopolitics: Militant Listening and the Sound of Life* (Fordham University Press, 2021), 15.

25. Peter Szendy, "*Parole, parole:* Tautegory and Musicology of the (Pop) Song," in *Speaking of Music: Addressing the Sonorous*, ed. Keith Chapin and Andrew H. Clark (Fordham University Press, 2013), 192.

26. Elio Baldi, *The Author in Criticism: Italo Calvino's Authorial Image in Italy, the United States, and the United Kingdom* (Fairleigh Dickinson University Press, 2022), 91. This tendency continues today, even among authors who are strongly sympathetic to Calvino, as in Domenico Scarpa's quite excellent *Calvino fa la conchiglia* (2023), whose title (Calvino makes a shell) and central argument reinforce the idea of the writer as a sensitive child perpetually in flight from the world, although Scarpa is one of the most nuanced contemporary readers of Calvino, and equally inclined to stress Calvino's simultaneous movement toward new spaces and possibilities.

27. Elio Baldi, "La sfida al labirinto sessuale: L'eros nell'opera di Italo Calvino," *Incontri* 27, no. 2 (2012): 60.

28. Jonathan Sterne, "Sonic Imaginations," in *The Sound Studies Reader*, ed. Jonathan Sterne (Routledge, 2012), 6.

29. I take it for granted that literature is an acoustic art, but this claim has proven somewhat controversial for some of my colleagues, who contend that prose at least is consumed silently and without attention to its sonic properties (something like a movie in which not only people and actions but even thoughts and concepts become visible to the mind's eye). I certainly read much faster than I could plausibly listen, but it's pretty clear that the acoustic character of written language always has the *potential* to emerge. No reader can read the opening lines of Nabokov's *Lolita*, for instance, and not also *hear* what is being said.

30. I leave open here the question of why so many of the book-length studies on sound and literature are about high modernism. Gellen and Napolin are examples, but one could also add Tyler Whitney's *Eardrums: Literary Modernism as Sonic Warfare* (2019) and Mark Christian Thompson's *Kafka's Blue: Figurations of Racial Blackness in the Construction of an Aesthetics* (2016) to the mix.

1 / Calvino's Voice: Stutter, Falsetto, Laughter

1. All citations to Calvino's fiction in Italian are to the three-volume Meridiani set of *Romanzi e racconti* (Novels and short stories); for details, see the "Titles and Citations" section at the end of the book.

2. All translations from Italian, unless otherwise noted, are mine (including this one); for details, see the "Titles and Citations" section at the end of the book. Calvino may very well have based this passage on one from Roland Barthes's "The Grain of the Voice," in which Barthes describes how he can sometimes hear the body within the voice, emerging from a "movement from deep down in the cavities, the muscles, the membranes, the cartilages" (in *Image—Music—Text*, ed. and trans. Stephen Heath [Fontana, 1977], 181). Calvino initially seems to stand on the side of Barthes and Cavarero, linking a unique voice to the materiality of the body—but as the story progresses, the King comes to doubt the idea that voices are truth, that they cannot be faked,

altered, and so on. It is not clear to me that Calvino takes a final position, beyond affirming that the notion of the unique, spontaneous, and natural voice is a compelling, even seductive, proposition—and that there is reason to doubt it all the same.

3. In Dolar's view, one can never perfectly distinguish between the signifier and the voice, but one can also never collapse them, since *something* always remains stubbornly unassimilated to the signifier (the *object a*, of course), but a something that remains also stubbornly resistant to definition or analysis. "Undecidability" and "indeterminacy . . . are the paramount features of the voice" (13).

4. Martha Feldman, "Voice Gap Crack Break," in *The Voice as Something More: Essays toward Materiality*, ed. Martha Feldman and Judith T. Zeitlin (University of Chicago Press, 2019), 188. In a more ordinary context, a speaker might deliberately crack their voice for comedic effect to indicate nervousness, anxiety or immaturity.

5. Karmen MacKendrick, *The Matter of Voice: Sensual Soundings* (Fordham University Press, 2016), 8.

6. Nina Sun Eidsheim, *The Race of Sound: Listening, Timbre and Vocality in African American Music* (Duke University Press, 2019), 3.

7. Intriguingly, uptalk is often associated with exaggerated femininity, an unconscious attempt to appear nonthreatening and unassertive by presenting statements as if they were questions. Vocal fry, however, is produced when one speaks in a *lower*-than-normal voice with the glottis loosely closed, and air rattling through in an irregular way (producing the popping, "frying" sound it is associated with).

8. Judith Butler, *Gender Trouble: Feminism and the Subversion of Identity* (Routledge, 1990), 33.

9. Katie McDonough ("Elizabeth Holmes's Fake Voice Is Actually Just 'Stupid Man' Voice," *Jezebel*, March 19, 2019) argues that Holmes's voice elicited such a visceral response because it "is the same voice that I (and maybe you) put on when making fun of very stupid men." Holmes may have meant it as an homage to Jobs, but it verged on unintentional parody.

10. Natalia Ginzburg, "Il sole e la luna," in *Italo Calvino: Enciclopedia: Arte, scienza e letteratura*, ed. Marco Belpoliti, special issue, *Riga*, no. 9 (Marcos y Marcos, 1995), 188.

11. The interview, "Franco Maria Ricci, l'editore di Babele," was directed by Nereo Rapetti for RSI (Radio Svizzera Italiana) and was released on May 26, 1974. It is worth noting that a phonetic transcription of most "normal" speakers would show quite a bit of repetition, false starts, and verbal fumbling, too, although not to this degree.

12. Domenico Scarpa, *Calvino fa la conchiglia: La costruzione di uno scrittore* (Hoepli, 2023), 608.

13. Marc Shell, *Stutter* (Harvard University Press, 2005), 92. Both Tia Basu ("Women Who Stutter: Media Depictions of Speech Impediments Are Usually of Men, Sidelining the Struggles of Women Who Stutter," *The Swaddle*, January 5, 2021) and Sophia Stewart ("Why Are Female Stutterers Such a Rarity in Literature?," *The Literary Hub*, April 2, 2019) separately note—and critique—the extreme disproportion of male and female stutterers in popular culture (stutterers are more likely to be male, but not nearly as much as in popular culture, where the proportion of male stutterers is close to 100 percent). Intriguingly, Jeffrey K. Johnson ("The Visualization of the Twisted Tongue: Portrayals of Stuttering in Film, Television, and Comic Books," *Journal of Popular Culture* 41, no. 2 [2008]: 245–61) does not appear to notice that all of the stutterers he discusses are male, an indication of how universally it is taken as a sign of specifically masculine weakness.

14. Elsa de' Giorgi, *Ho visto partire il tuo treno* (Feltrinelli, 2017), 36.

15. Chiara De Caprio, "Architettura," in *Le parole di Calvino*, ed. Matteo Motolese (Treccani, 2023), 17–30.

16. There are in fact some thirty-five wartime letters to Scalfari in the Meridiani edition of Calvino's letters (*Lettere, 1940–1985*), and they are (unsurprisingly) written in a direct, energetic, and colloquial style, but none of them is the letter that Perrella imagines.

17. We might recall that Benedetti, whose polemic against Calvino comes out the same year as Perrella's *Calvino*, refers to Calvino's "pulsione a . . . una voce fittizia" (107, drive toward a fictitious voice). Scarpa again repeats Perrella's language when he asserts that the wartime Calvino has "una voce che da lui non ascolteremo mai più: assoluta, frontale" (40, a voice that we'll never hear again from him: absolute, frontal).

18. Mutes are used on a number of instruments for special effects, but are probably best known with brass instruments, especially in jazz. A trumpet played with a mute, for example, has a mellower, less aggressively "brassy" sound. Ferrero also describes Calvino as placing his self "in sordina" (103, on mute), once again without mentioning Perrella.

19. James Butler, "Infinite Artichoke," *London Review of Books* 45, no 12, June 15, 2023, https://www.lrb.co.uk/the-paper/v45/n12/james-butler/infinite-artichoke.

20. Fabio Gambaro, *Lo scoiattolo sulla Senna: L'avventura di Calvino a Parigi* (Feltrinelli, 2023), 131.

21. Marc Matter, "Voices Up for Grabs," in *Grounds for Possible Music: On Gender, Voice, Language, and Identity*, ed. Julia Eckhardt (Errant Bodies, 2018), 51.

22. Cathy Lane, "Women as Animal, Women as Alien," in Eckardt, *Grounds for Possible Music*, 102.

23. Simon Ravens, *The Supernatural Voice: A History of High Male Singing* (Boydell, 2014), 183.

24. The suffix *-ista* is sometimes employed to designate a male singer who employs technique or artifice to sing in a given register, so that a *contraltista* or *sopranista* (male) is to be contrasted to a contralto or soprano (female), who sings in that range naturally. This is not true of the falsettist, however, since falsetto as a register is so strongly associated with the male voice. The effect of this usage is to assert a difference between what one *is* (a soprano) and what one *does* (a sopranist), a difference that once again suggests that there is an inauthenticity or artificiality to the "falsettist."

25. Susan McClary, *Feminine Endings: Music, Gender, and Sexuality* (University of Minnesota Press, 1991), 77.

26. Michel Chion, *Audio-Vision: Sound on Screen*, ed. and trans. Claudia Gorbman (Columbia University Press, 1994), 63.

27. Perrella returns to the lack of Calvino's "frontal" engagement throughout the book (see also 92, for example).

28. In Baldi's impressively encyclopedic *The Author in Criticism: Italo Calvino's Authorial Image* (Fairleigh Dickinson University Press, 2022), he mentions work in queer studies and disability, but his footnote is to two articles on disability. There does not appear to have been any work on queer Calvino until very recently (I know Alessandro Giammei has done some work in this direction), something that I hope this chapter and the one on jazz will change.

29. The original draft of Calvino's account of this experience (before he excised the reference to hemorrhoids) can be found today in *Lettere a Chichita, 1962–1963*, 33–45.

30. Calvino is quite clear that the ghosts in "Cibernetica e fantasmi" (*Saggi*, 205–25), for example, are the Freudian unconscious, as are the shadowy negative spaces of the *ubagu* (the opaque) in the essay "Dall'opaco" (*Romanzi e racconti*, III:89–101). We will also return to Freud in chapter 4.

31. The almost exclusive interest in the retentive type is already visible in Freud himself, who uses the general phrase "the anal character" to refer to the first, retentive type, and devotes little attention to the second, in both "Transformations of Instinct" (1917) and "Character and Anal Erotism" (1908), the first essay in which he develops the idea.

32. I might observe in passing that the paragon of Enlightenment thinking whom Calvino knew very well, Diderot, makes much the same anticonformist, antirational-ist gesture in *Le neveu di Rameau* (tellingly, a work about music, the dark other of the Enlightenment), when the nephew suddenly bursts out in praise of the anal expulsive: "Le point important est d'aller aisément, librement, agréablement, copieusement, tous les soirs à la garde-robe: *O stercus pretiosum!*" (61, the important point is to go easily, freely, happily, copiously, to the bathroom every evening: *O stercus pretiosum!* [Latin, Oh, precious turd]).

33. Thanks to Rebecca Falkoff, who reminded me that this theme was in fact widespread in Calvino, and pointed me toward "La poubelle" as a site worth further exploration of this theme. For those who think that "La poubelle" is "just" about trash and not about the body's excretions, attend to the final pages in which reading itself becomes "alimento" (food) that must be processed by "un metabolismo mentale" (3:79, a mental metabolism), leaving us with an undeniable if unspoken conclusion about what writing constitutes.

34. Signs of Perrella's fantasy are everywhere, from his claim that Pasolini was Calvino's "alter ego" (38), to his statement in the preface to the second edition that Cal-vino's falsetto exerts a powerful "fascino" (ix, fascination), but that there is "un rischio che si corre frequentandolo a lungo: il rischio di contrarre il virus della virtualità" (ix, a risk one runs spending too much time with him: the risk of contracting the virus of virtuality).

35. Paolo Monelli, *Ombre cinesi: Scrittori al girarrosto* (Mondadori, 1965), 175. Calvino's colleague at Einaudi, Ernesto Ferrero, gives a quite different account in *Italo* of how Calvino dressed in those years, namely, like a government functionary with absolutely no ambition: shrunken jackets, gray sweaters, out-of-date ties in geomet-ric patterns and lifeless colors. The only thing distinctive about his sartorial choices were his enormous tie knots, as if to "sottolineare il fastidio di un ingombro assurdo" (122, underline the annoyance of an absurd encumbrance). Ferrero repeats Monelli's story, but expresses a certain incredulity. It hardly matters if Monelli's account was accurate or—as seems likely—not: The point is that something about this image of Calvino resonated with Italian critics. Indeed, it is rather astonishing that Perrella takes Monelli's description of Calvino seriously. It is at odds with all photographic evidence and Monelli's subtitle (*Scrittori al girarrosto*—Writers on the roasting spit) clearly indicates his portraits of writers should be understood as polemical rather than factual. (As an indicator of his trustworthiness, Monelli also states flatly that Calvino's nurse in Cuba was a black cannibal [175], a claim astonishing, in equal parts, for its racism and its absurdity.)

36. Dumayet, evidently baffled by this response, appears to mutter "yes" in English, and ends the interview.

2 / An Echo-Logical Opera (in Headphones)

1. Richard Lord, "Hong Kong Architect William Lim and the Italo Calvino Novel That Changed His Life, *Invisible Cities*," *South China Morning Post*, August 4, 2018.

2. The unit was based on a seminar of the Yale National Initiative's National Fellows, and features ten articles by public school teachers covering multilingualism, disability, the intersections between geography and history, recovering the stories of lost communities, and more.

3. Except for Chowdhury's *Moving Cities*, I have not included these in the more formal bibliography, but Patricia Slavinski's *Invisible Cities* Gingerbread House Contest was in 2015 (twitter.com/msslavinski/status/677974734747774976); David Fleck does not give dates for his works, but they can be seen at davidfleck.co.uk/invisible-cities; Colleen Corradi Brannigan also does not date her work, although I've followed it for at least ten years (www.cittainvisibili.com/); Liu Wei has worked on her *Invisible Cities* sculptures for the last fifteen years, and brought them to the United States in 2019 (medium.com/cma-thinker/beijing-to-cleveland-liu-wei-reveals-invisible-cities-to -us-e681ac91506); Diana Al-Hadid's sculptures are from 2012–13 (www.dianaalhadid .com/exhibitions); Nadia Lakhani's *Invisible Cities* installation is from 2011 (www .nadialakhani.com/invisible-cities.html); Zoey Liangzhang's book design is undated (zoeyliangzhang.com/invisible-cities); and the Hotel Tres Sants in Menorca has recently redecorated and eliminated its *Invisible Cities* theme, but images of the original design from 2004 can still be found (www.architectureweek.com/2004/0121/design_1 -1.html).

4. Sonja Dragovic, "Discovering Calvino's 'Invisible Cities' in Brussels: September Salon 2017 (Part 1)," 4Cities website, October 5, 2017.

5. The 2011 Bucci and Kabutakapua documentary *(In)visible Cities* should not be confused with the 2009 documentary film by Hubert Davis, *Invisible City*, about the plight of young Black men in Toronto's Regent Park neighborhood. One can certainly see in the impulse behind both, however, that referring to Calvino's novel is an obvious gesture when discussing dispersed or marginalized groups that can be thought of as a city of their own.

6. The rhetoric of Calvino as visual is surprisingly pervasive, with a writer like Daniele Del Giudice referring to Calvino simply as "l'occhio che scrive" (the eye who writes; "L'occhio che scrive," in *Italo Calvino: Enciclopedia; arte, scienza e letteratura*, ed. Marco Belpoliti, [Marcos y Marcos, 1995], 176–79). Franco Ricci offers a more evenhanded rhetoric in his approach to the topic; he explores the visual, but is also very much aware of the "default concept" of Calvino as an author exclusively dominated by "one signifying structure: sight" (*Painting with Words, Writing with Pictures: Word and Image in the Work of Italo Calvino* [University of Toronto Press, 2001], 43). On the Italian side, Tommaso Pomilio ("Scrittura dell'ascolto: Calvino in Berio," in *Le théâtre musical de Luciano Berio: Actes de six journées d'études qui ont eu lieu à Paris et à Venise entre 2010 et 2013*, vol. 2, ed. Giordano Ferrari [L'Harmattan, 2016]) agrees that vision is, for Calvino, "fra i sensi, quello privilegiato" (137, the privileged among the senses), but argues that hearing has a dominant role—but dominant in the musical sense (*la dominante*), the V chord that in tonal harmony gives the strongest suggestion of tension (especially with an added seventh), longing to return to the root of I, the tonic; hearing is not so much the repressed, but rather the background field that allows the visual to take on such prominence. The insistence on Calvino as an eye, and as the author of an exclusively visual literature, however, has not diminished in most recent

criticism; Alberto Carli (*L'occhio e la voce: Pier Paolo Pasolini e Italo Calvino fra lettera-tura e antropologia* [Edizioni ETS, 2018]) repeats Carla Benedetti's claim that Calvino is "un occhio che osserva" (Carli, 9, an eye that observes; 144 in Benedetti, *Pasolini contro Calvino: Per una letteratura impura* [Bollati Boringhieri, 1998]), and the aptly named Andrea Mirabile argues that critics have not appreciated Calvino's visuality enough (*Piaceri invisibili: Retorica della cecità in D'Annunzio, Pasolini, Calvino* [Carocci editore, 2017], 30). By contrast, however, we should note not only Adriana Cavarero's work on Calvino and sound, but Ulla Musarra-Schrøder, who explores all five senses in Calvino's works, including a substantial section on sound (*Italo Calvino tra i cinque sensi* [F. Cesati, 2010], 115–88).

7. The obsessive critical identification of Pasolini with his voice (references to the "voce rauca" [hoarse voice] or "voce corsara" [pirate voice] are frequent in Pasolini criticism) is almost as symptomatic as that of Calvino with the eye.

8. I will generally give citations from Lacoue-Labarthe in the English translation, "The Echo of the Subject," in *Typography: Mimesis, Philosophy, Politics*, ed. Christopher Fynsk (Harvard University Press, 1989), 130–207; when I cite in French, the page numbers refer to the original French publication in *Le sujet de la philosophie: Typographies 1* (Aubier-Flammarion, 1979), 217–303.

9. For a scientific account of the "added information" to the echo, see Allan D. Pierce: "When a sound wave strikes a surface . . . , a reflected wave, or *echo*, results whose nature depends on the characteristics of the surface and of the adjoining substances" (115); in other words, every reflected sound carries information about the medium it is passing through, about the material it has struck, and about the materials that comprise the nearby space. That said, the majority of textbooks on acoustics tend to follow the historical arc that Emily Thompson describes, which is that, from the 1930s onward, we have tended to view reverberation as a nuisance in need of elimination: Stanley A. Gelfland (2010), for example, concentrates exclusively on how reverberation decreases speech comprehension or creates illusions in binaural hearing (which in fact depends on echoes in order to locate sound sources in space).

10. Brandon LaBelle, *Background Noise: Perspectives on Sound Art*, 2nd ed. (Bloomsbury, 2015), xi.

11. This would include the eerie sounds produced in anechoic chambers, which are sealed off from external sounds and have no reverberations at all, and hence are so quiet that you can hear your own blood flow (some have claimed they can hear the high-pitched electrical whine of their own nervous system, which I did not experience). What I can say from personal experience is that an anechoic chamber has an *extremely* distinct acoustic signature, a distinct (if eerie) sound of place, and not "no sound of place."

12. Emily Thompson, *The Soundscape of Modernity: Architectural Acoustics and the Culture of Listening in America, 1900–1933* (MIT Press, 2002), 3. Thompson's larger argument is that reverberation becomes increasingly undesirable, a characteristic of old buildings perhaps suited only to old music, and that the electronic era separates reverberation from space as reverb is introduced, modulated, and controlled artificially. It is certainly true that both transmission and recording of sound make extensive use of artificially controlled reverberation (modern music recording programs offer an effectively infinite range of possible reverberation characteristics), but after almost 100 years of listening to artificial reverberation, we still hear every reverberation as the sound of a given space—in other words, reverberation is space, whether it is created artificially or not.

13. The subtitle of Luca Di Bari's *Lo scoiattolo della penna* encapsulates this prevailing view perfectly: *Profilo di Italo Calvino dall'impegno politico alla rottura con il PCI* (Profile of Italo Calvino, from political engagement to the break with the PCI). The book (which is quite good) simply presumes as a tacit given that there can be no political commitment after a break with the Party. You are either politically committed to the Italian Communist Party, or you have given up on politics.

14. Lucia Re, "Pasolini vs. Calvino, One More Time: The Debate on the Role of Intellectuals and Postmodernism in Italy Today," *MLN* 129, no. 1 (2014): 99–117; Carla Benedetti, *Pasolini contro Calvino: Per una letteratura impura* (Bollati Boringhieri, 1998); Alessia Ricciardi, *After "La Dolce Vita": A Cultural Prehistory of Berlusconi's Italy* (Stanford University Press, 2012). An overview of the question of Italian "postmodern" writers and political commitment can be found in Jennifer Burns, *Fragments of Impegno: Interpretations of Commitment in Contemporary Italian Narrative, 1980–2000* (Northern Universities Press, 2001), with a more explicitly positive assessment in Pierpaolo Antonello and Florian Mussgnug, eds., *Postmodern Impegno: Ethics and Commitment in Contemporary Italian Culture* (Peter Lang, 2009). See, in that latter volume, Orsetta Innocenti's essay which posits even Calvino's later work as displaying a fundamental political commitment.

15. At first glance, it would appear that artificially generated voices like Siri, Apple's digital assistant, are a counter-example, but they in fact prove the point: We readily identify the gender, race, and geographical background of the voice—so much so that Apple provides male, female, and nonbinary voices, including voices that are coded as African American, not to mention Australian, British, and so on. We might not recognize as readily the physical space in which Siri is speaking, but I do: Siri is speaking in a professional sound studio, close-miked, with no audible reverberation. The absence of reverberation still marks a sound as taking place in a particular space.

16. Guido Almansi, "Il mondo binario di Italo Calvino." *Paragone,* no. 258 (1971): 95–110; Marco Belpoliti, *L'occhio di Calvino* (Einaudi, 1996) clearly admires Calvino very much, but this rhetoric is still surprisingly pervasive. Franco Ricci, *Painting with Words, Writing with Pictures: Word and Image in the Work of Italo Calvino* (University of Toronto Press, 2001) offers a more even-handed rhetoric in his approach to the topic—he explores the visual, but is also very much aware of the "default concept" of Calvino as an author exclusively dominated by "one signifying structure: sight" (43).

17. As Benedetti says, Calvino is "spaventato dalla complessità e dalle angosce del mondo" (frightened by the complexity and anguish of the world) and "finisce per rifugiarsi" (ends up seeking shelter) inside the comforting limits of his postmodern, self-reflective literary world (135).

18. Although the amount varies depending on the type of music, the normal range for reverberation time in concert halls "runs from 1.8 to 2.1 seconds" (Nina Sun Eidsheim, *Sensing Sound: Singing and Listening as Vibrational Practice* [Duke University Press, 2015], 64); although not every famous venue falls precisely into this range, most do. In her overview of the history of concert hall acoustics, Eidsheim ably shows how the rise of opera drove this "idealized" length of reverberation—longer echo times made the words unintelligible (62).

19. Modern digital reverb uses very few parameters to model a space: How much reverb vs. the original source (so-called wet and dry), how distant are the reflections, how close is the source of the sound, and what are the harmonic properties of the reflection (is more low-frequency reflected? More high-frequency?). Along with a few

other acoustic properties (like stereo panning—that is, whether the sound is located left, center, or right in the stereo field), it is almost entirely reverberation that gives us our sense of space in recorded music. This is my third mantra: "reverberation is space."

20. I've used several sources for Cerrone's opera, all of which are listed in the bibliography. It was performed in New York in 2009–10 in a rather different format, but attracted major media attention when it was restaged and reimagined in 2013 in Los Angeles in collaboration with The Industry, an experimental opera company headed by Yuval Sharon; a filmed version (directed by Joris Debeij, blending performance footage from the final LA performance with a staged version without an audience) was released on DVD, along with a sound recording of the work on CD (it is currently also available on most major streaming platforms). I have also consulted the score from the Library of Congress (a piano reduction with eight voices written out).

21. Erika Nadir observes that Cerrone is greatly influenced by Janet Cardiff's "audio walks" (which are something like a combination audio guide tour for a specific site and a soundtrack for the walk), and that a significant concern for both Cerrone and Sharon in staging the opera was making the actors mobile ("Prima la musica o prima la parola? Textual and Musical Intermedialities in Italian Literature and Film" [PhD diss., UCLA, 2017], 174–75).

22. Cerrone is a highly literate and literary composer with global tastes, referencing Borges, Rilke, Brecht, Calvino, Akutagawa, Franzen, Melville, and contemporary American poetry and prose (including the inimitable Lydia Davis), among others, in his compositions.

23. On the term "postminimalism," see Tristian Evans, *Shared Meanings in the Film Music of Philip Glass: Music, Multimedia and Postminimalism* (Ashgate, 2015), who has a nice overview of how the term came into use and scholarly debates around it, 5–11; Evans also contends that postminimalist music is much more associated with multimedia, including opera (13). Readers may be struck by a significant overlap between minimalist/postminimalist compositional techniques and the techniques that Calvino championed, particularly additive and subtractive processes and combinatorial techniques, both of which are especially visible in the complex and much-discussed structure of *Invisible Cities*. There have been some attempts to draw parallels between the minimalism/postminimalism divide and that of modernism/postmodernism (see Evans, 13–15), but the two divisions appear to map onto each other somewhat poorly, referring to quite different times and even styles. To take one obvious example of the poor fit, both minimalism and postminimalism are equally serious and sincere, untouched by postmodern irony; to take another clear example, no one would call the indisputably modernist *Finnegans Wake* "minimalist."

24. Dynamic markings indicate that the name is to be pronounced with a distinct "fade" each time, which enhances the echoing effect.

25. Cerrone says (personal communication) that this reference was "neither intentional nor unintentional," but that several of the singers also remarked on it. Although it does not appear in the score, the sound recording of the opera includes at this point the sound of waves, meant to recall Venice—or perhaps a backyard pool?

26. Eidsheim is absolutely correct to say that there are two acoustic worlds in conflict, but to some degree, this tension is also a tension between the visual and the acoustic—the idealized mix is not congruent with what I *see* (there are no instrumentalists in this space, just a singer), or I am witnessing a performance that is consistent but strangely partial. In this regard, the opera's experience of sound is in many ways

most reminiscent of film sound, with both "onscreen" and "offscreen" sources for sound, music that is both diegetic (being produced within the performance) and extradiegetic (coming from "outside," another, unseen dimension).

27. See, for example, Thor Steingraber, who says that at the end of the opera, he "removed [his] headset to hear the vocal harmonies reverberate live throughout the cavernous space. Relieved of the headset, [he] indulged in an unmediated musical experience that provided a moving closure to the performance" (https://artsmeme.com/2013/11/04/opera-occupies-union-station/, accessed May 17, 2019). See also Eidsheim, 87–90, on the constant choice between wearing and not wearing the headphones.

28. Shuhei Hosokawa, "The Walkman Effect," *Popular Music* 4 (1984): 175, and Michael Bull, *Sound Moves: iPod Culture and Urban Experience* (Routledge, 2007), 40.

29. Cerrone has in fact experimented with some of these unreal reverberations, as in the piano and electronics piece "Hoyt-Schermerhorn"—in the piece's second half, the performer utilizes electronic processing to give certain notes a massive reverb that eventually, after a long delay, begins to produce crackling repetitions, as if some distant cavern wall made of an exotic reflective material were repeating the note in its own voice.

30. See Christopher Cerrone and Tim Munro, "Rebuilding the Flute: Christopher Cerrone and Tim Munro Discuss 'Liminal Highway,'" *Classical Post*, August 21, 2020, classicalpost.com/read/chris-cerrone-and-tim-munro-liminal-highway. For the composition he discusses here, Cerrone made use of the longest-ever "naturally" produced reverb, about seventy seconds long; the echo was produced by firing a pistol inside enormous empty oil tanks.

31. Cerrone utilizes the sound of amplified human breathing in other works, as well, such as the wordless "How to Breathe Underwater," for male voice, clarinet, trumpet, trombone, and electronics. The end of the piece features the players blowing quietly through their instruments but without sounding notes, creating a pulse of rising and falling breath sounds.

32. The sound of an instrument will change depending on how far away the microphone is, and listeners are especially sensitive to this when it comes to voices. A close microphone, no reverb, and a whisper will tend to sound through headphones like someone is literally whispering in your ear, a sound that might be perceived as intimate or intrusive, depending on the context. Close miking is typical of so-called ASMR ("autonomous sensory meridian response") sounds that are supposed to promote a pleasurable relaxation.

33. In the audio recording of the opera, the "offstage" or "prerecorded" voices of Marco Polo and Kublai Khan are awash in reverb and faint, so they sound as if they are singing in a distant, cavernous space. They are also—unlike their voices normally— panned to one side or the other of the stereo mix, with Marco Polo on the right and Kublai Khan on the left, reinforcing the impression that they are "off stage." In the film of the opera, sometimes the camera uses these moments to explore Union Station (such as a female singer who stands, silent and motionless, in the center of the South Patio), and at other times, we actually see, say, Marco Polo, but visibly not singing even though we are hearing his voice.

34. Michel Chion, *Audio-Vision: Sound on Screen*, ed. and trans. Claudia Gorbman (Columbia University Press, 1994), 32, 71–73.

35. Serenella Iovino, *Gli animali di Calvino: Storie dall'Antropocene* (Treccani, 2023); Monica Seger, *Landscapes in Between: Environmental Change in Modern Italian*

Literature and Film (University of Toronto Press, 2015), 24–49; Adele Sanna, "The Hybrid 'Biocitizen' in Italo Calvino's *Marcovaldo or The Seasons in the City*," in *Ecocritical Approaches to Italian Culture and Literature: The Denatured Wild*, ed. Pasquale Verdicchio (Lexington Books, 2016); Angela M. Jeannet, *Under the Radiant Sun and the Crescent Moon: Italo Calvino's Storytelling* (University of Toronto Press, 2000), 134–54.

36. This is a long-standing problem (see Karin Bijsterveld, "Listening to Machines: Industrial Noise, Hearing Loss and the Cultural Meaning of Sound," *Interdisciplinary Science Reviews* 31, no. 4 (2006): 323–37 for an overview, both of the history of factory-induced deafness as well as the unexpected cultural value that it can have) that continues today: The National Institute for Occupational Safety and Health estimates that about 20 percent of manufacturing workers have hearing loss (likely related to the 24 percent of manufacturing workers who don't wear ear protection).

3 / A Jazz *Cosmicomics*

1. Ildiko Nemeth, quoted in Andy Horwitz, "Talking to Ildiko Nemeth About *Cosmicomics*," interview with Katy Einerson, *Culturebot: Maximum Performance*, March 31, 2014, www.culturebot.org/2014/03/21475/talking-to-ildiko-nemeth-about -cosmicomics/.

2. For Cavarero, the power of the voice is precisely in that it is a voice before it says anything at all, and its gesture toward sound (*phone*) rather than meaning (*logos*) indicates a repression of the material body's individual existence prior to discourse. That said, I would add a grain of salt that comes from my first chapter, on Calvino's voice; claims that sound is nonsemantic have a heuristic or pedagogical point, but they also all suffer from the same blind spot. Yes, a distorted electric guitar means things like rock and roll, rebellion, youthful energy, anger, while an exquisitely gentle and rounded Bösendorfer grand piano means "classical music"—but it also means money (they run from nearly $100,000 to almost half a million), class, privilege, Europe, etc. Vibrations may exist "by themselves," but sounds are always *heard* within a social milieu marked by race, class, gender, sexual orientation and other categories, and thus they mean all kinds of things, even when they don't precisely intend to.

3. In fact, the title of the symphony was in flux for some time, since Beethoven originally dedicated it to Napoleon, but was infuriated when Napoleon crowned himself emperor. One might always mis-read the title and imagine something very different—for years I was convinced that Beethoven's Third Symphony was known as the "Erotica."

4. Both Ellington albums feature a sincere interest in their subject matter, as well as a distinct jazz playfulness, a point I'll return to later. Track 3 of *Such Sweet Thunder* (the title is a citation from *A Midsummer Night's Dream*) is "Sonnet to Hank Cinq," a playful reference to Shakespeare's history play *Henry V*—one that plays across languages and cultural levels, since the English name "Hank" (an informal version of Henry) in fact rhymes with the French pronunciation of "cinq," the number five. *Suite Thursday* is already a play on the title of Steinbeck's novel *Sweet Thursday*, but the third movement of the suite continues this phonetic play, now in a buzzing, even more playful key: "Zweet Zurzday."

5. In the game, the detective (No Man) is in love with Miss Mass, who is tragically lost (indeed, murdered) in the Big Bang, and he strives to rewind the universe to its

initial state in order to get her back; Miss Mass is a jazz singer, and her killer (and former lover) is the saxophonist known as Golden Boy. Gameplay includes numerous acoustic elements (getting musicians to play, adjusting the resonant frequencies of the universe, playing specific notes, and so on).

6. There is general critical agreement that jazz is too historically varied for anything like a definition, but most critics agree that improvisation and rhythmic complexity (particularly swing) are among the most frequent and important elements (see Jonny King, *What Jazz Is: An Insider's Guide to Understanding and Listening to Jazz* (Walker, 1997), 5, 14; or Richard Lawn, *Experiencing Jazz*, 2nd ed. (Routledge, 2013), 7 on improvisation and swing as an often cited "core" of jazz). It's worth saying that my own musical experience is almost entirely in classical music and popular (rock) music. I understand some of the basics of jazz intellectually, but do not play it, and I'm sure that affects my expectations and analysis here.

7. Avril Dankworth, *Jazz: An Introduction to Its Musical Basis* (Oxford University Press, 1968).

8. As Gabriel Solis notes in *Monk's Music: Thelonious Monk and Jazz History in the Making* (University of California Press, 2007), the humorous and playful character of jazz, so evident to listeners and so evident in performances, is nonetheless understated (often dramatically) by musicologists who historically felt "the very real need to argue for the seriousness and intellectual rigor of jazz" (54) when it was regarded as "less" than classical music, a concern made more fraught by "racial stereotypes" (55) that inform the reception of jazz as an art form with deep African American roots. Solis discusses (49–56) both well-known examples of playful humor in jazz (Dizzy Gillespie) and the more complex negotiation of seriousness and play in Thelonious Monk.

9. For a much more literal version of this, see Stephon Alexander's *The Jazz of Physics* (Basic Books, 2016), in which he argues from the perspective of a theoretical physicist and jazz musician that there are deep analogies between theoretical physics and music, especially jazz.

10. Natalie Berkman, "Italo Calvino's Oulipian Clinamen," *MLN* 135, no .1 (2020): 255–80.

11. See in particular the essay "Cibernetica e fantasmi" (Cybernetics and ghosts) in *Saggi* (205–25), where Calvino affirms that a machine using statistical information and combinatorial logic (such as contemporary LLM, or Large Language Models like ChatGPT) could produce *writing*, but without an unconscious, it could not produce *literature*.

12. Dennis Duncan, "Calvino, Llull, Lucretius: Two Models of Literary Combinatorics," *Comparative Literature* 64, no. 1 (2012): 93–109; but see Calvino's letter to Sergio Solmi of November 6, 1977 (*Lettere*, 1353–55), where he gives some guidance about translating Raymond Queneau's *Petite cosmogonie portative*, a text that—like the *Cosmicomics*—imagines fantastic, farcical, and half-scientific, half-mythological origins of the world, life, the moon, etc. Calvino explains to Solmi why Queneau writes "l'immortel tartigrade" (the immortal *tartigrade* [*sic*]) rather than the correct spelling (as in English) "tardigrade": "direi che è solo una deformazione burlesca alla Jarry, da *tarte* o meglio ancora da *tartir* (in argot = cacare)" (*Lettere*, 1354, I'd say this is just a burlesque deformation in the style of Jarry, from *tarte* [cake] or better still from *tartir* (in French slang = to shit) [parentheses in original]). Once again, the switch of a single letter introduces the comic and scatological into the cosmological, and one is left with an immortal turdigrade.

13. The album received a fair amount of (positive) critical attention, and was featured on NPR's *Fresh Air* with jazz critic Kevin Whitehead.

14. Happily, this visual arrangement of the letter l's in the word "parallel" is the same in English and Italian.

15. Elio Baldi, "La sfida al labirinto sessuale: L'eros nell'opera di Italo Calvino," *Incontri* 27, no. 2 (2012): 60–68.

16. Benedetti's polemic against Calvino, *Pasolini contro Calvino: Per una letteratura impura*, from 1998, is careful—perhaps a little too careful—to avoid an explicit contrast of the two authors' sexuality (the only mention of Pasolini's homosexuality is inside a parenthesis in a footnote [14]), but her terms for discussing Calvino are nonetheless loaded; if Calvino has any sexuality outside the desire for a permanent "verginità artistica," it is a desire for death, from Calvino's "concezione cimiteriale della letteratura" (20, idea of literature as a cemetery) to his use of style, "un uso necrofilo" (53, a necrophiliac use). Hume—generally an astute and sympathetic reader of Calvino—in "Sensuality and the Senses in Calvino's Fiction," *MLN* 107, no. 1 (1992): 160–77, refers to Calvino's lifelong aversion to and fear of sexuality, while concluding it undergoes something of a shift when he works on his stories about the senses. Neither author ever offers any evidence for this supposed fear of sexuality—it is simply assumed as a given that any reasonable reader would see is intuitively true.

17. This reading is already complex enough, but I would be remiss if I didn't point out that much of the story is surprisingly structured by acoustic motifs, from Fenimore's tuneless whistling to the cries of pain and pleasure during the various erotic encounters that are—or are not—in unison.

18. Tommasina Gabriele, *Italo Calvino: Eros and Language* (Fairleigh Dickinson University Press, 1996), 38.

19. Domenico Scarpa, *Calvino fa la conchiglia: La costruzione di uno scrittore* (Hoepli, 2023), 529.

20. Pierpaolo Antonello, *Il ménage a quattro: Scienza, filosofia, tecnica nelle letteratura italiana del Novecento* (Le Monnier, 2005), 170.

21. Locrian is the rarest mode in music, the only mode with a fifth scale degree that is not a perfect fifth. Its root chord is thus neither major nor minor, but *diminished*, which is generally dissonant and eerie sounding, at least on its own. This unsettled sound evokes an unsettled acoustic universe, one with energy that will eventually seek resolution, but whose resolution may not be simple or easy.

4 / Desires and Fears: *Silent City*

1. Mimma was an ideal guide for many reasons, not least because she is very attuned to sound. As we proceeded through an ancient subterranean church, she commented on the acoustic properties of each room; before entering one chamber, she said it would be different and challenged me to figure out how. Remarkably, the next chamber we entered had virtually no reverberation at all, and was almost as dead as a modern anechoic chamber.

2. In English, the link between "city" and "citizen" is visible, but perhaps less evident than in the Italian *città* and *cittadino*. The word suggests the city much more strongly than the nation.

3. Michael Spitzer, "Hearing Postmemory" in *The Routledge Companion to Popular Music Analysis: Expanding Approaches* (Routledge, 2018), 401.

4. Marianne Hirsch, *The Generation of Postmemory: Writing and Visual Culture after the Holocaust* (Columbia University Press, 2012), 163.

5. In Italy, this territory can also be called "opera popolare," which nicely captures the mix of popular elements within a more elevated framework.

6. See Laura Parola Sarti, *Invito alla lettura di Rocco Scotellaro* (Mursia, 1992), 109–10, 113–14; and Dante Della Terza, introduction to *The Dawn Is Always New: Selected Poetry of Rocco Scotellaro*, trans. Ruth Feldman and Brian Swann (Princeton University Press, 1980), 7.

7. This emphatic rhythm is typical of pieces that are danced to, essentially all the portions of *Silent City* with vocals. Ali Farah uses a variety of metrical and poetic forms in the libretto, from hendecasyllables in *terza rima* (the form Dante uses throughout the *Divine Comedy*) to *settenari*, or seven-syllable lines that are also typical in Italian poetry. Ali Farah was at UCLA for a talk (April 12, 2024) on her latest novel appearing in translation, and we had the chance to discuss *Silent City* on that occasion.

8. Nigel Osborne, "Neuroscience and 'Real World' Practice: Music as a Therapeutic Resource for Children in Zones of Conflict," *Annals of the New York Academy of Sciences* 1252, no. 1 (2012): 69.

9. Cauzillo and I talked at several points in Matera, but in this chapter, I'm referring to our only formal sit-down conversation when we talked for about an hour about *Silent City* (December 14, 2023).

10. It is hard to overstate how unusual this is in Italy, where ancient infrastructure and uneven development make something like a universal Disabilities Act extremely challenging.

11. Benjamin Linder, *"Invisible Cities" and the Urban Imagination* (Palgrave Macmillan, 2022).

12. Georges Perec, "Approaches to What?," in *Species of Spaces and Other Pieces*, ed. and trans. John Sturrock (Penguin Books, 1999).

13. Guy Debord, "Theory of the Dérive," in *Situationist International Anthology*, rev. ed., ed. and trans. Ken Knabb (Bureau of Public Secrets, 2006). In its own way, the *dérive* (literally drift) is strongly similar to Lucretius's clinamen discussed in chapter 3—an unexpected and even irrational swerve away from the established and expected geometries of urban spacetime. Both are based on a disruption to the straight line, the obvious direct path.

14. The French *dérive* comes from precisely the same fluid metaphor as "derivative" (literally "from the river," here referring to motion away from the intended course alongside the riverbank).

15. Mladen Dolar, *A Voice and Nothing More* (MIT Press, 2006), 130–39.

16. Michel Chion, *Audio-Vision: Sound on Screen*, ed. and trans. Claudia Gorbman (Columbia University Press, 1994), 25–28.

17. During our conversation, Cauzillo told me the story of Mimmo, one of the older citizens of Matera who participated in the communal work on the opera (he served as the model for the character Domenico in the opera) and who was a child during the forced relocation. Rocco was based on one of Mimmo's childhood friends who limped, and who died in childhood.

5 / Dancing About Architecture

1. The epigraph to this chapter has been attributed to all manner of musical figures (Miles Davis, Thelonious Monk, Frank Zappa, David Byrne, Elvis Costello, and Laurie Anderson, among others) as well as comedians (George Carlin, Martin Mull, Steve Martin). Versions of it, however, were already in popular circulation at the start of the twentieth century. In all instances, however, it is meant to ridicule the idea that

one can *speak* meaningfully about music, whose experience is supposed to be purely sensual and emotional, and not semantic, and to make the point, the maxim turns to realms that are apparently even more comically incompatible: dance and architecture. Evidently, both of these realms of cultural expression are even more irreducible to logical analysis and the production of meaning. In this chapter, however, I am *still* writing about music, at the end of a whole book about the relationship of music to the written word, but now I am writing about the music of a dance that is incontestably based on a book very much about architecture, *Invisible Cities*. Why is it that we take it for granted that the visual image immediately submits to a semantic analysis, but that sound and the body resist it? At the conclusion of this chapter, however, I hope you will agree with me that not only *can* one dance about architecture, but it is possible that one can't dance about anything else.

2. Wayne Alan Brenner, "Sky Candy Takes on Italo Calvino's COSMICOMICS," *Austin Chronicle*, June 18, 2014, www.austinchronicle.com/daily/arts/2014-06-18/sky -candy-takes-on-italo-calvinos-cosmicomics/.

3. Jeff Davis, "A Chat with Joanna Wright on Sky Candy's COSMICOMICS," *Broadway World*, June 24, 2014, www.broadwayworld.com/austin/article/BWW-Interviews -A-Chat-with-Joanna-Wright-on-Sky-Can.

4. "Baron in the Trees," *New Grounds*, February 17, 2023; "Internationally-Acclaimed Lost in Translation Circus Swing into 10th Anniversary Year with Exciting London Tour," *Theatre Weekly*, May 21, 2021, https://theatreweekly.com/internationally -acclaimed-lost-in-translation-circus-swing-into-10th-anniversary-year-with-exciting -london-tour/.

5. For the record, the robot, a Unimation PUMA 560 model designed for both industrial and surgical operations, portrayed Kublai Khan (as in Chris Cerrone's opera, Kublai Khan was limited in movement); the robot used was nicknamed "Howard." Brenda Way was the choreographer, and Gayle Curtis handled the robotics. The entire performance is archived at Michael McNabb's website.

6. See the Moving Cities website, https://www.moving-cities.com/. Chowdhury's dance films express a powerful sense of both energetic vitality and the many different spaces in the cities he selects.

7. See the 59Productions website, 59productions.co.uk/project/invisible-cities/, as well as Sanjoy Roy's review in *The Guardian*, "Fantasy, Folly and Fancy Footwork: Cosmic Dance Comes to Manchester," *Guardian*, July 7, 2019.

8. "Dance Theater: 'Invisible Cities 2.022,'" *Smart Shanghai*, May 2023, accessed May 27, 2023, www.smartshanghai.com/event/72985.

9. Jerome Lewis, "A Cross-Cultural Perspective on the Significance of Music and Dance to Culture and Society: Insight from BaYaka Pygmies," in *Language, Music, and the Brain: A Mysterious Relationship*, ed. Michael A. Arbib (MIT Press, 2013), 46.

10. Ethan Philbrick, *Group Works: Art, Politics, and Collective Ambivalence* (Fordham University Press, 2023), 28, 31.

11. John Martin, *The Modern Dance* (Dance Horizons, 1935), 13.

12. Karen Barbour and Alexandra Hitchmough, "Experiencing Affect Through Site-Specific Dance," *Emotion, Space and Society* 12, no. 1 (2014): 63–72. The notion of a kinesthetic empathy between dancer and audience is extremely widespread, especially among practicing dancers and choreographers; see Karen Barbour, for example, who says that her "choreographic strategies were to use gestural, pedestrian or everyday movement designed to enhance kinesthetic empathy with the dancer" (*Dancing Across

the Page: Narrative and Embodied Ways of Knowing [Intellect, 2011], 76), with the ultimate goal of creating a meaning that has a personal resonance for the viewer. Graham McFee, writing as a philosopher of dance, rejects the idea as hopelessly subjective, allowing anything that is "brought to mind" by a movement to be equally valid (*Understanding Dance* [Routledge, 1992], 271–72). I think this largely misses the larger points that we know the world not only through our minds, but also through our bodies, and that feelings about art are at least as important as thoughts about art, which is not the same as saying they are all the same.

13. For a specific application of mirror neurons to dance (by way of philosopher Antonio Damasio), see Susan Pashman, "Feeling Is Movement: Damasio's Neural Model of Dance Expression," *Dance Research: The Journal of the Society for Dance Research* 35, no. 2 (2017): 258–73; for a broader discussion of mirror neurons, collective movement, and shared meaning, see Leonardo Fogassi, "Shared Meaning, Mirroring, and Joint Action," in *Language, Music, and the Brain: A Mysterious Relationship*, ed. Michael A. Arbib (MIT Press, 2013), who tellingly refers to these behaviors, along with many other scientists, as "resonance behaviors"; Fogassi also addresses dance directly (101–2), and its "capacity to resonate" (102) with its viewers.

14. The three women together are the Ragamala Dance Company. For the purposes of this chapter, if I say simply "Ramaswamy," I am referring to Ashwini Ramaswamy.

15. I've had the chance to talk with Ramaswamy in person about her work on several occasions, including a public forum on "dance and Calvino" at UCLA in 2023. I note in the text whenever I am quoting from her artist statements or programs—otherwise, quotations are from our conversations. I also had the opportunity to meet and talk with most of the other dancers, particularly Joe Tran.

16. See, for example, Laban Movement Analysis, which aims to give an abstract description of all the ways that the body can move, categorized by their movements (called "efforts") in *space* (direct or indirect), their *weight* (strong or light), their *time* (sudden or sustained), and their *flow* (bound or free, that is, a movement with a single, clear terminus vs. one that continues on). Laban analysis, in various forms, is used in dance, acting, music, athletics, and more. I don't use Laban terminology here, but it provides the kind of general framework that one could use to show the ways that different styles of dancing are both different and equivalent, in its etymological sense.

17. Sondra Fraleigh, "A Vulnerable Glance: Seeing Dance Through Phenomenology," *Dance Research Journal* 23, no. 1 (1991): 11.

18. Kerry Francksen, "The Implications of Technology in Dance: A Dancer's Perspective of Moving in Media-Rich Environments," in *Digital Echoes: Spaces for Intangible and Performance-Based Cultural Heritage*, ed. Sarah Whatley et al. (Palgrave, 2018), 58. Francksen's own position is that technology becomes part of the "vibrant life of the dance itself" (76), but certainly the Ramaswamy and Mourad collaboration preserves the sense of "liveness" that is so essential to the performing arts.

19. Dana Mills, *Dance and Politics: Moving Beyond Boundaries* (Manchester University Press, 2016), 3.

20. Is it ironic that the visual artist rejected the static image of the city as the inspirational source of the project, and turned instead to the more abstract formalism of Polo and Khan's conversations? Perhaps not: From the beginning, Mourad and Ramaswamy planned on making use of images in motion, images that the dancers could interact with, and that would respond to the dancers' movements. All of Mourad's images shift and change over time.

21. See, for example, the explanatory note that accompanies the table of contents in *Mr. Palomar* (2:872).

22. Alessia Ricciardi, "Lightness and Gravity: Calvino, Pynchon, and Postmodernity," *MLN* 114, no. 5 (1999): 1073–74.

23. Chiara De Caprio, "Architettura," in *Le parole di Calvino*, ed. Matteo Motolese (Treccani, 2023), 26.

24. One can foresee an immediate objection here, namely that kinesthetic sympathy implicitly depends on a normative body, and that it not only does not account for the disabled body, but even depends on rendering bodies that don't fulfill normative ideals (one with no legs, for example) absent and invisible. This is certainly true at first glance, but it depends enormously on the dance and on the dancers. That is, not every dance represents a body that is healthy and whole, and modern dance is perfectly capable of making me consider the ways that my body might limp, tremble, or stumble. It might very well bring me to recognize and feel my own body's disabilities, both potential and actual. Moreover, there are many dancers with disabilities whose movements surely make a wide variety of spectators feel a bodily kinship, even if we see them less often onstage. On disability and kinesthetic empathy, see Michelle Duffy et al., "Thresholds of Representation: Physical Disability in Dance and Perceptions of the Moving Body," in *Non-Representational Theory and the Creative Arts*, ed. Candice P. Boyd and Christian Edwardes (Palgrave Macmillan, 2019), who argue that, while kinesthetic empathy with the disabled dancer is perhaps less automatic for a normative audience, it is still very much possible (in many ways, however, it is the reverse situation that is perhaps more problematic: able-bodied dancers and disabled spectators).

25. Eugenie Brinkema, *Life-Destroying Diagrams* (Duke University Press, 2022), 65–68.

26. For different performances, Ramaswamy adapts the "maximalist" staging for the venue—for the 2024 performance at the Michael Kohler Center in Wisconsin, for example, the number of dancers was slightly reduced and the interactive layer of digital artistry was removed: that is, the live materials projected onto the front screen; the pre-made animations were still projected onto the rear screen. The length was the same, however, as was the mix of different dance styles, and with very few changes, the choreography as well. Irene Fiordilino's dance and multimedia production of *Invisible Cities* from 2021 is quite similar in its use of multimedia (music, dance, live drawing), but much, much smaller in scope: two dancers and an overhead projector. See Irene Fiordilino, "*Invisible Cities*: A Performative Adaptation," in *Circulation, Translation and Reception Across Borders: Italo Calvino's "Invisible Cities" Around the World*, ed. Elio Baldi and Cecilia Schwartz (Routledge, 2023), 245–55.

27. Scott Simon, "HBO's 'White Lotus' Soundtrack Haunts the Show and People's Lives." Cristobal Tapia de Veer, interviewed by Scott Simon, National Public Radio, *Weekend Edition*, August 21, 2021, www.npr.org/2021/08/21/1029957360/music-moment-white-lotus-composer.

28. Domenico Scarpa, *Calvino fa la conchiglia: La costruzione di uno scrittore* (Hoepli, 2023), 574.

29. "Negli ultimi anni, la letteratura di Calvino era diventata una cosmopolita esperienza narrativa" (in his later years, Calvino's literature had become a cosmopolitan narrative experience), notes Francesca Serra, *Calvino* (Salerno, 2006), 347—a cosmopolitan experience of the city, but also of space more generally.

30. Saraswati is part of the Tridevi, the female trinity that parallels the Trimurti of Brahma, Shiva, and Vishnu. The Tridevi (Saraswati, Lakshmi, and Parvati) are understood to be the wives, consorts, or perhaps the female forms of the Trimurti. Saraswati is associated with wisdom and the arts.

31. Rome's position as the nation's capital and largest city is complicated by its long history prior to the Risorgimento as a relatively poor and largely deserted provincial space (its population declined from over one million inhabitants in the ancient world to around 25,000 during the seventeenth century—it is just under 3 million today).

32. These larger categories have always had an unclear meaning, and as a result, evoke pure form more than anything else. The numbered sections of *Invisible Cities* do shape the novel into a clear beginning (section 1), middle (sections 2–8), and end (section 9), but there does not seem to be any special value to the number of cities (55), and many cities bear only a minimal relationship to the "category" they ostensibly belong to. Many scholars have suggested that the novel's fifty-five cities plus its nine sections sum to sixty-four, the number of squares on a chessboard (see, for example, Mario Barenghi's note in *Romanzi e racconti*, 2:1359), but this has always felt like a reading that is labored, unproductive, and ultimately rather implausible—surely Calvino would have chosen 64 cities if he had wanted to develop this structural analogy. Even if true, however, this too would gesture more toward pure form, form *as* form, rather than the form of a specific narrative or history. Somewhat more persuasive is Milanini's suggestion (125) that the fifty-five cities are a reference to the fifty-*four* cities in Sir Thomas More's *Utopia*, although this requires him to argue that Bauci, the center of the fifty-five cities, is in some sense a non-city, or an "empty" city. My own guess is that fifty-five cities and eleven categories are both arbitrary numbers that produced a set large enough for significant variations but small enough to not become tedious and labored; their greater value is in the attention they call to formal structure of the novel *as* form, not a reference to an external interpretive key.

33. See "L'italiano, una lingua tra le altre lingue" (*Saggi*, 146–53) and "L'antilingua" (*Saggi*, 154–59) for Calvino's part; the whole debate (in Italian), with many participants, was collected in Oronzo Parlangeli, *La nuova questione della lingua: Saggi raccolti da O. Parlangeli* (Paideia, 1971).

34. On the complex history of Bharatanatyam as a transnational dance form, see Avanthi Meduri, "Bharatanatyam as a Global Dance: Some Issues in Research, Teaching, and Practice," *Dance Research Journal* 36, no. 2 (2004), who laments that Bharatanatyam is often understood by scholars exclusively within a context of "Indian nationalism" and "local modernity" while in fact global modernity equally "defined the history and identity of Bharatanatyam since the nineteenth century, continuing into the present" (12). In reality, Meduri argues, Rukmini Devi conceived of Bharatanatyam in exactly the same way Westerners understand ballet (14), which is as a global dance form that "just happens" to have Italian, French, and Russian roots. Rumya Sree Putcha offers a very different (and largely negative) take on global Bharatanatyam in *The Dancer's Voice: Performance and Womanhood in Transnational India* (Duke University Press, 2023), where she sees it as the vehicle for the "gendered imperatives of Hindu nationalism" (91) that "cater to the white Euro-American gaze" (93)—in short, as a way of policing gender, race, and caste norms in a larger global context for a diasporic Indian community. This disagreement underlines a perpetual issue with the cosmopolitan impulse, namely that cosmopolitanism almost always means incorporating diversity,

but in a way that does not threaten dominant groups—a way that keeps it as a kind of luxury or privilege for dominant groups.

35. For the Kohler performance, the venue was not equipped with a front projection screen—the visuals were less complex as a result, but also at times clearer: The city does disappear, leaving only an increasingly majestic tree behind.

Coda: Invisible Dialogues

1. See Peter Szendy, "*Parole, parole:* Tautegory and Musicology of the (Pop) Song," in *Speaking of Music: Addressing the Sonorous,* ed. Keith Chapin and Andrew H. Clark (Fordham University Press, 2013), 186–92.

2. This is possible because strings, somewhat counterintuitively, actually vibrate not only across their whole length, but also at every integer division (½, ⅓, ¼, and so on) of that length. (These "fractional vibrations" produce the overtone series and are largely responsible for the distinctive timbre of the instrument.) If you lightly touch and quickly release a vibrating string at one of these nodal, integer division points, you will instantly hear a harmonic at a higher pitch.

Bibliography

Alexander, Stephon. *The Jazz of Physics.* Basic Books, 2016.

Almansi, Guido. "Il mondo binario di Italo Calvino." *Paragone,* no. 258 (1971): 95–110.

Angeleri, Claudio. *Music from the Castle of Crossed Destinies.* Dodicilune Music Ed507, 2021, compact disc.

Antonello, Pierpaolo. *Il ménage a quattro: Scienza, filosofia, tecnica nelle letteratura italiana del Novecento.* Le Monnier, 2005.

Antonello, Pierpaolo, and Florian Mussgnug, eds. *Postmodern Impegno: Ethics and Commitment in Contemporary Italian Culture.* Peter Lang, 2009.

St. Augustine. *Confessions.* Translated by Alfred Chadwick. Oxford University Press, 1991.

Aviram, Amittai F. *Telling Rhythm: Body and Meaning in Poetry.* University of Michigan Press, 1994.

Baldi, Elio. *The Author in Criticism: Italo Calvino's Authorial Image in Italy, the United States, and the United Kingdom.* Fairleigh Dickinson University Press, 2022.

Baldi, Elio. "La sfida al labirinto sessuale: L'eros nell'opera di Italo Calvino." *Incontri* 27, no. 2 (2012): 60–68.

Baldi, Elio, and Cecilia Schwartz. Introduction to *Circulation, Translation and Reception Across Borders: Italo Calvino's "Invisible Cities" Around the World,* edited by Elio Baldi and Cecilia Schwartz, 1–20. Routledge, 2023.

Barbour, Karen. *Dancing Across the Page: Narrative and Embodied Ways of Knowing.* Intellect, 2011.

Barbour, Karen, and Alexandra Hitchmough. "Experiencing Affect Through Site-Specific Dance." *Emotion, Space and Society* 12, no. 1 (2014): 63–72.

"Baron in the Trees." *New Grounds*, February 17, 2023. https://www.facebook
.com/events/1045505433032487?_rdr.

Barthes, Roland. "The Grain of the Voice." In *Image—Music—Text*, edited and
translated by Stephen Heath, 179–89. Fontana, 1977.

Barthes, Roland. "Listening." In *The Responsibility of Forms: Critical Essays on
Music, Art, and Representation*, translated by Richard Howard, 245–60. Hill
and Wang, 1985.

Basu, Tia. "Women Who Stutter: Media Depictions of Speech Impediments Are
Usually of Men, Sidelining the Struggles of Women Who Stutter." *The Swaddle*, January 5, 2021. theswaddle.com/depictions-of-speech-impediments-are
-usually-of-men-sidelining-the-struggles-and-triumphs-of-women-who
-stutter/.

Belpoliti, Marco. *L'occhio di Calvino*. Einaudi, 1996.

Beltrami, Marzia. *Spatial Plots: Virtuality and the Embodied Mind in Baricco,
Camilleri and Calvino*. Legenda, 2021.

Benadon, Fernando. "Cosmicomics." *delight/delirium*. Illinois Modern Ensemble with Stephen Andrew Taylor. New Focus Recordings, 2017.

Benedetti, Carla. *Pasolini contro Calvino: Per una letteratura impura*. Bollati
Boringhieri, 1998.

Benjamin, Walter. *The Arcades Project*. Translated by Howard Eiland and Kevin
McLaughlin. Harvard University Press, 1999.

Berkman, Natalie. "Italo Calvino's Oulipian Clinamen." *MLN* 135, no .1 (2020):
255–80.

Bijsterveld, Karin. "Listening to Machines: Industrial Noise, Hearing Loss and
the Cultural Meaning of Sound." *Interdisciplinary Science Reviews* 31, no. 4
(2006): 323–37.

Bloom, Harold. *The Anxiety of Influence*. 2nd ed. Oxford University Press, 1997.

Bogart, Anne. *The Art of Resonance*. Methuen Drama (Bloomsbury), 2021.

Botta, Anna. "Calvino and the Oulipo: An Italian Ghost in the Combinatory
Machine?" *MLN* 112, no. 1 (1997): 81–89.

Brenner, Wayne Alan. "Sky Candy Takes on Italo Calvino's COSMICOMICS."
Austin Chronicle, June 18, 2014. www.austinchronicle.com/daily/arts/2014-06
-18/sky-candy-takes-on-italo-calvinos-cosmicomics/.

Brinkema, Eugenie. *Life-Destroying Diagrams*. Duke University Press, 2022.

Bucci, Gianpaolo, and Beatrice Ngalula Kabutakapua. *(In)visible Cities*. Film.
Bucci and Kabutakapua, 2011.

Bull, Michael. *Sound Moves: iPod Culture and Urban Experience*. Routledge,
2007.

Burns, Jennifer. *Fragments of Impegno: Interpretations of Commitment in Contemporary Italian Narrative, 1980–2000*. Northern Universities Press, 2001.

Butler, James. "Infinite Artichoke." *London Review of Books* 45, no 12, June
15, 2023. https://www.lrb.co.uk/the-paper/v45/n12/james-butler/infinite
-artichoke.

Butler, Judith. *Gender Trouble: Feminism and the Subversion of Identity*. Routledge, 1990.

Byström, Britta. "Invisible Cities." *Invisible Cities*. Daphne Records, 2014.

Calvino, Italo. *Invisible Cities*. Translated by William Weaver. Harcourt, Brace, Jovanovich, 1974.

Calvino, Italo. "La foresta-radice-labirinto." In *Il teatro dei ventagli*, 31–54. Mondadori, 2023.

Calvino, Italo. *Lettere, 1940–1985*. Edited by Luca Baranelli, directed by Claudio Milanini. "I Meridiani." Mondadori, 2000.

Calvino, Italo. *Lettere a Chichita, 1962–1963*. Mondadori, 2023.

Calvino, Italo. *Ottimista in America*. Mondadori, 2019.

Calvino, Italo. *Romanzi e racconti*. Edited by Mario Barenghi and Bruno Falcetto, directed by Claudio Milanini. 3 vols. "I Meridiani." Mondadori, 1994.

Calvino, Italo. *Saggi*. Edited by Mario Barenghi, directed by Claudio Milanini. "I Meridiani." Mondadori, 1995.

Calvino, Italo. *Sono nato in America... Interviste 1951–1985*. Edited by Luca Baranelli. Mondadori, 2012.

Carli, Alberto. *L'occhio e la voce: Pier Paolo Pasolini e Italo Calvino fra letteratura e antropologia*. Edizioni ETS, 2018.

Carson, Rachel. *Silent Spring*. Mariner Books, 2002.

Cavarero, Adriana. *A più voci: Filosofia dell'espressione vocale*. Feltrinelli, 2003.

Cavarero, Adriana. *For More Than One Voice: Toward a Philosophy of Vocal Expression*. Translated by Paul A. Kottman. Stanford University Press, 2005.

Cavarero, Adriana. *Relating Narratives: Storytelling and Selfhood*. Translated by Paul A. Kottman. Routledge, 2000.

Cavarero, Adriana. *Tu che mi guardi, tu che mi racconti*. Feltrinelli, 1998.

Cerrone, Christopher. "How to Breathe Underwater." YouTube, uploaded by Chris Cerrone, December 22, 2014. Performed by Loadbang, directed by Jonathan Maurer. www.youtube.com/watch?v=s-ex3ieO1xc.

Cerrone, Christopher. "Hoyt-Schermerhorn." Performed by Vicky Chow. *Aorta*. New Amsterdam, 2016.

Cerrone, Christopher. *Invisible Cities*. The Industry Records, 2014.

Cerrone, Christopher. *Invisible Cities: An Opera in One Act Based on the Novel by Italo Calvino*. Outburst-Inburst Musics, 2013.

Cerrone, Christopher. "Reading a Wave." *Vimeo*, uploaded March 20, 2010, by Red Light New Music. vimeo.com/10311294.

Cerrone, Christopher, and Tim Munro. "Rebuilding the Flute: Christopher Cerrone and Tim Munro Discuss 'Liminal Highway.'" *Classical Post*, August 21, 2020. classicalpost.com/read/chris-cerrone-and-tim-munro-liminal -highway.

Chan, Sheryl. "Invisible Cities Linkup: Pros & Cons of Living with Chronic Illness in Your City." *A Chronic Voice*, September 14, 2018. www.achronicvoice .com/2018/09/14/invisible-cities-linkup/.

Chatel, François, dir. "Italo Calvino et l'amour." Interview with Bernard Pivot. Antenne 2, 1981. *L'INA éclaire l'actu.* Accessed January 16, 2023. https://www.ina.fr/ina-eclaire-actu/video/i08018800/italo-calvino-et-l-amour.

Chiarini, Duccio. *Italo Calvino: Lo scrittore sugli alberi.* Panamafilm, Les Films d'Ici e Luce Cinecittà, 2023.

Chion, Michel. *Audio-Vision: Sound on Screen.* Edited and translated by Claudia Gorbman. Columbia University Press, 1994.

Chowdhury, Jevan. *Moving Cities.* Accessed April 8, 2024. www.moving-cities.com.Cravenne, Marcel, dir. "Italo Calvino à propos de ses livres *Le Baron perché* et *Le Vicomte pourfendu.*" Office national de radiodiffusion télévision française, 1960. Accessed January 16, 2023. www.ina.fr/ina-eclaire-actu/video/i00018194/italo-calvino-a-propos-de-ses-livres-le-baron-perche-et-le-vicomte-pourfendu.

"Dance Theater: 'Invisible Cities 2.022.'" *Smart Shanghai,* May 2023. Accessed May 27, 2023. www.smartshanghai.com/event/72985.

Dankworth, Avril. *Jazz: An Introduction to Its Musical Basis.* Oxford University Press, 1968.

Davis, Hubert. *Invisible City.* National Film Board of Canada, 2009.

Davis, Jeff. "A Chat with Joanna Wright on Sky Candy's COSMICOM-ICS." *Broadway World,* June 24, 2014. www.broadwayworld.com/austin/article/BWW-Interviews-A-Chat-with-Joanna-Wright-on-Sky-Candys-COSMICOMICS-20140624.

de Blasio, Bill. "Transcript: Mayor de Blasio Delivers Remarks at the Regional Planning [*sic*] Association Luncheon." NYC: The Official Website of the City of New York, April 25, 2014. www.nyc.gov/office-of-the-mayor/news/183-14/transcript-mayor-de-blasio-delivers-remarks-the-regional-planning-association-luncheon#/0.

De Caprio, Chiara. "Architettura." In *Le parole di Calvino,* edited by Matteo Motolese, 17–30. Treccani, 2023.

De Certeau, Michel. *The Practice of Everyday Life.* University of California Press, 1984.

de' Giorgi, Elsa. *Ho visto partire il tuo treno.* Feltrinelli, 2017.

Debord, Guy. "Theory of the Dérive." In *Situationist International Anthology,* rev. ed., edited and translated by Ken Knabb. Bureau of Public Secrets, 2006.

Del Giudice, Daniele. "L'occhio che scrive." In *Italo Calvino: Enciclopedia; arte, scienza e letteratura,* edited by Marco Belpoliti, 176–79. Marcos y Marcos, 1995.

Della Terza, Dante. Introduction to *The Dawn Is Always New: Selected Poetry of Rocco Scotellaro,* translated by Ruth Feldman and Brian Swann, 3–14. Princeton University Press, 1980.

Di Bari, Luca. *Lo scoiattolo della penna: Profilo di Italo Calvino dall'impegno politico alla rottura con il PCI.* Pensa MultiMedia, 2009.

di Buduo, Pino, dir. *Città invisibili.* Accessed September 4, 2024. www
.teatropotlach.org/citta-invisibili.

Diderot, Denis. *Le neveu de Rameau.* Garnier Flammarion, 1967.

distanza della luna, La. *La distanza della luna.* Bassa Fedeltà Records, 2015.

Dolar, Mladen. *A Voice and Nothing More.* MIT Press, 2006.

Dos Monos. "Ra Cosmicomiche (Race for Space) [feat. JAZZ DOMMU-
NIUSTERS]." *Dos Siki Second Season.* Warner Music Japan, 2021.

Dragovic, Sonja. "Discovering Calvino's 'Invisible Cities' in Brussels: September Salon 2017 (Part 1)." 4Cities website, October 5, 2017. www.4cities.eu/
discovering-calvinos-invisible-cities-in-brussels-september-salon-2017
-part-i/.

Duffy, Michelle, Paul Atkinson, and Nicola Wood. "Thresholds of Representa-
tion: Physical Disability in Dance and Perceptions of the Moving Body."
In *Non-Representational Theory and the Creative Arts*, edited by Candice P.
Boyd and Christian Edwardes, 243–62. Palgrave Macmillan, 2019.

Duncan, Dennis. "Calvino, Llull, Lucretius: Two Models of Literary Combinatorics." *Comparative Literature* 64, no. 1 (2012): 93–109.

Eagle, Chris. *Dysfluencies: On Speech Disorders in Modern Literature.* Bloomsbury, 2014.

Eidsheim, Nina Sun. *The Race of Sound: Listening, Timbre and Vocality in African American Music.* Duke University Press, 2019.

Eidsheim, Nina Sun. *Sensing Sound: Singing and Listening as Vibrational Practice.* Duke University Press, 2015.

Ellington, Duke. *Such Sweet Thunder.* Columbia Records, 1957.

Ellington, Duke, and Billy Strayhorn. "Suite Thursday." *Swinging Suites by Edward G. & Edward E.* Columbia Records, 1961.

Evans, Tristian. *Shared Meanings in the Film Music of Philip Glass: Music, Multimedia and Postminimalism.* Ashgate, 2015.

Feldman, Martha. "Voice Gap Crack Break." In *The Voice as Something More:
Essays Toward Materiality*, edited by Martha Feldman and Judith T. Zeitlin,
188–208. Chicago University Press, 2019.

Feral Cat Den. *Genesis Noir.* MacOS version. Fellow Traveller Games, 2021.

Fernandez, James W. *Persuasions and Performances: The Play of Tropes in Culture.* Indiana University Press, 1986.

Ferrero, Ernesto. *Italo.* Einaudi, 2023.

Fiordilino, Irene. "*Invisible Cities:* A Performative Adaptation." In *Circulation,
Translation and Reception Across Borders: Italo Calvino's "Invisible Cities"
Around the World*, edited by Elio Baldi and Cecilia Schwartz, 245–55. Rout-
ledge, 2023.

Fogassi, Leonardo. "Shared Meaning, Mirroring, and Joint Action." In *Language, Music, and the Brain: A Mysterious Relationship*, edited by Michael A.
Arbib, 83–106. MIT Press, 2013.

Fortini, Franco. *L'ospite ingrato.* Marietti, 1985.

4th World Orchestra. "Cosmicomics." *Sound Reasons*. Sound Reasons Records, 2012.

Fraleigh, Sondra. "A Vulnerable Glance: Seeing Dance Through Phenomenology." *Dance Research Journal* 23, no. 1 (1991): 11–16.

Francksen, Kerry. "The Implications of Technology in Dance: A Dancer's Perspective of Moving in Media-Rich Environments." In *Digital Echoes: Spaces for Intangible and Performance-Based Cultural Heritage*, edited by Sarah Whatley, Rosamaria Cisneros, and Amalia Sabiescu, 57–80. Palgrave, 2018.

Frattarola, Angela. *Modernist Soundscapes: Auditory Technology and the Novel.* University Press of Florida, 2018.

Freud, Sigmund. "Character and Anal Erotism." In *The Standard Edition of the Complete Psychological Works of Sigmund Freud*, edited by James Strachey, vol. 9, 167–76. Hogarth, 1959.

Freud, Sigmund. *The Interpretation of Dreams (First Part)*. In *The Standard Edition of the Complete Psychological Works of Sigmund Freud*, edited by James Strachey, vol. 4. Hogarth, 1953.

Freud, Sigmund. "On Transformations of Instinct as Exemplified in Anal Erotism." In *The Standard Edition of the Complete Psychological Works of Sigmund Freud*, edited by James Strachey, vol. 17, 125–34. Hogarth, 1955.

Gabriele, Tommasina. *Italo Calvino: Eros and Language.* Fairleigh Dickinson University Press, 1996.

Gambaro, Fabio. *Lo scoiattolo sulla Senna: L'avventura di Calvino a Parigi.* Feltrinelli, 2023.

Gelfland, Stanley A. *Hearing: An Introduction to Psychological and Physiological Acoustics.* 5th ed. Informa Healthcare, 2010.

Gellen, Kata. *Kafka and Noise: The Discovery of Cinematic Sound in Literary Modernism.* Northwestern University Press, 2019.

Gillette, Kyle. *The Invisible City: Travel, Attention, and Performance.* Routledge, 2020.

Ginzburg, Natalia. "Il sole e la luna." In *Italo Calvino: Enciclopedia: Arte, scienza e letteratura*, edited by Marco Belpoliti, 188–91. Special issue, *Riga*, no. 9. Marcos y Marcos, 1995.

Goss, Stephen. "Dialogues from *Invisible Cities*." Doberman-Yppan, 2022.

Goss, Stephen. *Invisible Cities*, featuring the Boulder Philharmonic and soloists Nicolò Spera (guitar) and Charles Wetherbee (violin). SoundCloud, uploaded by Stephen Goss, March 5, 2021. soundcloud.com/stevegoss/sets/invisible-cities.

Grossi, Lina. *Italo Calvino: Il sapore del racconto (Le ricette delle fiabe italiane).* Il leone verde, 2011.

Grundtvig, Birgitte, Martin McLaughlin, and Lene Waage Petersen, eds. *Image, Eye and Art in Calvino: Writing Visibility.* Legenda, 2007.

Halles, Les. "Elsewhere Is a Negative Mirror." *Elsewhere Is a Negative Mirror.* Constellation Tatsu, 2022. Accessed April 13, 2024. halles.bandcamp.com/album/elsewhere-is-a-negative-mirror-compilation.

Hirsch, Marianne. *The Generation of Postmemory: Writing and Visual Culture after the Holocaust*. Columbia University Press, 2012.

Horwitz, Andy. "Talking to Ildiko Nemeth About *Cosmicomics*." Interview with Katy Einerson. *Culturebot: Maximum Performance*, March 31, 2014. www.culturebot.org/2014/03/21475/talking-to-ildiko-nemeth-about-cosmicomics/.

Hosokawa, Shuhei. "The Walkman Effect." *Popular Music* 4 (1984): 165–80.

Houston, Whitney. "I Will Always Love You." Composed by Dolly Parton. *The Bodyguard: Original Soundtrack Album*. Arista and BMG, 1992.

Hume, Kathryn. "Sensuality and the Senses in Calvino's Fiction." *MLN* 107, no. 1 (1992): 160–77.

Innocenti, Orsetta. "La trasformazione dell'intimità: Anthony Giddens e il *romance* dell'impegno." In *Postmodern Impegno: Ethics and Commitment in Contemporary Italian Culture*, edited by Pierpaolo Antonello and Florian Mussgnug, 121–46. Peter Lang, 2009.

"Internationally-Acclaimed Lost in Translation Circus Swing into 10th Anniversary Year with Exciting London Tour." *Theatre Weekly*, May 21, 2021. https://theatreweekly.com/internationally-acclaimed-lost-in-translation-circus-swing-into-10th-anniversary-year-with-exciting-london-tour/.

Invisible Cities, "a social enterprise that trains people who have experienced homelessness" as tour guides to their cities. Accessed May 10, 2024. https://invisible-cities.org.

"Invisible Cities." *Artbound*. KCET. Original airdate: January 4, 2015. www.kcet.org/shows/artbound/artbound-special-episode-invisible-cities. Accessed May 21, 2019.

"Invisible Cities: Composing an Opera for Headphones." *Artbound*. KCET. Original airdate: October 22, 2013. www.kcet.org/shows/artbound/invisible-cities-composing-an-opera-for-headphones. Accessed May 21, 2019.

Invisible Cities. Film of the Christopher Cerrone opera, directed by Joris Debeij for KCET's "Artbound" series (opera direction by Yuval Sharon, Marc Lowenstein conducting, and Danielle Agami, choreography). The Industry Productions, 2015.

Invisible Cities Studio, collaborative design studio. https://www.invisiblecitiesstudio.com/. Accessed Feb 10, 2019, but now defunct. See Moody, John.

Iovino, Serenella. *Gli animali di Calvino: Storie dall'Antropocene*. Treccani, 2023.

Iovino, Serenella. "Italo Calvino and the Landscapes of the Anthropocene: A Narrative Stratigraphy." In *Italy and the Environmental Humanities: Landscapes, Natures, Ecologies*, edited by Serenella Iovino, Enrico Cesaretti, and Elena Past, 67–77. University of Virginia Press, 2018.

Iovino, Serenella. *Italo Calvino's Animals: Anthropocene Stories*. Cambridge University Press, 2021.

Ivasiuc, Ana. "Desires and Fears in the Invisible Eternal City: An Ethnography of All Urban Ethnographies." In *"Invisible Cities" and the Urban Imagination*, edited by Benjamin Linder, 329–35. Palgrave Macmillan, 2022.

Jeannet, Angela M. *Under the Radiant Sun and the Crescent Moon: Italo Calvino's Storytelling.* University of Toronto Press, 2000.

Johnson, Jeffrey K. "The Visualization of the Twisted Tongue: Portrayals of Stuttering in Film, Television, and Comic Books." *Journal of Popular Culture* 41, no. 2 (2008): 245–61.

King, Jonny. *What Jazz Is: An Insider's Guide to Understanding and Listening to Jazz.* Walker, 1997.

Kourlas, Gia. "Review: Three Dancers, One Solo. How Do They Make It Their Own?" *New York Times*, April 14, 2022. https://www.nytimes.com/2022/04/14/arts/dance/review-let-the-crows-come-ashwini-ramaswamy.html.

Kramer, Lawrence. *Musical Meaning: Toward a Critical History.* University of California Press, 2002.

Kramer, Lawrence. *The Thought of Music.* University of California Press, 2016.

Krohn, Leena. *Tainaron: Mail from Another City.* Translated by Hildi Hawkins. In *Collected Fiction*, 67–148. Cheeky Frawg Books, 2015.

LaBelle, Brandon. *Background Noise: Perspectives on Sound Art.* 2nd ed. Bloomsbury, 2015.

Lacoue-Labarthe, Philippe. "The Echo of the Subject." In *Typography: Mimesis, Philosophy, Politics*, edited by Christopher Fynsk, 130–207. Harvard University Press, 1989.

Lacoue-Labarthe, Philippe. "L'écho du sujet." In *Le sujet de la philosophie: Typographies 1*, 217–303. Aubier-Flammarion, 1979.

Lahiri, Jhumpa. *Translating Myself and Others.* Princeton University Press, 2022.

Lakoff, George, and Mark Johnson. *Metaphors We Live By.* University of Chicago Press, 1980.

Lane, Cathy. "Women as Animal, Women as Alien." In *Grounds for Possible Music: On Gender, Voice, Language and Identity*, edited by Julia Eckhardt, 98–103. Errant Bodies, 2018.

Lawn, Richard. *Experiencing Jazz.* 2nd ed. Routledge, 2013.

Lecavalier, Louise. "Mille batailles." *Quebec danse*, September 21, 2019. www.quebecdanse.org/agenda/mille-batailles-louise-lecavalier-6/.

Lewis, Jerome. "A Cross-Cultural Perspective on the Significance of Music and Dance to Culture and Society: Insight from BaYaka Pygmies." In *Language, Music, and the Brain: A Mysterious Relationship*, edited by Michael A. Arbib, 45–66. MIT Press, 2013.

Lightman, Alan. *Einstein's Dreams.* Vintage, 1992.

Linder, Benjamin. *"Invisible Cities" and the Urban Imagination.* Palgrave Macmillan, 2022.

Lisa Mezzacappa Six. *Cosmicomics.* Queen Bee Records, 2020.

Liturri, Vito. *Desires and Fears.* DodiciLune Records, 2022.

Lord, Richard. "Hong Kong Architect William Lim and the Italo Calvino Novel That Changed His Life, *Invisible Cities*." *South China Morning Post*, August 4, 2018. www.scmp.com/magazines/post-magazine/books/article/2158081/hong-kong-architect-william-lim-and-italo-calvino.

Lucier, Alvin. "I am sitting in a room." *Alvin Lucier: Two Circles*. Mode Records, 2017.

Lucier, Alvin. "I am sitting in a room." *I am sitting in a room*. Lovely Music, 1990.

Lucretius. *De rerum natura*. Translated by W. H. D. Rouse. Harvard University Press, 1924.

MacKendrick, Karmen. *The Matter of Voice: Sensual Soundings*. Fordham University Press, 2016.

Manning, Erin. *Politics of Touch: Sense, Movement, Sovereignty*. University of Minnesota Press, 2007.

Margolies, Dany. "Site-Specific Opera 'Invisible Cities' Brings Headphone-Wearing Audiences to Union Station." *Los Angeles Downtown News*, October 16, 2013. www.ladowntownnews.com/arts_and_entertainment/site-specific -opera-invisible-cities-brings-headphone-wearing-audiences-to/article _b7349d12-3680-11e3-84f3-0019bb2963f4.html.

Martin, John. *The Modern Dance*. Dance Horizons, 1935.

Matter, Marc. "Voices Up for Grabs." In *Grounds for Possible Music: On Gender, Voice, Language, and Identity*, edited by Julia Eckhardt, 45–51. Errant Bodies, 2018.

McClary, Susan. *Feminine Endings: Music, Gender, and Sexuality*. University of Minnesota Press, 1991.

McDonough, Katie. "Elizabeth Holmes's Fake Voice Is Actually Just 'Stupid Man' Voice." *Jezebel*, March 19, 2019. jezebel.com/elizabeth-holmess-fake -voice-is-actually-just-stupid-ma-1833402366.

McFee, Graham. *Understanding Dance*. Routledge, 1992.

McNabb, Michael. *Invisible Cities*, 1985. Accessed April 8, 2024. https://www .mcnabb.com/music/invisiblecities/.

Medhi, Areej. "Elsewhere Is a Negative Mirror." *Networks and the Creative Process* (blog). Georgetown University, Spring 2015. Accessed April 13, 2024. blogs.commons.georgetown.edu/cctp-728-spring2015/2015/02/04/elsewhere -is-a-negative-mirror/.

Meduri, Avanthi. "Bharatanatyam as a Global Dance: Some Issues in Research, Teaching, and Practice." *Dance Research Journal* 36, no. 2 (2004): 11–29.

Miano, Tonino, and ensemble. "The Moon Like a Mushroom." *Roulette*, April 4, 1998. roulette.org/event/tonino-miano-2/.

Migrantour. "Le nostre città invisibili." Accessed May 10, 2024. migrantour.org/ en/le-nostre-citta-invisibili/.

Milanini, Claudio. *L'utopia discontinua: Saggi su Italo Calvino*. Carocci Editore, 2022.

Mills, Dana. *Dance and Politics: Moving Beyond Boundaries*. Manchester University Press, 2016.

Mirabile, Andrea. *Piaceri invisibili: Retorica della cecità in D'Annunzio, Pasolini, Calvino*. Carocci editore, 2017.

Modena, Letizia. *Italo Calvino's Architecture of Lightness: The Utopian Imagination in an Age of Urban Crisis*. Routledge, 2011.

Monelli, Paolo. *Ombre cinesi: Scrittori al girarrosto*. Mondadori, 1965.

Moody, John. (Urban designer, founder of Invisible Cities Design Studio.) Accessed May 10, 2024. https://moody.studio/about.

Musarra-Schrøder, Ulla. *Italo Calvino tra i cinque sensi*. F. Cesati, 2010.

Musin, Nicholas. "Archipelago." *Théâtre National Populaire*, November 2021. Accessed May 27, 2023. www.tnp-villeurbanne.com/cms/wp-content/uploads/2021/11/dosprod_archipel_va-novembre21.pdf.

Nadir, Erika. "Prima la musica o prima la parola? Textual and Musical Intermedialities in Italian Literature and Film." PhD diss., UCLA, 2017.

Napolin, Julie Beth. *The Fact of Resonance: Modernist Acoustics and Narrative Form*. Fordham University Press, 2020.

Nemeth, Idilko. *Cosmicomics*. New Stage Theatre Company, accessed April 8, 2024. newstagetheatre.org/production/cosmicomics/.

Nilsson, Ivo. *Lunaria. Lunaria*, with Ensemble MA. Blue Music Group, 2021.

Œ. "Cosmicomics." *Sainte Pop II*. La Souterraine, 2018.

Osborne, Nigel. "Galanthus nivalis." *Insomniac: New Noise*, with Joby Burgess and Janey Miller. NNLrecords, 2003.

Osborne, Nigel. "Neuroscience and 'Real World' Practice: Music as a Therapeutic Resource for Children in Zones of Conflict." *Annals of the New York Academy of Sciences* 1252, no. 1 (2012): 69–76.

Parlangeli, Oronzo. *La nuova questione della lingua: Saggi raccolti da O. Parlangeli*. Paideia, 1971.

Pashman, Susan. "Feeling Is Movement: Damasio's Neural Model of Dance Expression." *Dance Research: The Journal of the Society for Dance Research* 35, no. 2 (2017): 258–73.

Perec, Georges. "Approaches to What?" In *Species of Spaces and Other Pieces*, edited and translated by John Sturrock. Penguin Books, 1999.

Perrella, Silvio. *Calvino*. Laterza, 1999.

Perrella, Silvio. "Italo Calvino raccontato da Silvio Perrella." *Wikiradio*, RAI, October 15, 2019. www.raiplaysound.it/audio/2019/10/WIKIRADIO-2cbd0e4e-f07f-4b07-8b72-f35e049ce30e.html.

Pettigrew, Damian, dir. *Dans la peau d'Italo Calvino*. Portrait, 2012.

Philbrick, Ethan. *Group Works: Art, Politics, and Collective Ambivalence*. Fordham University Press, 2023.

Pierce, Allan D. *Acoustics: An Introduction to Its Physical Principles and Applications*. 3rd ed. Springer, 2019.

Pomilio, Tommaso. "Scrittura dell'ascolto: Calvino in Berio." In *Le théâtre musical de Luciano Berio: Actes de six journées d'études qui ont eu lieu à Paris et à Venise entre 2010 et 2013*, edited by Giordano Ferrari, vol. 2, 117–43. L'Harmattan, 2016.

Prencipe, Andrea, and Massimo Sideri. *L'innovatore rampante: L'ultima lezione di Italo Calvino*. Luiss University Press, 2022.

Pritchard, Alwynne. "Invisible Cities." *Invisible Cities*. Metier, 2013.

Putcha, Rumya Sree. *The Dancer's Voice: Performance and Womanhood in Transnational India*. Duke University Press, 2023.

Rapetti, Nereo, dir. "Franco Maria Ricci, l'editore di Babele," interview with Valerio Riva for Radio Televisione Svizzera Italiana ca. 1972. RSI (Radio Svizzera Italiana). https://www.rsi.ch/play/tv/-/video/franco-maria-ricci -leditore-di-babele?urn=urn:rsi:video:1650757.

Ravens, Simon. *The Supernatural Voice: A History of High Male Singing*. Boydell, 2014.

Re, Lucia. "Pasolini vs. Calvino, One More Time: The Debate on the Role of Intellectuals and Postmodernism in Italy Today." *MLN* 129, no. 1 (2014): 99–117.

Ricci, Franco. *Painting with Words, Writing with Pictures: Word and Image in the Work of Italo Calvino*. University of Toronto Press, 2001.

Ricciardi, Alessia. *After "La Dolce Vita": A Cultural Prehistory of Berlusconi's Italy*. Stanford University Press, 2012.

Ricciardi, Alessia. "Lightness and Gravity: Calvino, Pynchon, and Postmodernity." *MLN* 114, no. 5 (1999): 1062–77.

Rimondi, Giorgio. *La scrittura sincopata: Jazz e letteratura nel Novecento italiano*. Mondadori, 1999.

Romaniello, Giuseppe. *Six Memos in Jazz*. Conti (Morgex), 2014.

Roy, Sanjoy. "Fantasy, Folly and Fancy Footwork: Cosmic Dance Comes to Manchester." *Guardian*, July 7, 2019. https://www.theguardian.com/stage/ 2019/jul/07/invisible-cities-alphabus-manchester-international-festival -review.

Rubini, Francesca. "Italo Calvino in Other Languages—Part Three." *New Italian Books*, December 12, 2023. www.newitalianbooks.it/italo-calvino-in -translation-part-three/.

Rubini, Francesca. *Italo Calvino nel mondo: Opere, lingue, paesi (1955–2020)*. Carocci editore, 2023.

Rueb, Teri. "Invisible Cities: Sounding Baltimore." *Consciousness Reframed 2002 Sonic Space-Time: Sound Installation and Secondary Orality*. Artist's website, 2002. Accessed May 21, 2019. http://terirueb.net/wp-content/uploads/2018/ 03/caiia.pdf.

Rushing, Robert. "Calvino, Cerrone, and the Catacoustic: An 'Echo-Logical' Reading." *Italian Culture* 39 no. 2 (2021): 115–35.

Rushing, Robert. "Dialogues from *Invisible Cities*." Recording of Stephen Goss's composition. SoundCloud, uploaded by Robert Rushing, December 1, 2023. soundcloud.com/robushing/sets/invisible-dialogues.

Ryder-Jones, Bill. *If. …* Double Six Records, 2024.

Sabatino, Lorenzo. "Centenary Calvino, *Here and Elsewhere*." *Textual Cultures* 16, no. 2 (2023): 283–89.

Sanchez, Telesmar. *Cosmic Music*. Telesmar Sanchez, 2021.

Sanna, Adele. "The Hybrid 'Biocitizen' in Italo Calvino's *Marcovaldo or The Seasons in the City*." In *Ecocritical Approaches to Italian Culture and Literature:*

The Denatured Wild, edited by Pasquale Verdicchio, 31–42. Lexington Books, 2016.

Sarti, Laura Parola. *Invito alla lettura di Rocco Scotellaro*. Mursia, 1992.

Scaffai, Niccolò. *Letteratura e ecologia: Forme e temi di una relazione narrativa*. Carocci, 2017.

Scarpa, Domenico. *Calvino fa la conchiglia: La costruzione di uno scrittore*. Hoepli, 2023.

Schmidt, Christian Marc, and Xia Liangjie. "Invisible Cities: Representing Social Networks in an Urban Context." *Parsons Journal for Information Mapping* 3, no. 1 (2011): 1–6.

Seger, Monica. *Landscapes in Between: Environmental Change in Modern Italian Literature and Film*. University of Toronto Press, 2015.

Serra, Francesca. *Calvino*. Salerno, 2006.

Shell, Marc. *Stutter*. Harvard University Press, 2005.

Simon, Scott. "HBO's 'White Lotus' Soundtrack Haunts the Show and People's Lives." Cristobal Tapia de Veer, interviewed by Scott Simon. National Public Radio, *Weekend Edition*, August 21, 2021. www.npr.org/2021/08/21/1029957360/music-moment-white-lotus-composer.

Solis, Gabriel. *Monk's Music: Thelonious Monk and Jazz History in the Making*. University of California Press, 2007.

Spitzer, Michael. "Hearing Postmemory: Anne Frank in Neutral Milk Hotel's *In the Aeroplane over the Sea*." In *The Routledge Companion to Popular Music Analysis: Expanding Approaches*, edited by Ciro Scotto, Kenneth Smith, and John Brackett, 400–415. Routledge, 2018.

Steingraber, Thor. "Opera Occupies Union Station." *Arts•Meme*, November 4, 2013. https://artsmeme.com/2013/11/04/opera-occupies-union-station/.

Sterne, Jonathan. "Sonic Imaginations." In *The Sound Studies Reader*, edited by Jonathan Sterne, 1–17. Routledge, 2012.

Stewart, Sophia. "Why Are Female Stutterers Such a Rarity in Literature?" *The Literary Hub*, April 2, 2019. lithub.com/why-are-female-stutterers-such-a-rarity-in-literature/.

St. Terrible. "Cosmicomics." *The Wonderful End of the World: Side A*. Records DK, 2021.

Summers, Andy. "Invisible Cities." *Synaesthesia*. CMP Records, 1996.

Szendy, Peter. "*Parole, parole*: Tautegory and Musicology of the (Pop) Song." In *Speaking of Music: Addressing the Sonorous*, edited by Keith Chapin and Andrew H. Clark, 186–92. Fordham University Press, 2013.

Thompson, Emily. *The Soundscape of Modernity: Architectural Acoustics and the Culture of Listening in America, 1900–1933*. MIT Press, 2002.

Thompson, Mark Christian. *Kafka's Blues: Figurations of Racial Blackness in the Construction of an Aesthetic*. Northwestern University Press, 2016.

Tufte, Edward R. *Envisioning Information*. Graphics, 1990.

Vellum/LA + SuperRare. *Elsewhere Is a Negative Mirror: Spatiality and the Architectural Imaginary in Digital Art*. Accessed April 13, 2024. www.vellumla.com/elsewhere-is-a-negative-mirror.

Vernon, Mark. *Elsewhere Is a Negative Mirror*. Granny Records, 2022. Accessed April 13, 2024. grannyrecords.bandcamp.com/album/elsewhere-is-a-negative -mirror.

Waltham-Smith, Naomi. *Shattering Biopolitics: Militant Listening and the Sound of Life*. Fordham University Press, 2021.

Warner, Leo. "*Invisible Cities*: Manchester International Festival 2019." 59 web-site, accessed April 8, 2024. 59productions.co.uk/project/invisible-cities/.

Whitney, Tyler. *Eardrums: Literary Modernism as Sonic Warfare*. Northwestern University Press, 2019.

Yale National Initiative. *Invisible Cities: The Arts and Renewable Community*. 2013. Accessed May 21, 2019. https://teachers.yale.edu/curriculum/volumes/ 2013/4/13_04_intro.

Zac, Pino, dir. *Il cavaliere inesistente*. Istituto Luce, 1971.

Robert A. Rushing is Professor of European Languages and Transcultural Studies at UCLA, where he also holds an affiliate appointment in Film, Television and Digital Media. He is the author of *Resisting Arrest: Detective Fiction and Popular Culture* (2007) and *Descended from Hercules: Biopolitics and the Muscled Male Body on Screen*, winner of the 2016 AAIS (American Association for Italian Studies) Film/Media book prize. He is coeditor of two volumes on North American television: *Mad Men, Mad World* (2011) and *Orphan Black* (2018), and has published widely on Italian literature and cinema, especially popular genres and, of course, Italo Calvino.

www.ingramcontent.com/pod-product-compliance
Ingram Content Group UK Ltd.
Pitfield, Milton Keynes, MK11 3LW, UK
UKHW011352220126
467228UK00004BB/308